T0306707

Pressure Point Fighting Secrets of Ryukyu Kempo

George A. Dillman with Chris Thomas

A George Dillman Karate International Book

First published in 2012 by:
George Dillman Karate International
251 Mt. View Rd, (Grill)
Reading, PA 19607
USA

Copyright 2012 George Dillman Karate International

All rights reserved
First edition, 2012

ISBN 978-1-889267-14-2

5,000 copies in print

No part of this publication may be reproduced,
stored in a retrieval system or transmitted in any form or by any means,
electronic, mechanical, photocopying, recording, or otherwise,
without the written permission of the copyright holders.

A NOTE TO THE READER

This book is written as a means of preserving a vital, historical aspect of the martial arts. George Dillman Karate International Publishers and the authors make no representation, warranty or guarantee that the techniques described and illustrated in this book will be effective or safe in any self-defense situation or otherwise. You may be injured, or you may injure someone else if you train in the techniques presented within. We therefore suggest that you practice only under the supervision of a qualified instructor and exercise the utmost restraint in training. The George Dillman Karate International Publishers and the authors are in no way responsible for any injuries which may result from the practice or use of the techniques presented within. Some self-defense applications illustrated may not be justified in some circumstances under applicable federal, state or local law. Neither George Dillman Karate International, nor the authors make any representation or warranty regarding the legal or ethical appropriateness of any technique found in this book.

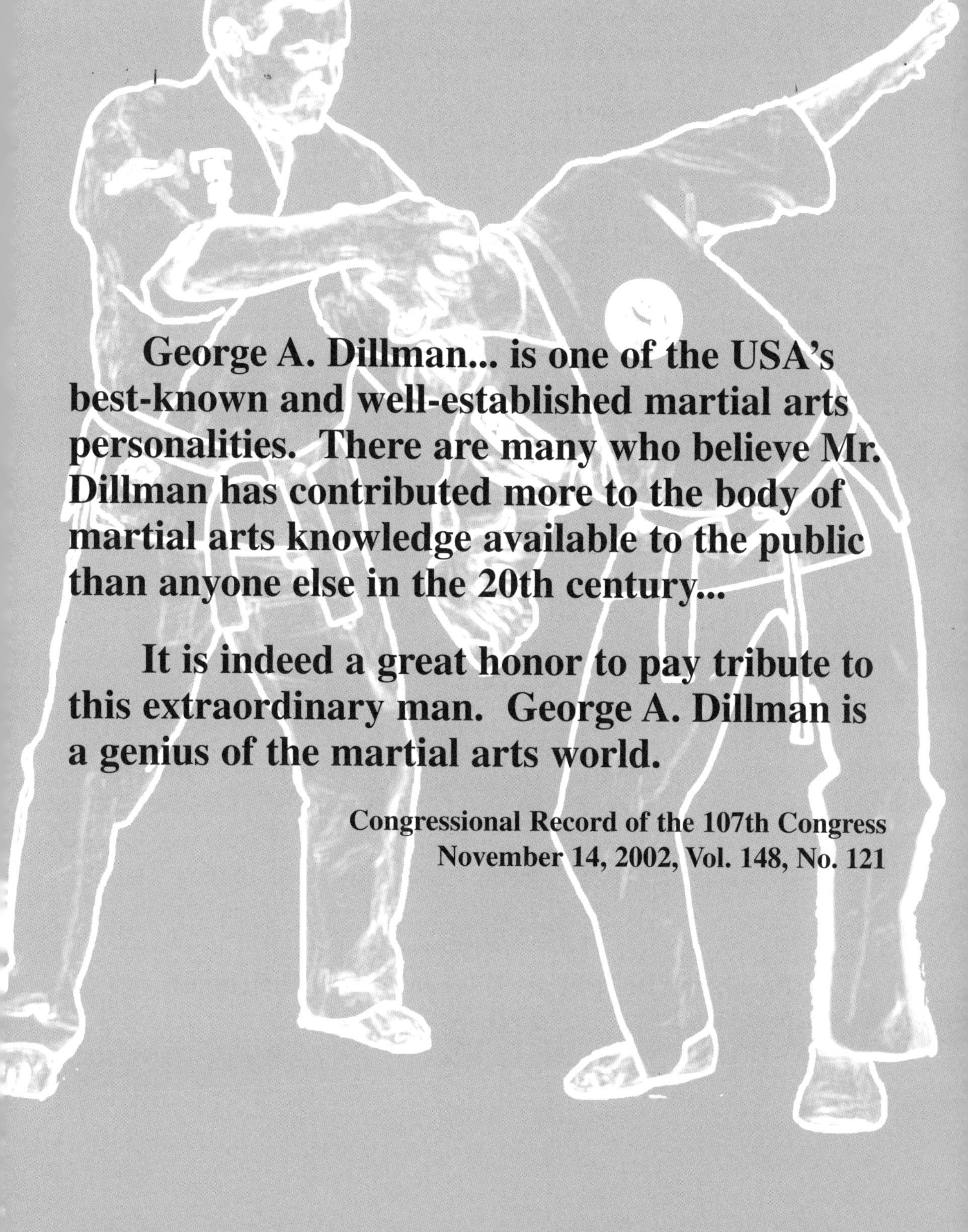

George A. Dillman... is one of the USA's best-known and well-established martial arts personalities. There are many who believe Mr. Dillman has contributed more to the body of martial arts knowledge available to the public than anyone else in the 20th century...

It is indeed a great honor to pay tribute to this extraordinary man. George A. Dillman is a genius of the martial arts world.

**Congressional Record of the 107th Congress
November 14, 2002, Vol. 148, No. 121**

ACKNOWLEDGMENTS

We would like to thank the many people who have made this book a reality. Thanks to Tom Countryman for principal photography; layout and artwork, and to Kim Foreman for photography, and proof-reading. To April Taylor, Wendy Countryman and Tammy Janke for additional photography. Thanks to those who appear in the photos: Barb Baran, Lloyd Brown, Bill Burch, Mike Christie, Greg Dillon, Harvey Flesburg, Kim Foreman, Rick Fryer, Bruce Fronk, Blythe Holmes, Shad Janke, Dave Kuske, Ed Lake, Chris Martingilio, Ken Moreno, Travis Pobuda, Dave Poirier, Steve Schreiner, Dustin Seale. Will Higginbotham, Thanks to Joe Swift and Patrick McCarthy for their help in obtaining certain historical source materials, and for their contributions as karate historians. Special thanks to Wally Jay, Taika Oyata (a.k.a. Seiyu Oyata), Hohan Soken, and Remy Presas, for the knowledge they have shared. And thank you to all the members of Dillman Karate International world-wide for your support and encouragement.

Dedicated to the memory of our dear friends

Remy Presas

Wally Jay

Gordon Travers

and

Elizabeth "Betty" Cart Dillman Mengle Hollenbush

1927-2008

INTRODUCTION

Our Second book, Advanced Pressure Point Fighting of RYUKYU KEMPO was produced using technology that has become outdated, and we are no longer able to reprint it. Not wanting that material to be lost to the martial arts community, we considered rebuilding the book from scratch. However, in the intervening years we have compiled more examples of pressure point applications and a greater understanding of the art we cherish. So, we have decided to produce a new book – one which retains content from Advanced Pressure Point Fighting of RYUKYU KEMPO, but also greatly expands on that content in both breadth and depth. This is that book. We have rescanned the original negatives and graphics, re-editted the original manusrcipt, added more points, more techniques and deeper knowledge.

Because this work represents nearly 20 years of training and development, and many different photo shoots conducted over those 20 years, you will notice differences in lighting, background, clothing, hairlines and waistlines in the many sequences presented. We hope you have fun seeing how young (and thin) we used to be, and how much we have grayed. And we also hope it will serve as an encouragement to see it so graphically illustrated that the art we practice is a life-long study.

This book contains detailed information about the location and use of many of the most important pressure points. It explains in detail both the performance and the application of the kata Naihanchi Shodan, as well as the energetic qualities of stances. But, most importantly, we are presenting principles to help you, the reader, in your own personal search for a greater knowledge and understanding of the classical martial arts. If after reading this book you have a greater appreciation for your own art (whether Ryukyu kempo or not), and a deeper insight into its true use, then our effort will be proven worthwhile.

Chris Thomas

It was grandmaster Hohan Soken who first itroduced George Dillman to pressure points, giving Dillman pressure point charts, and an impromptu 4 hour private training session.

Photos by Kim Foreman

Hohan Soken was well known for his skill with the kama (sickle).

Soken-sensei was also famed for his knowledge of empty hand kata.

George Dillman, Hohan Soken, Daniel K. Pai.

Photos by Kim Foreman

Hohan Soken and George Dillman.

Photos by Kim Foreman

Fusei Kise and George Dillman. Kise-sensei was a senior student of Hohan Soken.

Eizo Shimabukuro, George Dillman.

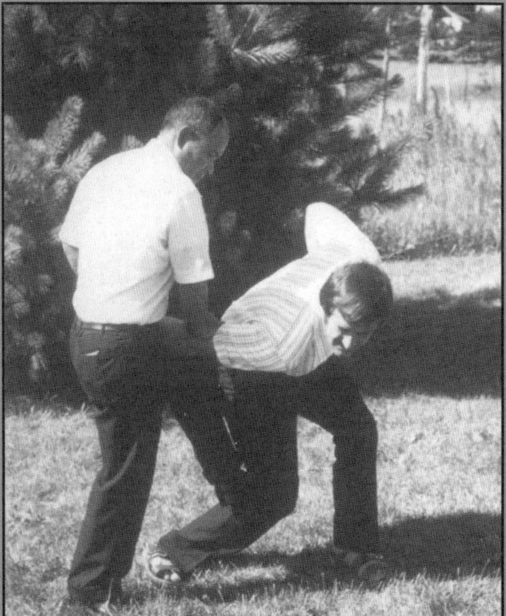

Eizo Shimabukuro demonstrating technique on George Dillman.

Eizo Shimabukuro and George Dillman in weapons practice.

Photos by Kim Foreman

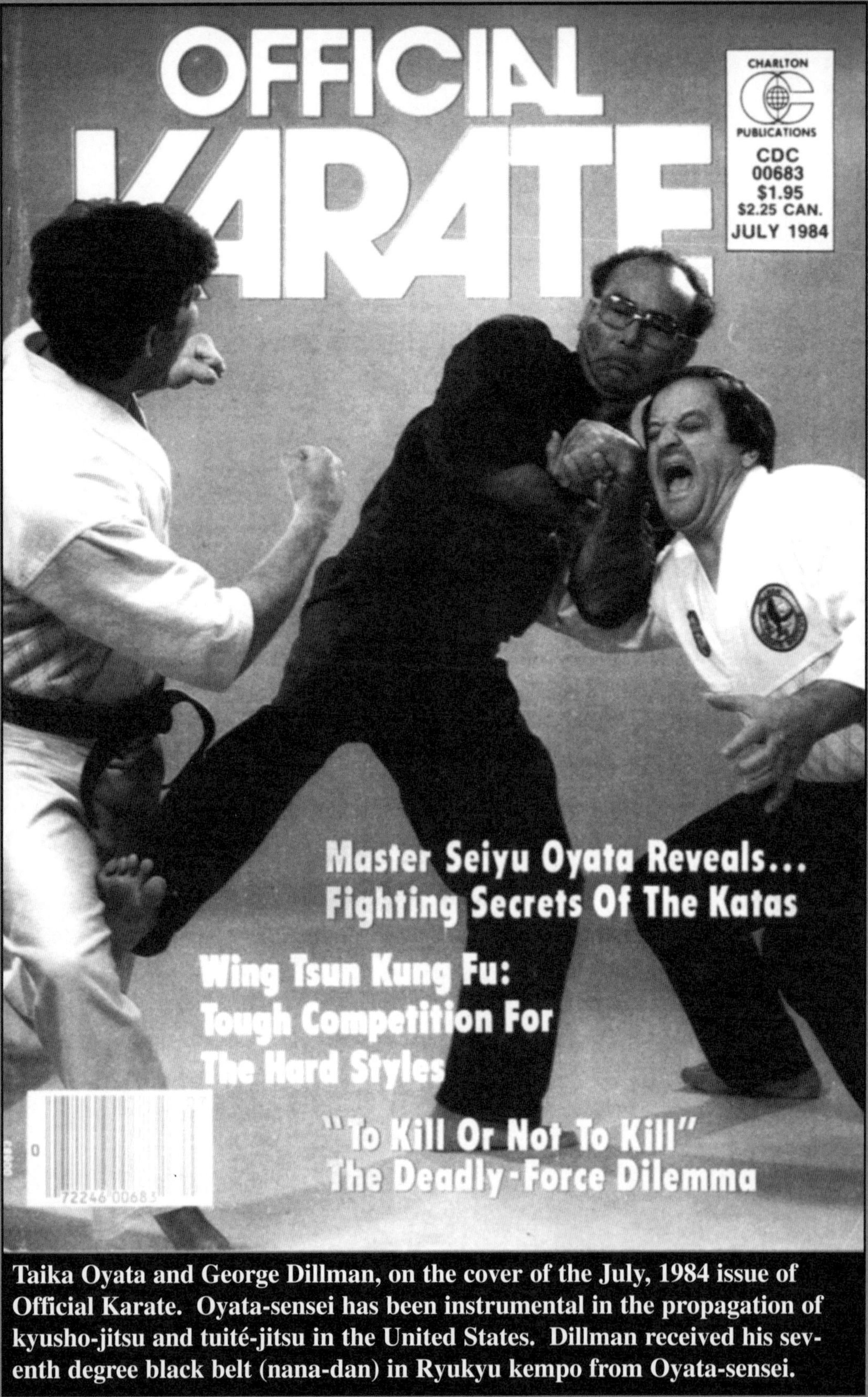

Taika Oyata and George Dillman, on the cover of the July, 1984 issue of Official Karate. Oyata-sensei has been instrumental in the propagation of kyusho-jitsu and tuité-jitsu in the United States. Dillman received his seventh degree black belt (nana-dan) in Ryukyu kempo from Oyata-sensei.

Photo by Sandra Schlessman

Author George Dillman is knocked out by Oyata-sensei. Experiencing pressure point techniques is an important part of learning them.

George Dillman's 7th dan diploma from Oyata-sensei, dated October 23, 1983.

Photo by Kim Foreman

These 3 photos by Sandra Schlessman

Oyata-sensei demonstrates the tuité maneuver called palm turn (te-hira-gatame) on author George Dillman.

Oyata-sensei demonstrating a technique from the kata Tomari Bassai. Author George Dillman is on the right.

Oyata-sensei teaching at George Dillman's school in Reading, PA.

Photos by Kim Foreman

Author George Dillman's first appearance on the cover of Black Belt Magazine, January, 1990. In 1997, Dillman was named the Black Belt Hall of Fame Instructor of the Year. In addition to Black Belt, Dillman has been featured on the covers of many martial arts magazines around the world.

Suzanne and George Dillman (2011).

Photo by Kim Foreman

Will Higginbotham teaching at the Martial Arts Training Camp, in Deer Lake, PA.

Photo by Wendy Countryman

Author Chris Thomas demonstrating effective, if unsophisticated, bunkai in the pages of Black Belt Magazine (1981).

Mickey Wittekiend training active duty U.S. Marines in Dillman Pressure Point Method.

Author Chris Thomas training a police Emergency Response Team (ERT) in Dillman Pressure Point Method.

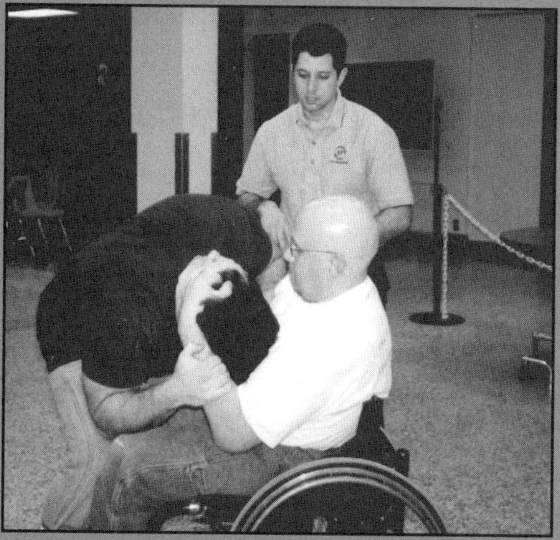

Mark Gridley teaching Dillman Pressure Point Method to a class of wheel-chair bound adults.

Photo by Kim Foreman

From left to right, Wally Jay, Linda Lee Caldwell, Remy Presas, George Dillman. This photo was taken at Wally Jay's 83rd Birthday celebration, in 2000. Professor Presas died in 2003. Professor Jay died in 2011.

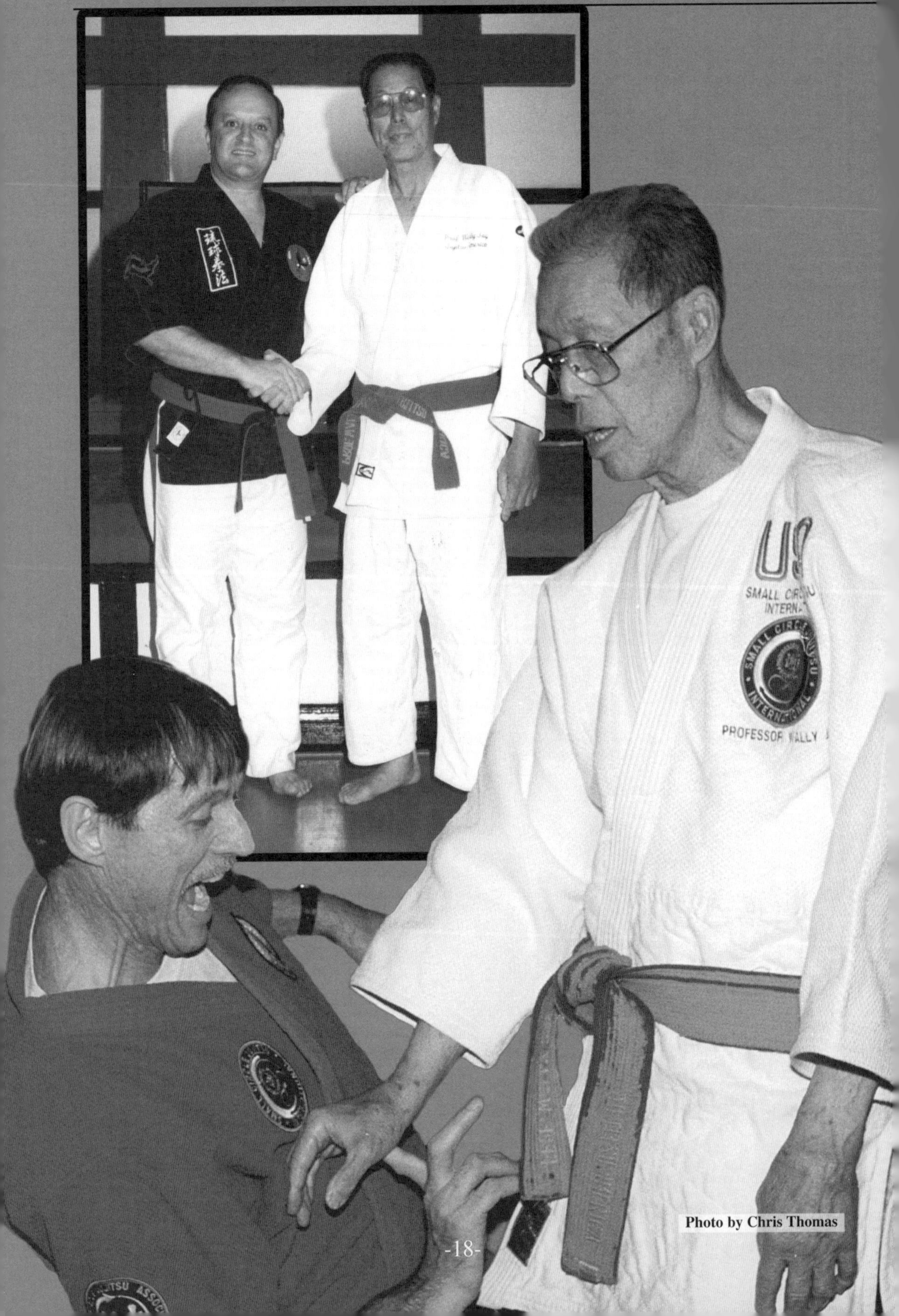

Photo by Chris Thomas

Photo by Kim Foreman

Professor Wally Jay

June 16, 1917 - May 29, 2011

Photo by Chris Thomas

Photo by Kim Foreman

Bruce Lee and Daniel K. Pai with author George Dillman.

Daniel K. Pai and author George Dillman working with traditional weapons – the long staff (bo) and the side-handle baton (tonfa).

Photos by Kim Foreman

George Dillman knocks Ed Lake unconscious during a demonstration of *toate-jitsu*, the art of no-touch fighting.

Paul Bowman, Larry Holmes and George Dillman at Paul Bowman's 60th birthday celebration.

George Dillman with Mike Douglas and Bernadette Peters during an appearance on the Mike Douglas Show.

Allen & George Dillman.

Black Belt Magazine photo by Rick Hustead

成都王府井电影城 影城年度 共享夜宴
美国奇幻冒险动作大片 冯小刚电影
X战警III 夜宴
最后的战斗 正在热映 隆重巨献 正在热映
正在热映《东京审判》《赛车总动员》《加菲猫》 电话：86512628

“阿里出快拳 李小

拳王阿里的保镖昨现身成都 讲述其与李小龙、拳

·面对面·

专访乔治·迪欧曼

作为一代巨星，李小龙以及拳王阿里的故事永远都不乏听众。记者在专访迪欧曼时，他介绍了一些关于两位武打巨星鲜为人知的故事。

年轻时与李小龙的合影（翻拍）

·关于李小龙· **他教我出快拳**

记者：对李小龙的印象如何？

迪欧曼：1967年，我在华盛顿开了一家空手道馆，当时通过一位美国的武术爱好者认识了大名鼎鼎的李小龙，他不仅人长得帅，拳也打得好，是当时全世界最优秀、最伟大的拳手。

记者：与李小龙的技术交流，你从中吸取了哪些精华？

迪欧曼：认识李小龙以前，我出拳虽然有力量，但没有足够的杀伤力。李小龙将出快拳的技巧传授给我，让我的拳既快又有力量，且大大增加了杀伤力。我做了4年拳王阿里的保镖，我后来也将这种

Author George Dillman visiting the DKI-affiliate school in mainland China.

已经63
力，对手立
即在其肩
说：“这就
示迪欧曼
道馆交流
据了解
其中年龄
行为期两
迪欧曼曾
韩回成都
邀请，迪
差武艺。
乔治·迪欧曼是本次活动的组织者，也是国际迪欧曼琉球拳
会到创始
三次与国际
的技术传授给拳王阿里。为了证实迪欧曼身份的真实性，记者
览了迪欧曼留下的网址，上面有他在美国做武术教练方面的
绍，以及与阿里关系的简短介绍。

，我太太
，李小龙一
完了。但
意见：“我只
去的。希望
人就是太客

关

子，很多人
是因为打拳
森病，现在

武术

国武术的人
而不能叫武
术，武术是能自救救旁的，我的拳法就是中国传统拳法，所以
没有见到过
在成都见到的这么多美女，我吃到了全世界最美味的火锅和川菜。”采访结束前，迪欧曼还留言向成都晚报读者问好。

本报记者 李寰 摄影 冯石

CAUTION

The pressure point methods and applications demonstrated in this book are serious self-defense techniques. Many are capable of causing severe bodily harm. The utmost restraint and care must be taken whenever practicing martial arts skills in general, and pressure point techniques in particular.

To receive the maximum benefit from your study, train under the supervision of a qualified instructor of the Dillman Pressure Point Method.

Rules for Safe Pressure Point Practice

1. Train only under a qualified instructor.

2. Do not work on pressure points for more than fifteen minutes per week.

3. When training, do not switch sides. Only strike on one side of the body in any given training session.

4. Do not apply cross-body techniques, that is: do not strike corresponding points on opposite sides of your partner's body.

5. Be sure to learn proper revival techniques.

6. Do not work pressure points on persons with health problems, or people over the age of 40, or people on drugs (legal or otherwise).

7. Use the utmost restraint at all times. It is not necessary to knock someone out cold to see the effect of a pressure point. Usually a light blow is sufficient to demonstrate effectiveness.

TABLE OF CONTENTS

photo by Kim Foreman

Author George Dillman and Muhammad Ali at Ali's Deer Lake training camp in the early 70's. In 1997, Dillman purchased Ali's camp and restored it to pristine condition. It is now the Martial Arts Training Camp.

Gordon Travers.

photo by Kim Foreman

George Dillman, jr., Wally Jay & author George Dillman.

photo by Kim Foreman

Long time friends, and Black Belt Magazine Hall of Fame members, George Dillman & Leo Fong.

Chapter One: Understanding & Interpreting Kata

Kata are prearranged sequences of movements which contain the essential knowledge for mastery of the martial arts. Codified over the centuries, they have been passed down through generations of practitioners to the present. Virtually every martial art includes some form of kata in its training regimen. But, for most practitioners of these beloved and ancient forms, the actual meaning – the combative use of the techniques – is either lost, or grossly misunderstood.

Think of a song. The meaning of a song is stated in the lyrics and expressed in the melody. If the lyrics are sad, the melody is haunting; if the lyrics are noble, the melody is bold. But, what if the lyrics of the song are in a foreign language? Without knowing the meaning of the words, how is it possible to truly comprehend the song?

Similarly, the meaning of kata is in its application for real fighting, the expression of that application is in the physical movements of the form. For most students of the martial arts, kata is like a song whose lyrics have not been explained. They can appreciate its beauty and power. They have a feel for its rhythms and dynamics. They may even catch some vague sense of its purpose, but without understanding the actual application of the techniques, they cannot truly comprehend the fullness of the meaning.

Unfortunately, most karate instructors have not understood the meanings of their own kata, even though they have committed their time and effort to perfecting their performance. Since they can do the kata so well, and since they have found value in the effort, they have decided the question of meaning is not appropriate. They have told their students, "This is traditional, don't ask, don't think too much, just do."

However, for the ancient masters of karate, kata was the very essence of combat because they knew not only the outward form but also the application. The kata was alive for these masters because they saw in their minds the exact application of the movements as they performed them. In this way, mental image and physical performance together insured that the masters were truly able to fight.

This is why the martial artists of old always insisted that kata alone was sufficient, and that competetive sparring was unnecessary. Kata alone was sufficient because they knew what they were doing. But, they had no desire to pass on a precious legacy to those who would have no appreciation of what it truly represented. Karate was the ancient Okinawan secret to surviving with strength, dignity, and the ability to defend oneself and one's family in times of foreign occupation.

The Japanese had controlled and militarily occupied Okinawa from 1609. This was the context in which karate developed. The art was practiced and taught in the utmost secrecy due to the threat of reprisals by armed samurai. In fact, the only reason karate went public in 1903 was because of societal pressures.

In 1891, so the story goes, two young Ryukyu kempo experts, Chomo

Hanashiro (1869-1945) and Kentsu Yabu (1866-1937) – students of Sokon "Bushi" Matsumura (1809-1901), and later of Anko Itosu (1832-1916) – took their army physicals. As this was a time of military expansionism, Japan was vigorously recruiting Okinawan men into the army. The military doctors noticed that, unlike their contemporaries, Hanashiro and Yabu were exceptionally robust. The two credited their kempo training for their health and vigor. This prompted an investigation into whether Ryukyu kempo might be used to improve the quality of Okinawan conscripts.

Around the turn of the century, in response to this interest by the Japanese military, Anko Itosu (who was also one of Matsumura's students) began a program to teach Ryukyu kempo in elementary school. Itosu detailed his plan for teaching Ryukyu kempo tode-jitsu to children in a letter to the Prefectural Education Department. The letter states, in part, "The purpose of tode (another term for Ryukyu kempo) is to make the body hard like stones and iron; hands and feet should used like the points of arrows; hearts should be strong and brave. If children were to practice tode from elementary-school days, they would be well prepared for military service... This will be a great asset to our militaristic society."

Since, however, kempo was considered far too hazardous for children, Itosu modified the art so that they could not hurt each other. Some of these modifications involved changing the manner in which certain techniques were performed so that they could cause no injury -- in effect blunting the weapons. Itosu also deleted all teaching of the core methods of Ryukyu kempo, removing both kyusho-jitsu and tuite-jitsu from the curriculum. Instead, he taught the children to punch and block.

After WW II the Americans became the occupying political and military presence. The American invasion, like all invasions, had resulted in the deaths of many non-combatants. Certainly the Okinawan populace would be wary of such people. Not only that, but unwittingly, American forces had committed serious cultural crimes. For example, many of the Okinawan mausoleums were destroyed by U.S. personnel who mistook them for military bunkers. Think of how such desecration of tombs would be understood by a people who practice veneration of their ancestors!

But, the American sevice personal were far from home, in a strange culture, and looking for some meaningful practice. So, they began to practice Ryukyu kempo, which, by that time, had come to be generally known as karate. Because times were hard for the Okinawan people, it was a great financial boon if one had enough expertise in karate to charge money and teach the G.I.s. But it would be naive to assume that knowledgeable Okinawan masters gladly exchanged their most treasured secrets for a few American dollars, especially when the Americans happily forked over the cash for far less. Because of the nature of kata, it was a simple matter to teach the outward form of karate, and so, appear to be sharing a great treasure with American students, while withholding the hidden, but essential, meaning. But the Americans happily paid, and happily learned the kata sequences, imagining that somehow, they were learning deep and ancient secrets. And, in a way, they were. Contained in the old kata are the secrets of presure point fighting, secrets so treasured, that even to this day there are masters who go to their graves, without ever finding a student they consider worthy of teaching.

Concerned about the loss of such important knowledge, we have devoted ourselves to the recovery, preservation and dissemination of this treasured knowledge. And because of the openness of a few willing teachers who did not want these secrets to become lost, and our determined application of the principles they revealed, we have recovered the meaning of kata. In short, kata contains the information of kyusho-jitsu, mapping out the location and application, angle and direction for pressure points combat.

We can easily detail actual combative applications for kata movements (called *bunkai*, which literally means “breakdown”). But, if all you do is try to remember our examples, you will never be a true martial artist, you will only be a martial mimic. What is important is for you to understand the principles at work, so that you can apply those principles and all kinds of settings. This is a sound truth of martial arts: If you can perform one technique, you have one technique; if you understand the principles which underly one technique, you have 1,000 techniques. So, before we will show you any kata, and any explanations for kata movements, we will explain the principles of interpretation, the principles of pressure point methods, and, in the appendix, advanced principles of stance energetics.

PRINCIPLES OF KATA INTERPRETATION

1. Kata must be interpreted against real-world attacks.

When kata is explained in most martial arts schools, it is explained as a series of responses to completely ridiculous situations. For example, kata movements are repeatedly interpreted as defending against a lunge punch. The lunge punch involves stepping forward boldly into a front stance, and performing a straight punch with the lead hand. When done in class, one lunge punch can cover a large distance. So, the typical kata explanation involves one student charging at another with a punch that starts from 6 to 9 feet away. However, in the real world no one initiates a punch in this manner. So, no matter how good one becomes at defending against a lunge punch, all that practice is pointless because you will never be attacked that way.

To make sense of kata, the attacks must first be real. So, how do people attack in real life? One common form of attack is a sucker punch, which is usually a right cross, hook or haymaker. Another tactic is to grab the opponent with the one hand (to stabilize the target) and pummel him with the other. Attackers will frequently grab the lapel with one or two hands, or push and shove an opponent with one or two hands. If the intended victim is armed, it will be common to see the wrists and forearms being grabbed (to prevent the drawing of a weapon).

Just as empty hand attacks must be realistic, so too must weapon attacks. It is very typical in training to see the attacker step forward and stab with a knife as if performing a fencer's thrust. But in actual knife attacks, the assailant will usually slide in with his weak side forward, grab hold of the opponent with his empty hand, and then stab with the knife. The same can be seen in stick attacks. The attacker will generally try to grab the opponent with his free hand while clubbing away with the stick. All of this means that the person who wishes to truly understand kata must seek to become a student of the most common types of assaults. Only with a realistic attack, can one begin to seek for truly practical applications.

2. The movements of kata do not contain any blocks.

A large number of traditional martial arts movements are taught as methods for blocking this or that. However, if you are walking down the street and somebody throws a ball at your head, you will not perform an upward block, or a knife hand block. You will simply throw your hands up in a spontaneous warding-off gesture before you have had time to think. Blocking is an entirely natural reflex, so there is no point in learning "how" to block. (However, training in defensive skills can improve your reaction time, and reduce the delay between your initial reflex and your first conscious action.)

The main problem with interpreting any kata movement as a block is that the act of blocking does nothing to progress the fight toward a favorable conclusion for you. The opponent grabs you and throws a punch at your head, you block his punch, so he just winds up and punches again. All blocking does is reset the game. But, an important rule of strategy is, *win the fight with your first move!* You should seek to make your victory a foregone conclusion with the very first thing you do in response to an attack.

The movements in kata need to be interpreted as ways of immediately controlling the opponent and rendering him harmless before you finish him off. (This, by the way, creates the possibility for ethical action in the midst of self-defense. If you have neutralized an attacker, you will have the opportunity to choose an appropriate and suitable response.)

3. Kata is completely practical.

The first rule of violent encounters is this, *under stress you regress.* Part of what this means is that you lose fine motor control during stressful situations. So, it follows that a complicated and intricate breakdown of the kata will probably fail in the real world. Therefore, kata application must first be clearly workable solutions. One of the ways to scrutinize the practicality of any technique is to ask, "How badly must I screw this up before it doesn't work?" A good technique adheres to this concept: when done well it's amazing, and when done poorly it's still pretty good. This is the tactical quality called **redundancy**.

Now, it is important to point out that the purpose of training is to enable a person to perform high skill tasks under stress. So, the practice of increasingly complex and intricate kata interpretations as a means of developing oneself as a martial artist is very valuable – provided the advanced skills are built on a foundation of simple and fool-proof methods. This is especially important because, *under stress you regress*, also means that you will regress to what you learned first, your foundation and base. It you tried to learn useless "traditional" block and counter applications, that is what you will attempt – and fail at – in a real-world encounter. If, however, your base, your foundational techniques and understandings, are practical and effective, simple and reliable, the stress of a violent encounter will cause you to regress to something that works.

4. Many movements in kata are informational.

In many places, kata reveals some important information about a technique. In other words, the kata tells you something you need to know, rather than rehearsing the movement you need to perform. Two of the most prominent examples of this are the **mapping rule** and the **direction = orientation rule**.

In this movement from Pinan Shodan, the left hand indicates the H-2/*Qingling* point on the right arm.

Here the same movement is interpreted as a palm strike to point H-2/*Qingling* on the opponent's right arm. This follows the **mapping rule** of kata analysis.

The **mapping rule** states that any movement which involves you pointing towards or touching some part of your own anatomy can be interpreted as "mapping out" your target. There are many examples of these movements, and one can be found in the kata Pinan Shodan. A right hand strike is performed with the fingertips of the left hand lightly touching the extended right arm at pressure point H-2/*Qingling*. Following the mapping rule, this move can be interpreted as indicating a strike to the opponent's H-2/*Qingling*.

Key to the interpretation of mapping movements is the understanding that the kata does not only show which point to attack, it also shows the correct angle required to effectively activate that point. In the example from Pinan Shodan, the left hand is placed at a 90° angle to the pressure point – the correct angle for attacking H-2/*Qingling*.

The **direction = orientation rule** is about the meaning of various angles of movement. Kata steps generally follow the 8 compass points. In the typical interpretation of kata, the performer is pictured as wandering through a field of opponents, moving to meet attacks coming from varying directions. However, for this to have any basis in reality, the martial artist would need the psychic ability to anticipate attacks from impossible angles.

The majority of real-world confrontations come from an opponent standing directly in front of their intended victim, and so, effective bunkai interprets the attacks accordingly. As a result, the angle of a movement in the kata does not represent the direction from which an attack originates. It reveals the orientation that the defender must attain in relation to the attacker for a given response to work effectively. So, a movement along a 45° angle in the kata is interpreted to mean that one must move to the attacker's diagonal when applying the technique.

4. The technique lies between the postures.

When looking at photos of kata in a book, one sees a series of postures.

In this movement from Naihanchi Shodan, a strike with the right fist is performed on a diagonal.

Here the movement is for striking the opponent under the ear at TW-17/*Yifeng*. In order to strike the point properly, the defender must be on the diagonal with respect to the attacker. This follows the **direction = orientation rule**.

These are not the techniques of the kata. The techniques are what happens between the postures. When a final position has been reached, the technique is long over.

Failure to understand this concept will lead to poor kata interpretation. What will generally occur is that kata will be interpreted with the idea that the opponent is somehow engaged at the end of the movement, at the point of the posture. In fact, the opponent is engaged in the middle of the movement, on the way to the posture. An example of this is a movement from Naihanchi Nidan which involves performing a left cross-over step, while bringing the fists up in front of the chest.

In application, the step is not a step, but the follow-through of a low kicking movement aimed to a pressure point just above and inside the attacker's ankle. Similarly, the final hand position is where the fists end up after hitting through the attacker's rib cage. In the actual application of this movement, one may never actually reach the final kata posture, because of the presence of the opponent's body between the fists.

In Naihanchi Nidan, one performs a left cross-step, while bringing the fists up in front of the chest.

In practical application, the left foot kicks Sp-6/*Sanyinjiao* during the cross step, and the fists strike Sp-21/*Dabao* as they move up toward the chest. This is an illustration the principle that **the technique occurs between the postures**.

5. There is more than one correct way to interpret a movement, so there is more than one correct way to perform a kata.

One of the most difficult ideas for many martial artists to comprehend is that there is more than one legitimate way of performing any given move or any given kata. Many people want a single, uniform method, but this is simply not practical.

Consider what it would mean if there was only one way to perform a certain technique. It would mean that particular technique could only be used in a single way. And so, it would be a useless technique unless an assailant just happened to attack in the exact manner required for that particular move. But, if a movement can be interpreted any number of ways, then the movement becomes very useful and effective. However, performance of the kata will be altered by whatever particular interpretation is being envisioned at the time. This means that the performance of kata necessarily changes in a manner consistent with the interpretation given.

Still, many people ask, "What is the correct way to perform the kata?' To this we counter, "Do you have a practical and effective interpretation for what you are doing?" If the answer is, "No," we respond, "Then what difference does it make how you do the kata, since you don't know what you're doing?"

However, if the answer is, "Yes," we respond, "Then what difference does it make how you do the kata, since you are doing something truly effective and practical?" As a result, we hold to a performance standard for any given kata which accommodates a great degree of individual variation, and only broadly represents some accepted (one might say, "orthodox") method of practice. Our primary criteria is that the performance must be based on demonstrably sound bunkai.

Since the goal of training is freedom and spontaneity, we resist any attempt to define the "correct" bunkai, insisting only that bunkai adhere to these sound principles of effectiveness: a) kata gives good answers to common and specific real-world self-defense situations; b) those answers reveal principles which are transferable to a wide variety of situations; and c) every element in the kata is there for a reason.

KATA TRAINING

An old piece of wisdom handed down from the masters of old, which never made sense, is this: when performing a kata, always visualize the opponent. But, what good did it do to visualize an opponent when the interpretations of the kata movements were so completely useless? But, with proper understanding of the kata, visualization not only makes sense, it is absolutely essential. Kata is not primarily a physical exercise; it is primarily a mental one. Through the process of visualizing the exact location of pressure points, and the proper method of activation (including angle and direction) the mind is trained to instantly and accurately respond. The physical actions of the kata close the loop, uniting body and mind in the process of rehearsing and ingraining real combat skills.

It is also important to work with a partner, practicing the various applications. This allows one to get a tactile sense of how it feels to apply a technique, and this is added to the visualization process. Obviously, working with a partner is a good method of insuring that the applications will really work. However, we have found that by visualization alone we are able to develop and use new techniques effectively the first time we try them on someone. The old masters were right when they insisted that kata training -- proper and complete kata training -- was all that was necessary.

It is important to always bear in mind this important reality: If you are attacked, your teacher is not going to miraculously appear and fight for you. As a result you are ultimately responsible for your own martial art. And this means that you are ultimately responsible for your own interpretation of the kata you practice. Now, this does not mean that you should ignore good applications which are shared with you by others in some vain belief that you ought to think up something better. What it means is that, ultimately, you are responsible for insuring that the applications which you envision during solo performance, and practice in partner training, are applications which make sense to you and which you yourself can confidently perform under stress. This is part of how you can take responsibility for your own martial art.

The kata performance and interpretations which we present in these pages are intended to assist you as you explore your own understandings. Some of these interpretations will work well for you and they can become yours. Others will seem impractical for you and you can ignore them. And some (and this is the best outcome) will trigger an idea which will lead to you discovering something for yourself.

Attendees at the Martial Arts Training Camps, October, 2004.

photo by Chris Thomas

Dusty Seale demonstrating kata bunkai.

Author Chris Thomas teaching pressure point fighting in Germany.

Photo by Wendy Countryman

Chapter Two: Pressure Point Theory

Principles, Location, & Usage

Since Asian martial arts are inseparably bound to Asian culture, it is to be expected that the arts would conform, both superficially and substantively with the Asian world view. Arts with strong roots in taoist thinking (tai chi, hsing-i, etc.) are characterized by the concepts of yin and yang, the five elements and so on. Among arts of buddhist origin (e.g. shaolin-chuan) we find buddhist concepts and elements. In the same way, it is to be expected that kyusho-jitsu, or pressure point combat, would be based on eastern concepts. If this art had developed in the west we would expect nerve plexii and baro-receptors, motor-nerve points and neural pathways to be the descriptive language employed. Since this is an Asian art, and the primary medical practice in that part of the world historically is acupuncture, we find, as expected, that acupuncture terminology and concepts form the theoretical basis for kyusho-jitsu.

Traditional eastern medicine, unlike modern western medicine, is based on clinical observation, rather than controlled experimentation. The Asian clinicians carefully observed the results of certain actions, but did not experiment to determine the mechanisms at work. Instead, they formed theories about what was happening using concepts from their philosophical cosmology -- a cosmology based on a unity (the One, or the Tao) which becomes the duality (Yin and Yang), which in turn generates the five fundamental elements (Earth, Metal, Water, Wood, Fire).

This means that the traditional explanation for a given effect of acupuncture or kyusho-jitsu may or may not express concepts which are scientifically meaningful. There may be no western equivalent for the acupuncture interpretations. For example, acupuncture anesthesia is explained as energy flow and the interaction of the five elements. But, in western thinking anesthesia effect is understood as the release of endogenous morphine (endorphines) in the brain as a result of needling.

However, from our perspective as martial artists, what is important is the outcome which we achieve. We are interested in results, even if we do not have western scientific language to explain the mechanisms which produce those results. In our search for deeper interpretations and applications of classical movements, it is not so important whether "Fire" actually melts "Metal" (see below). What is important is that this general framework can predict what will happen when we perform some particular technique, and can guide us in successfully discovering deeper meanings for techniques.

By using the language and principles of acupuncture as the theoretical basis for our study, we are better able to understand what the founders of our method intended in their kata. It isn't important for our purposes if the acupuncture explanation for an event is meaningful to western science, so long as the principle provides an algorithm for successfully solving combative and strategic problems – in other words, that it works. And our experience shows that it does work.

In order to perform a kyusho-jitsu technique it is only necessary to know the proper point combination and the proper angle and direction. After adequate practice of kata (with visualization) and bunkai, these techniques can successfully be applied. However, to be better able to analyze kata in order to gain deeper insights into the art and develop additional pressure point techniques, one should become familiar with the general principles of acupuncture and how those principles relate to combat.

The Eastern medical viewpoint is a holistic one. The body is understood as a wholly interactive, interrelated and integrated organism. The health of each part of the body depends on the wellness of the whole. In fact, health is defined as the proper balance of intrinsic energy, or life force.

This energy, called *ki* in Japanese and Korean, and *qi (chi)* in Chinese, flows through the body along pathways or channels called meridians. Along the meridians are discreet points which serve as gateways or valves by which the flow of energy can be controlled. These points are known as tsubo (a shiatsu term which roughly means "pressure point") or kyusho (which roughly means "vulnerable point").

The healer manipulates these points with fingertip pressure (shiatsu) or needles (acupuncture) in an effort to restore and maintain a proper balance of energy in the body. The kyusho-jitsu exponent attacks these points in order to disrupt the balance of energy.

There are 361 "regular" points which are scattered across 14 meridian channels. There are also some 391 "extraordinary" points which have been identified, but which are not as widely used in medicine. The meridians upon which the points are found are related to the various organs of the body. These associations are determined through clinical observation that stimulating the points on a particular meridian had a noticeable effect on the corresponding organ.

Meridians are also classified in two other ways. In oriental thinking there are two polar opposites which together make-up all things. These are the yin and the yang, the negative and positive, the spiritual and substantial, the female and male. Each channel is either yin or yang, according to its energy flow. Also, in oriental philosophy there are five elements which describe the physical characteristics of all things. These elements are Earth, Metal, Water, Wood, and Fire, and each meridian is characterized by one of these elements.

Therefore, to understand kyusho-jitsu it is necessary to be generally familiar with the meridians (and know four important features of each: 1. To what organ does it relate? 2. What is its polarity, yin or yang? 3. What element characterizes it? 4. Where is each meridian located?). And, obviously, it is necessary to know the pressure points themselves (understanding location, angle of attack, mode of activation, and special characteristics). Finally, it is necessary to know the 5 rules of point selection (1. Attack along the meridian; 2. Attack yin and yang; 3. Attack in accordance with the diurnal cycle; 4. Attack in the cycle of destruction; 5. Rule of the special points.)

THE MERIDIANS

There are 14 primary meridians. 12 of them are bilateral, meaning that they are mirrored on the right and left sides of the body. The other two are along the centerline, front and back. The 12 bilateral meridians are related to the organs of the body, though the concept of *organ* in acupuncture includes more than the anatomical part we think of as *organ* in western medicine. And, in the case of the Triple Warmer meridian, the meaning of *organ* in acupuncture does not have an equivalent in western thinking.

LUNG MERIDIAN (L) The Lung Meridian begins at the upper corner of the chest and proceeds down the inner aspect of the arm on the thumb side, ending in the tip of the thumb. It is a yin meridian with 11 points. Its element is Metal.

LARGE INTESTINE MERIDIAN (LI) The Large Intestine Meridian begins at the tip of the index finger and travels up the outer aspect of the arm on the thumb side, across the shoulders and the neck to end at the corner of the nose. It is a yang meridian with 20 points. Its element is Metal. In some acupuncture books, this meridian is designated *Colon.*

STOMACH (S) The Stomach Meridian begins directly under the eye and proceeds down the neck, torso, the outside of the leg, ending at the tip of the second toe. It is a yang meridian with 45 points. Its element is Earth.

SPLEEN (Sp) The Spleen Meridian originates at the tip of the big toe and moves upward along the inside of the leg and up to the torso to end at the side of the body. It is a yin meridian with 21 points, and its element is Earth. In some acupuncture books, this meridian is designated *Spleen/Pancreas.*

HEART (H) The Heart meridian starts in the armpit and travels down the inside of the arm on the little finger side, terminating at the tip of the little finger. It is a yin meridian with 9 points, and its element is Fire.

SMALL INTESTINE (SI) The Small Intestine Meridian begins at the tip of the little finger and runs up the outer aspect of the arm on the little finger side, across the shoulder and onto the side of the head, where it ends at the ear. It is a yang meridian, having 19 points, and its element is Fire.

BLADDER (B) The Bladder Meridian originates at the inner corner of the eye, moves up over the head, then down the back in two lines running parallel to the spine. It then follows down the back of the leg and terminates at the little toe. It is a yang meridian with 67 points, and its element is Water. In some acupuncture books, this meridian is designated *Urinary Bladder.*

KIDNEY (K) The Kidney Meridian begins in the sole of the foot, and travels up the inside of the leg, past the genitals and up the torso just beside the mid-line, to terminate just below the collar bone. It is a yin meridian with 27 points and its element is Water.

PERICARDIUM (P) The Pericardium Meridian begins on the chest, near the nipple, from there it flows up to the shoulder, then down the inside of the arm to end at the tip of the middle finger. It is a yin meridian with 9 points. Its element is Fire. In some acupuncture books, this meridian is designated *Governor of the Heart.*

TRIPLE WARMER (TW) The Triple Warmer meridian originates at the tip of the ring (fourth) finger, and follows the back of the arm along the mid-line, up to the shoulder. It continues across the back surface of the shoulder, then onto the head, where it flows around the border of the ear to end at the temple. It is a yang meridian with 23 points, and its element is Fire. In some acupuncture books, this meridian is variously designated *Triple Burner, Triple Heater, Triple Energizer, The Three Fires, Sanjiao, Thyroid, Circulation/Sex.*

GALL BLADDER (GB) The Gall Bladder meridian begins at the outer corner of the eye, then follows a zig-zag route around the ear, back to the forehead, across the top of the head and down the rear side of the neck. From there it travels down the side of the body to end at the tip of the fourth toe. It is a yang meridian with 44 points and its element is Wood.

LIVER (Li) The Liver meridian begins at the tip of the big toe, and follows upward along the inside of the leg, and onto the abdomen to terminate at the border of the rib cage. It is a yin meridian with 14 points. Its element is Wood.

CONCEPTION (C) The two centerline meridians (Conception and Governor) are not related to any specific organ, but are important in the regulation of ki. The Conception Meridian begins in the crotch, midway between the anus and the scrotum on men, and midway between the anus and the commisura labiorum on women. It travels up the front of the body, along the centerline to end just below the lower lip. This meridian is the primary source line of yin-ki (yin energy) and all yin-meridians are related to it. The Conception channel has 24 points. In some acupuncture books, this meridian is designated *Ren.*

GOVERNOR (G) The Governor meridian begins at the tip of tail-bone and travels upward along the spine, over the head to terminate inside the top lip. This meridian is the "governor" of yang-ki (yang energy) and all yang meridians are related to it. The Governor channel has 28 points. In some acupuncture books, this meridian is designated *Du.*

Meridian	*Alarm Point*
Lung	L-1/Zhongfu
Large Intestine	St-25/Tianshu
Stomach	Co-12/Zhongwan
Spleen	Li-13/Zhangmen
Heart	Co-14/Juque
Small Intestine	Co-4/Guanyuan
Bladder	Co-3/Zhongji
Kidney	GB-25/Jingmen
Pericardium	Co-17/Shanzhong
Triple Warmer	Co-5/Shimen
Gall Bladder	GB-24/Riyue
Liver	Li-14/Qimen

The Special Points include Alarm, Associated and Meeting points, as well as individual points with unique functions, and a number of non-meridian points.

Meridian	*Associated Point*
Lung	B-13/Feishu
Large Intestine	B-25/Dachangshu
Stomach	B-21/Weishu
Spleen	B-20/Pishu
Heart	B-15/Xinshu
Small Intestine	B-27/Xiaochangshu
Bladder	B-28/Pangguangshu
Kidney	B-23/Shenshu
Pericardium	B-14/Jueyinshu
Triple Warmer	B-22/Sanjiaoshu
Gall Bladder	B-19/Danshu
Liver	B-18/Ganshu

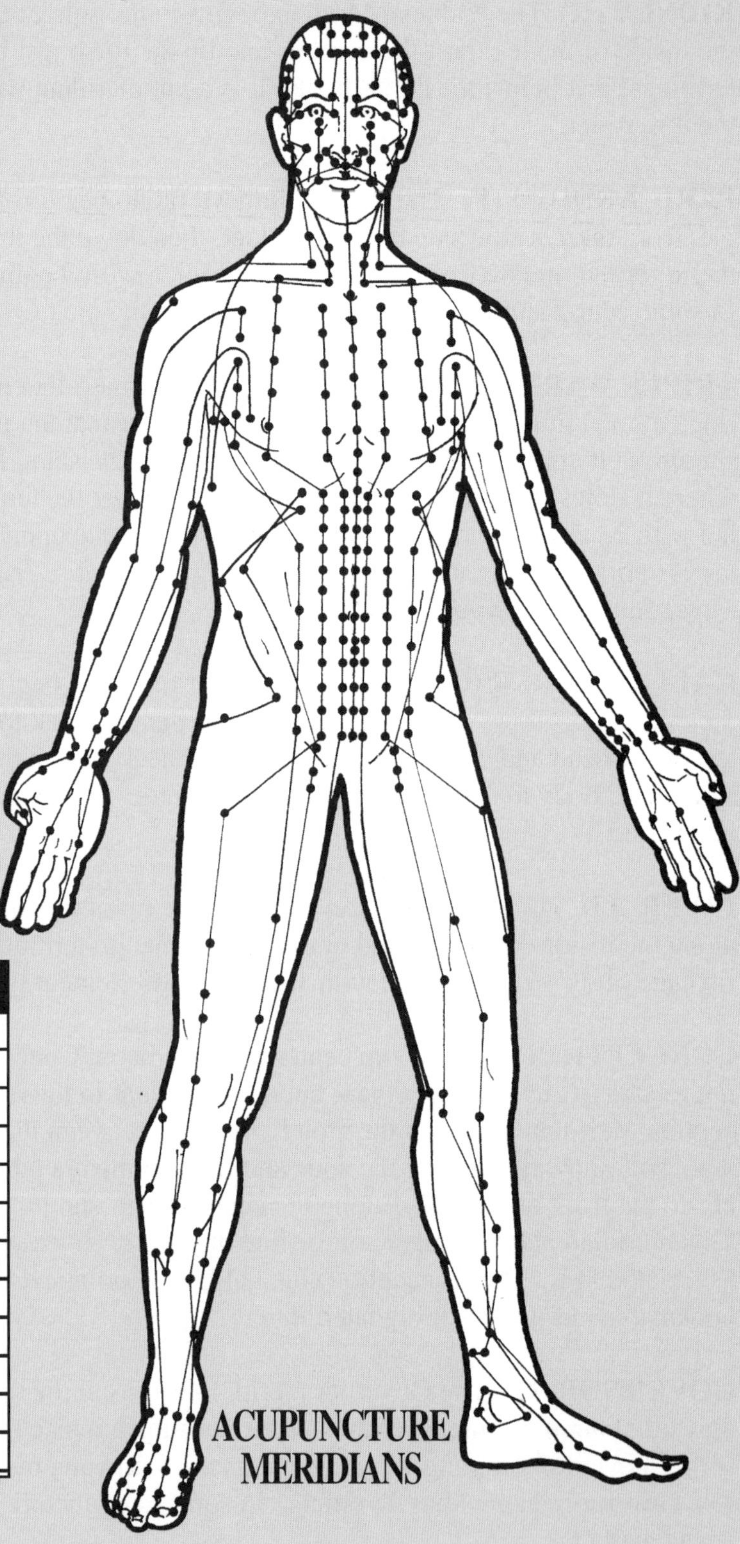

ACUPUNCTURE MERIDIANS

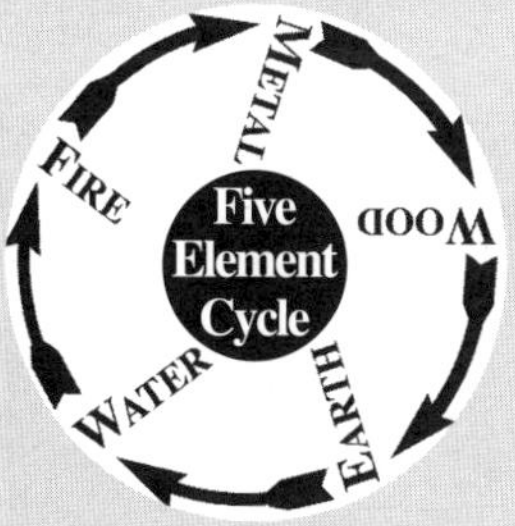

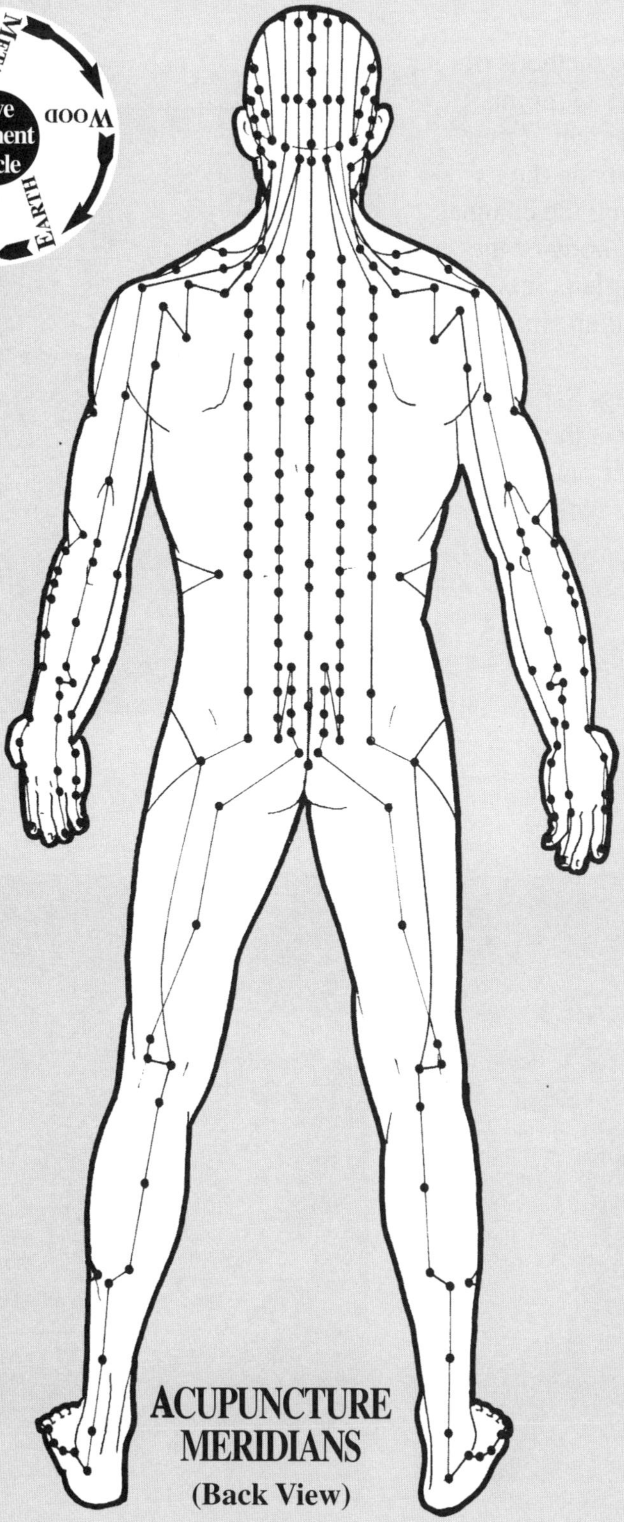

ACUPUNCTURE MERIDIANS
(Back View)

Channel	Element
Lung	Metal
Large Intestine	
Stomach	Earth
Spleen	
Heart	Fire
Small Intestine	
Bladder	Water
Kidney	
Pericardium	Fire
Triple Warmer	
Gall Bladder	Wood
Liver	

Yang Channels	Yin Channels
Large Intestine	Lung
Stomach	Spleen
Small Intestine	Heart
Bladder	Kidney
Triple Warmer	Pericardium
Gall Bladder	Liver
Governor	Conception

DIURNAL CYCLE

Lung
Large Intestine
Stomach
Spleen
Heart
Small Intestine
Bladder
Kidney
Pericardium
Triple Warmer
Gall Bladder
Liver
Lung

RULE OF THE MERIDIAN

One of the most basic methods of kyusho-jitsu is to attack points along any particular meridian. Often, this will begin with points on the extremities, then move along the channel to finish at points on the body or the head. Alternately, multiple points can be attacked on one meridian simultaneously.

For example, press S-12/*Quepen* and S-4/*Dicang* at the same time to produce a level of pain which exceeds what is possible with either point alone (1,2).

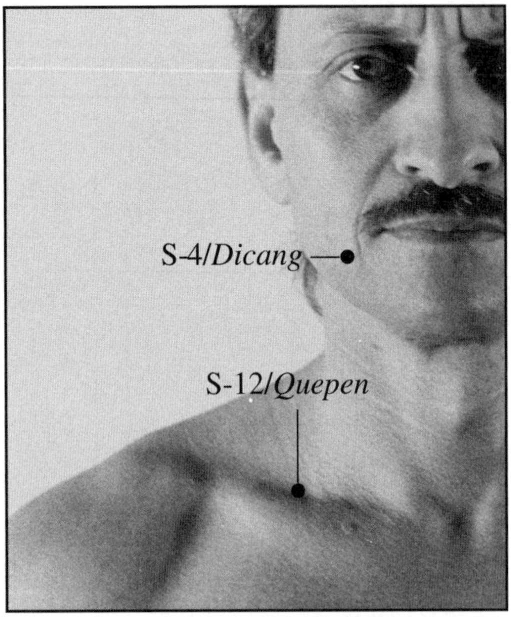

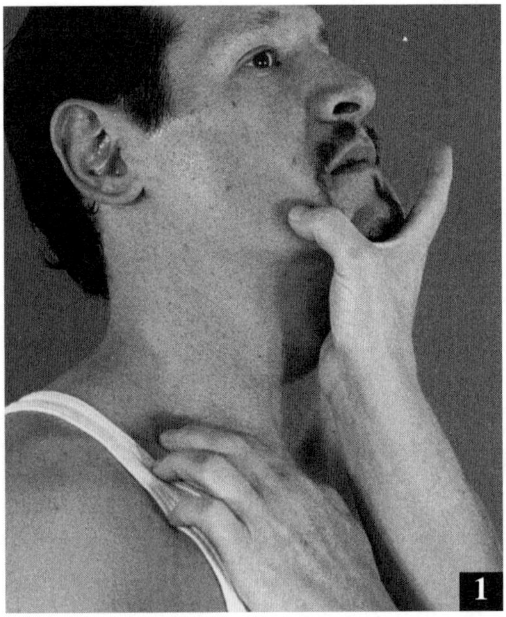
1

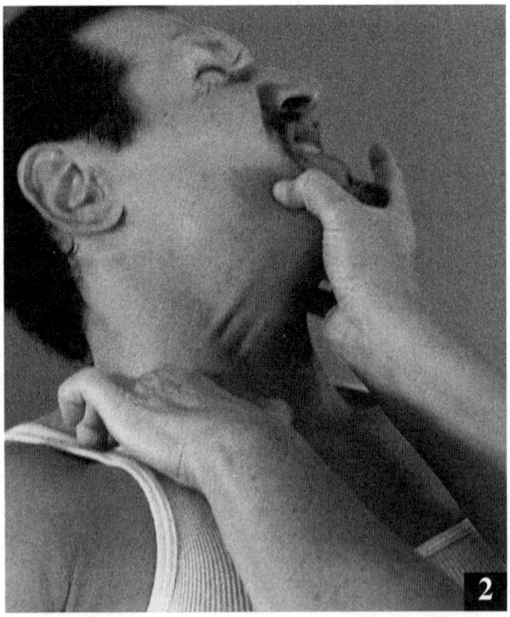
2

RULE OF YIN AND YANG

Each meridian is either yin or yang, depending on the direction of the energy flow. Since yin and yang are intended to coexist in balance and harmony, it is clear that each yin must have a balancing yang. In acupuncture this balance of yin and yang is quite specific. All meridians are paired in circuits, which might be compared to electrical wiring. There is a positive and a negative wire and both are needed for the electric current to flow. For example energy flows down the inside of the arm to the tip of the little finger in the heart channel, then it flows up from the little finger on the outside of the arm along the Small Intestine meridian. These circuits are known in healing as the *feng-shu* relationship.

In kyusho-jitsu, this circuit can be used in ways similar to the rule of the meridians. Rather than striking along one single meridian, it is possible to use two meridians in a circuit. Striking along the Lung channel effects the Large Intestine line, and vice-versa. For example, manipulating the index finger affects the Large Intestine (yang) meridian (especially through LI-3/*Sanjian*). The Lung is the corresponding yin organ. So, while manipulating the index finger, attack with a punch to L-1/*Zhongfu*, the first point on the Lung channel.

Attacking yin and yang can also be understood in a more general manner. The front of the body can be designated as yin, the back as yang. The left side is yin, the right yang (for males, the opposite for female). above the waist is yang, below the waist is yin. This means that pressure point techniques which cross the body -- front to back, side to side, top to bottom, or diagonally, as in right upper back to left lower front -- are applying the yin/yang principle.

RULE OF THE DIURNAL CYCLE

One aspect of pressure point fighting most people have encountered is the principle of the Diurnal Cycle, or "time of day." Many old accounts of pressure point techniques insist that points must be attacked at certain times in order to be effective. The theory is that certain targets are especially vulnerable to attack during a specific zodiac-hour (a zodiac hour is 2 hours by a western clock) of the day. For example, the document the *Bubishi* contains a set of 12 drawings depicting pressure points to attack during each zodiac- hour.

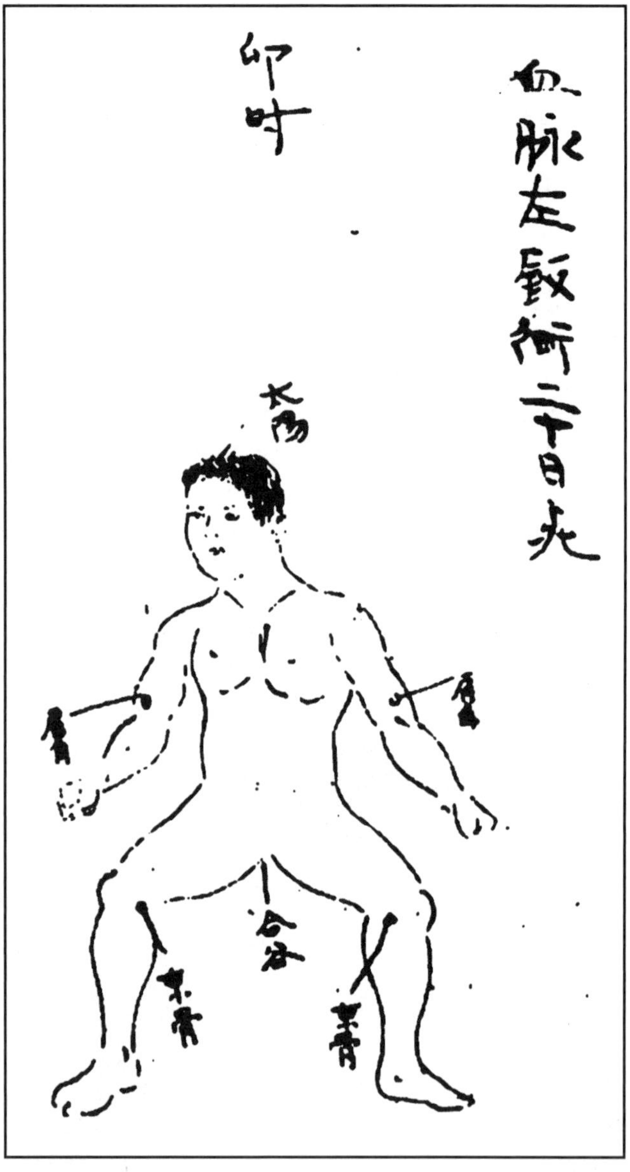

This theory is supported in Oriental medicine, where it is said that energy flows through the body from meridian to meridian, completing one cycle every day. Each meridian is particularly active during a particular zodiac-hour. There is evidence for this view in western medicine as well. Chrono-biology is the study of circadian rhythms. Research in this field has shown that the majority of asthma attacks take place between 3:00 and 5:00 a.m., the precise zodiac-hour the Lung meridian is most active. Interestingly, however, the majority of heart attacks take place between 9:00 and 11:00 a.m., the zodiac-hour immediately preceding the active time for the Heart meridian.

This apparent discrepancy suggests a theory of energy flow: namely that the zodiac-hour of activity in a meridian is preceded by a zodiac-hour of depressed energy in that meridian. The mental picture is that there is a wave of energy flowing through the body. As in the ocean, the water recedes before the wave crashes. However, there are other theories about how energy circulates through the body.

One is that the flow of energy is like the tide. High tide corresponds to the zodiac-hour of activity, low tide is twelve hours (six zodiac-hours) later. Another theory is that the zodiac-hour of fullness in a meridian is followed by a period of emptiness. The problem is that there has been (at least as far as we are aware) no comprehensive research to accurately measure this phenomenon.

Even if we did know exactly how energy flows through the body, we would be left with one fundamental problem: to use time of day techniques requires knowing what time it is. In other words, a martial artist would need to be constantly looking at a clock and thinking, "Ok, now it's the hour of the Rat, so I want to attack the Gall Bladder meridian in particular." Clearly, this is impractical. So, kyusho-jitsu employs a much simpler method.

Since energy flows through the body continuously, we simply "follow the *ki*." In other words, we would follow an attack to the Large Intestine meridian with an attack to the Stomach meridian, and an attack to the Triple Warmer meridian is followed by an attack to the Gall Bladder meridian. So, while it is true that the effects are more dramatic on specific meridians at specific times, the body's natural current of energy can be utilized throughout the day, without having to know the exact time.

Channel	Zodiac-Hour	Clock Time
Lung	Tiger	3 a.m. - 5 a.m.
Large Intestine	Rabbit	5 a.m. - 7 a.m.
Stomach	Dragon	7 a.m. - 9 a.m.
Spleen	Snake	9 a.m. - 11 a.m.
Heart	Horse	11 a.m. - 1 p.m.
Small Intestine	Ram	1 p.m. - 3 p.m.
Bladder	Monkey	3 p.m. - 5 p.m.
Kidney	Rooster	5 p.m. - 7 p.m.
Pericardium	Dog	7 p.m. - 9 p.m.
Triple Warmer	Boar	9 p.m. - 11 p.m.
Gall Bladder	Rat	11 p.m. - 1 a.m
Liver	Ox	1 a.m. - 3 a.m.

RULE OF THE DIURNAL CYCLE (cont.)

1-3. When an opponent grabs your lapels, a strike against LI-10/*Shousanli* will bring his head forward in such a manner that the point S-5/*Daying* along the jaw becomes vulnerable.

NOTE: Stomach meridian follows Large Intestine in the diurnal cycle.

4-7. When performing an armbar, strike TW-12/*Xiaoluo*, which causes the opponent's head to turn, exposing GB-20/*Fengchi* to a palm strike.

NOTE: Gall Bladder meridian follows Triple Warmer in the diurnal cycle.

2

3

6

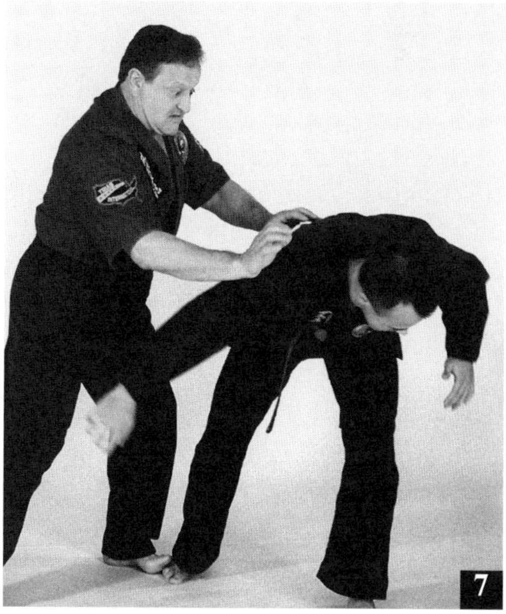
7

RULE OF THE CYCLE OF DESTRUCTION

In oriental thought, everything begins as a void (the One) which becomes a singularity (the Tao), which differentiates into two (yin/yang) which then becomes five elements, which then give rise to the "myriad of things." The five elements are Fire, Earth, Metal, Water, Wood. Since these "elements" are regarded as essential and primordial, they are often used as a way of describing how things interrelate. Each of the twelve bilateral organ related meridians is assigned one of the five elements. So, for example, the Stomach Meridian is said to be Earth, while the Gall Bladder Meridian is designated as Wood.

Now "Earth" and "Wood" should not be taken literally. This language is used to describe relationships rather than essence. Stomach isn't actually Earth, and Gall Bladder isn't actually Wood, but there is a relationship between them which is characterized by the interaction of Earth and Wood. There are two primary relationships which the elements describe – the first is called the Cycle of Creation, and the second is called the Cycle of Destruction. The cycle of creation is as follows: Fire *creates* Earth (think of the dirty ashes of a camp fire); Earth *creates* Metal (visualize iron "clinkers" found in the cold ashes of the fire); Metal *creates* Water (think of condensation on a metal container); Water *creates* Wood (visualize rain in a forest); Wood *creates* Fire (think of burning logs in camp fire).

The cycle of destruction is as follows: Fire *destroys* Metal (imagine metal melting in a furnace); Metal *destroys* Wood (picture an ax chopping through a log); Wood *destroys* Earth (think of the roots of a tree penetrating into the ground); Earth *destroys* Water (visualize an earthen dam); Water *destroys* Fire (as water quenches the blaze).

The concept of Creation is also referred to in acupuncture as "tonification." The idea is that stimulating a point on, say, a Wood meridian (such as Gall Bladder), will increase the activity and level of energy (*ki* or *chi/qi*) in a Fire meridian (such as Heart). In therapeutic application, this approach is applied if a meridian is underfunctioning. Destruction is also called "sedation." In this case, stimulating a point on a Wood meridian, such as Gall Bladder, will decrease the energetic level of an Earth meridian like Stomach. This would be used if a meridian is over-functioning. It is this destructive cycle which is extensively applied in pressure point fighting. The theory is that after striking a point on one meridian, one should follow up by striking a point on a meridian which has been adversely affected (sedated).

In kyusho-jitsu, the cycle of destruction is used against the opponent and the cycle of creation is used within one's self (for more on using the cycle of creation, see the appendix on stances and in particular the section on transmutation of stance).

ELEMENTAL CYCLES OF CREATION & DESTRUCTION

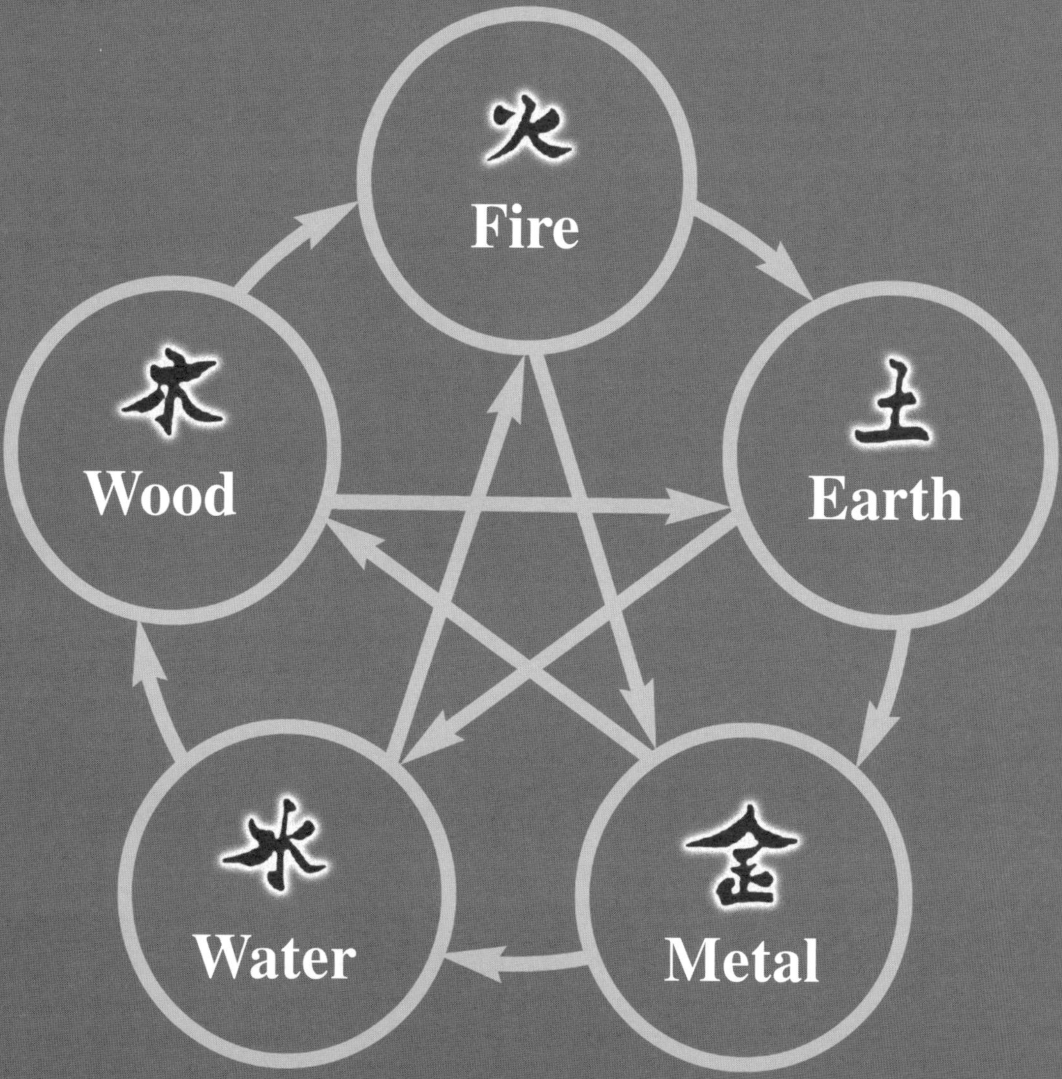

Circular arrows indicate the cycle of creation.
Straight arrows indicate the cycle of destruction.

RULE OF THE CYCLE OF DESTRUCTION (cont.)

1. An attacker grabs your lapel with his right hand.

2. With your right hand strike the attacker near the wrist at L-7/*Lieque*, while cutting across the opponent's forearm at the "Triple Warmer Triangle" (see below about point cluster TW-6/*Zhigou,* TW-7/*Huizong,* TW-8/*Sanyangluo).*

4-6. Trap the attacker's right arm against your body with your left forearm, as you strike him with your right hand, hitting GB-20/*Fengchi* at the back of his head.

NOTE: Fire (Triple Warmer) weakens Metal (Lung). This in turn weakens and exposes Wood (Gall Bladder).

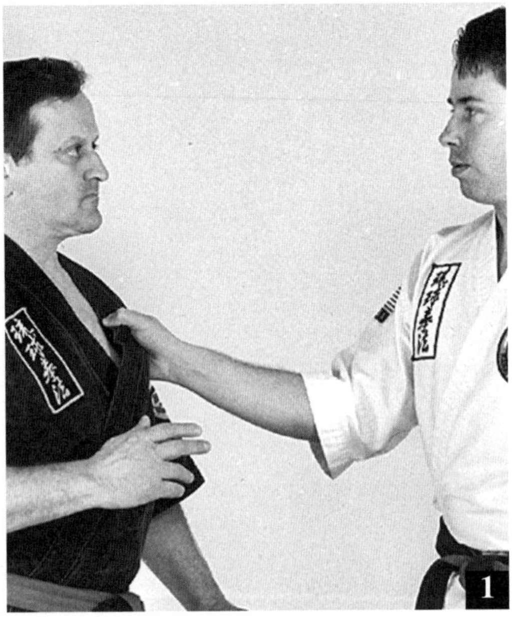

1

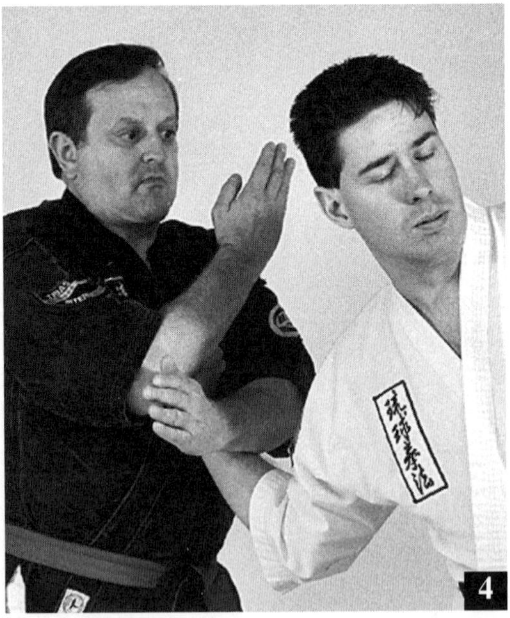

4

2

3

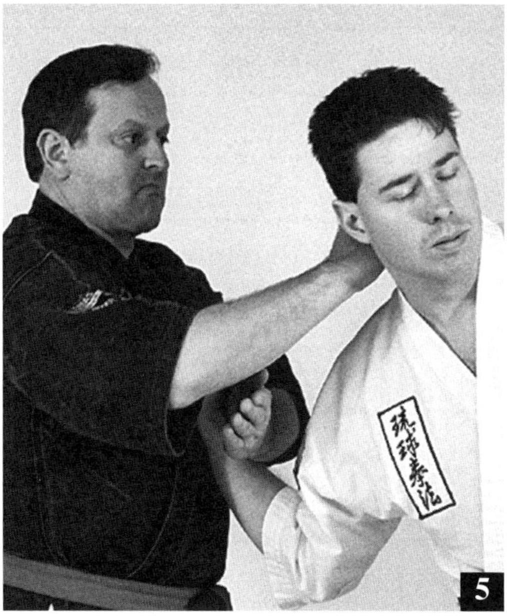
5

6

RULE OF THE SPECIAL POINTS

There are a variety of special points which must be learned on a case by case basis. For example, there are 100 Meeting Points, many of which are very practical for use in fighting. There are also points which lie outside the meridian system called Extraordinary Points, many of which we describe in this chapter.

Among the most useful of the special points are those called the Front Alarm and Back Associated points. These points are related to specific bodily organs. In healing arts they are useful diagnostically because they become painful when there is a problem with the corresponding organ. In pressure point fighting they are used as a means to directly affect an organ. The Back Associated points are also used in pressure point revival, especially if a subject has been the victim of a technique which depends heavily on the transmission of *ki.*

Meeting Points are another very useful type of the special points. These are locations where different meridians connect to each other. A Meeting Point can be treated as if it belonged to each of the meridians which intersect there. An example

Meridian	*Alarm Point*	*Associated Point*
Lung	L-1/Zhongfu	B-13/Feishu
Large Intestine	St-25/Tianshu	B-25/Dachangshu
Stomach	Co-12/Zhongwan	B-21/Weishu
Spleen	Li-13/Zhangmen	B-20/Pishu
Heart	Co-14/Juque	B-15/Xinshu
Small Intestine	Co-4/Guanyuan	B-27/Xiaochangshu
Bladder	Co-3/Zhongji	B-28/Pangguangshu
Kidney	GB-25/Jingmen	B-23/Shenshu
Pericardium	Co-17/Shanzhong	B-14/Jueyinshu
Triple Warmer	Co-5/Shimen	B-22/Sanjiaoshu
Gall Bladder	GB-24/Riyue	B-19/Danshu
Liver	Li-14/Qimen	B-18/Ganshu

of this is S-12/*Quepen*. It is located behind the collarbone, and is the Meeting Point of the Large Intestine, Small Intestine, Triple Warmer (Sanjiao), and Gall Bladder meridians with the Stomach meridian.

For example, normally, one would not think of starting with an attack to the Triple Warmer meridian, then following with a point on the Stomach meridian, since Stomach is actually strengthened (Earth element) by the input of energy into a Fire meridian. But, the point S-12/*Quepen* is a direct link to the Triple Warmer meridian, a meeting point, so it uniquely can be attacked following a setup on the Triple Warmer meridian.

1. When an opponent grabs your lapel with his right hand, press your left palm against the "Triple Warmer Triangle" (TW-6/*Zhigou,* TW-7/*Huizong,* TW-8/*Sanyangluo),* while striking with a single knuckle fist to P-6/*Neiguan.*

2. Immediately dig with fingertips into S-12/*Quepen* behind the opponent's right collarbone.

NOTE: Attacking P-6/Neiguan in conjunction with "Triple Warmer Triangle" (TW-6/Zhigou, TW-7/Huizong, TW-8/Sanyangluo) is an example of the Rule of Yin and Yang (Pericardium is Yin to Triple Warmer Yang). Attacking next to S-12/Quepen is the Rule of the Special Points.

Since the central rule of kata interpretation is that virtually every action is applied against pressure points, familiarity with pressure points is essential for truly understanding the kata. Throughout this book points are designated using both common alpha-numeric labels as well as their common Chinese names. This is to assist the reader to research further by referring to texts on acupuncture. In a few cases so-called "Miscellaneous and New Points" – those not lying on the 14 regular meridians – are mentioned. These points are only found in the most complete acupuncture texts.

It also needs to be mentioned that the English translations of the various channel names are not always consistent from text to text. In particular, the Triple Warmer is variously identified as the Triple Burner, Three Metabolisms, Three Fires, Thyroid, or Sanjiao channel. And the Pericardium is often called the Governor of the Heart.

In describing point location, the designation AU will often appear. AU stands for Anatomical Unit. This is what is sometimes called a "body inch" or *cun* in Chinese. The AU is different for every person, but the average length is 1 AU = 1/2 - 1 inch. One AU is equal to the width of the thumb at the joint.

The best process for locating points is to begin by locating them on oneself using AU measurements and finger-tip pressure. Generally, you will be able to feel when you are on a point. Once you are familiar with the location of points on your own body, practice locating them on the bodies of various training partners. Do not underestimate the importance of this step: accuracy is everything in kyusho-jitsu.

POINT CLUSTERS

A casual glance at an acupuncture chart can give the impression that there are countless places on the body where several points can be struck with one hand. However, this is somewhat misleading. For example, below we describe three points in a row on the side of the neck, S-9/*Renying*, LI-18/*Futu* and SI-16/*Tianchuang*. Clearly a palm up knife-hand strike could hit all three points simultaneously. However, these points must each be struck from a different angle and direction. S-9/*Renying* is hit diagonally front to back, LI-18/*Futu* from the side and SI-16/*Tianchuang* diagonally from back to front. This means that even if a blow lands on all three points, only one will be activated depending on the angle of impact.

There are certain places on the body where two or more points exist in a group having the following characteristics: 1. The points are discreet from one another (they do not have overlapping areas of activation); 2. The points respond to the same type of method (rub, touch, strike, knead); 3. The points have the same angle and direction of activation; 4. The points can be reached with one hand (or foot). In the course of describing pressure points, we will provide special information on these point clusters and their use.

POINTS ON THE UPPER EXTREMITIES

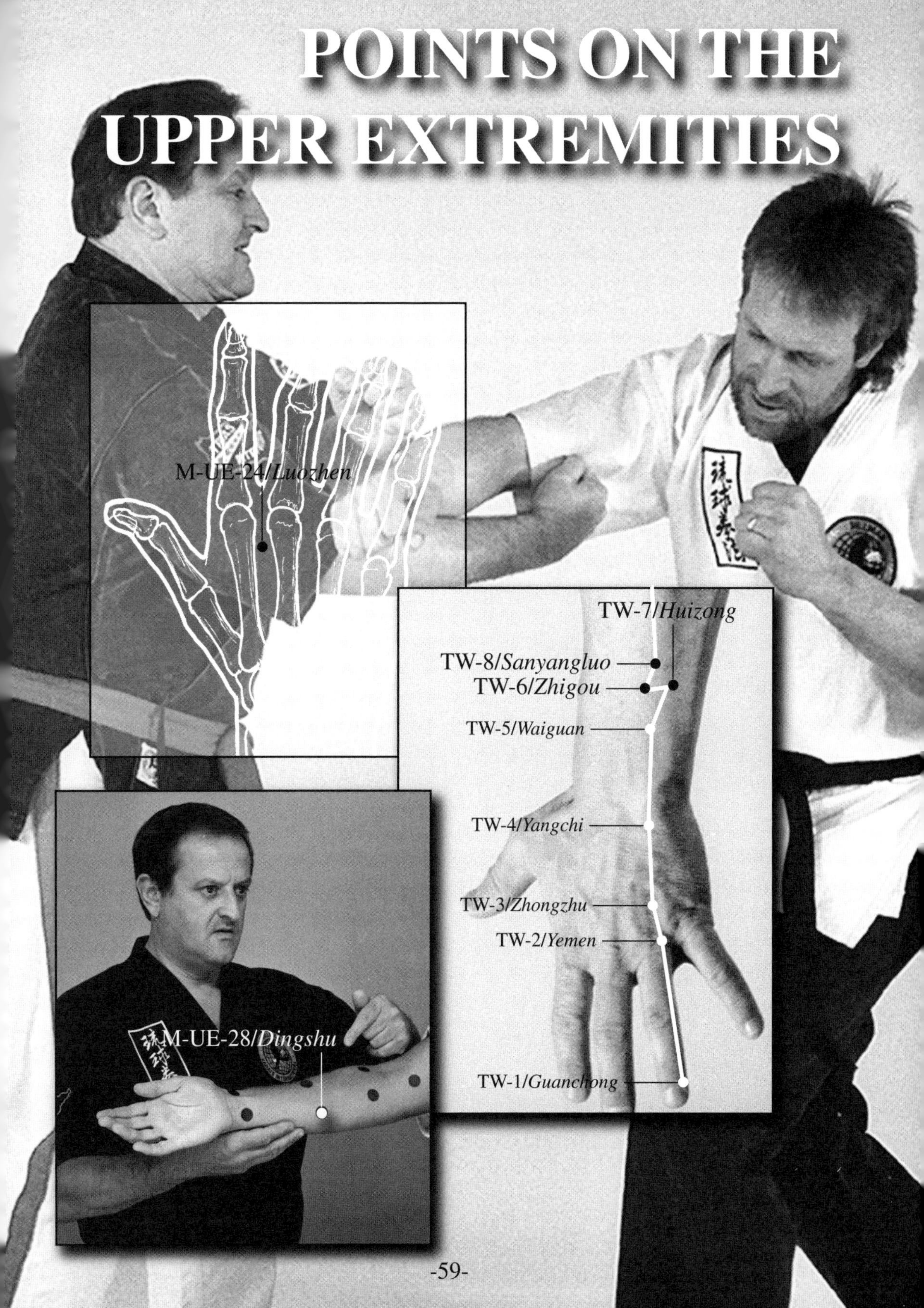

POINTS ON THE UPPER EXTREMITIES

Point Name: LI-2/*Erjian*

Location: On the side of the index finger, just distal to the metacarpalphalangeal (knuckle).

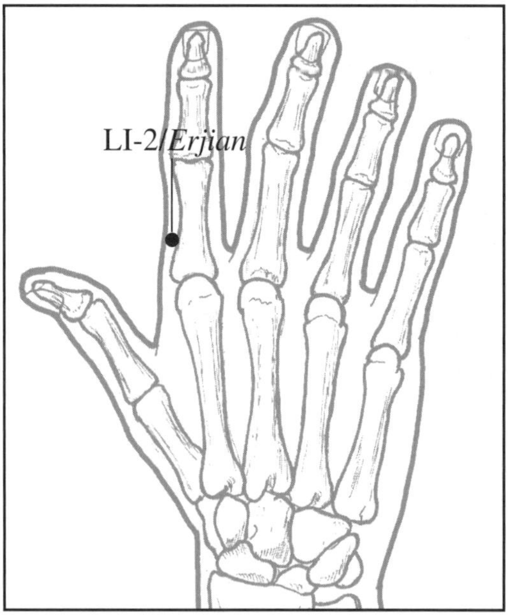

Anatomy: The dorsal digital branch of the radial nerve, the proper palmar digital branch of the median nerve, and the muscular branches of the median nerve.

Method & Usage: Press against the underlying bone to fold the hand inward when applying tuité (1 & 2).

Comments: Water point of the Large Intestine meridian.

Point Name: LI-3/*Sanjian*

Location: On the side of the index finger, just proximal to the metacarpalphalangeal (knuckle).

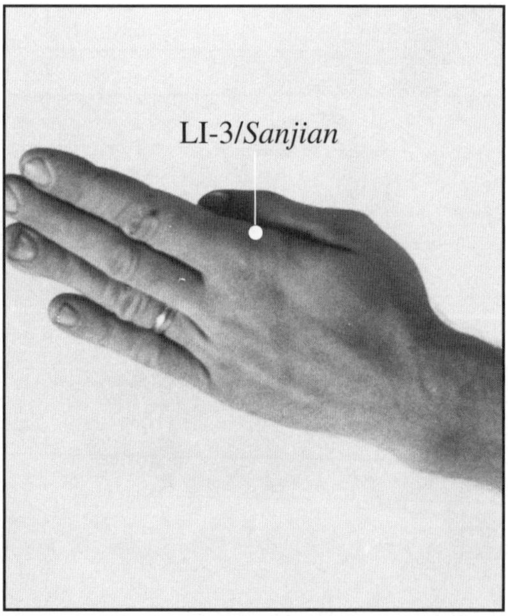

Anatomy: The dorsal digital branch of the radial nerve and the proper palmar digital branch of the median nerve, the deep branches of the ulnar nerve and the muscular branches of the median nerve.

Method & Usage: Press along an imaginary X through the joint to manipulate the index finger.

Comments: Wood point of the Large Intestine meridian.

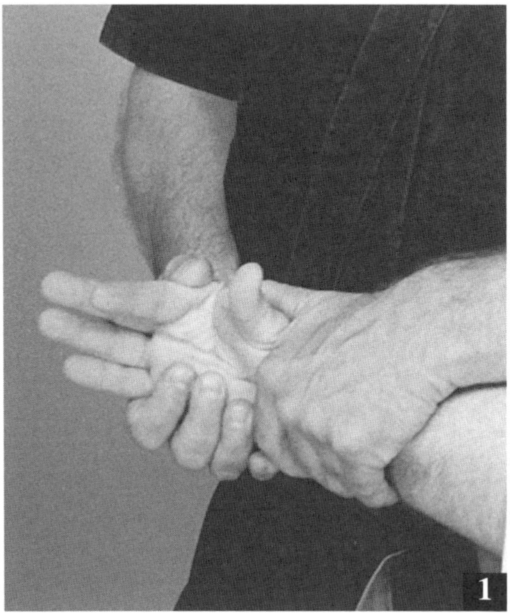
1

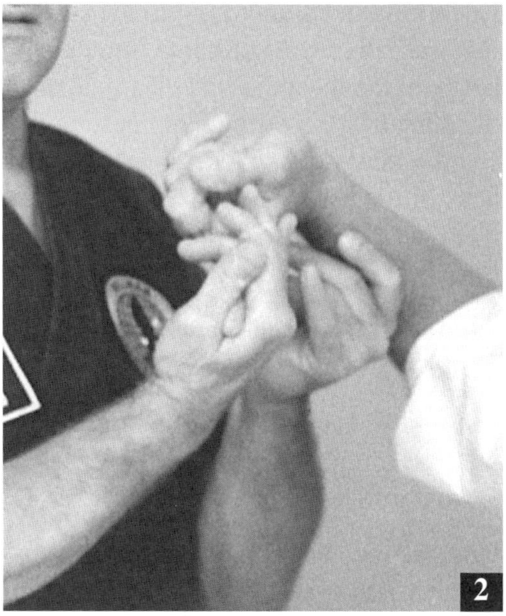
2

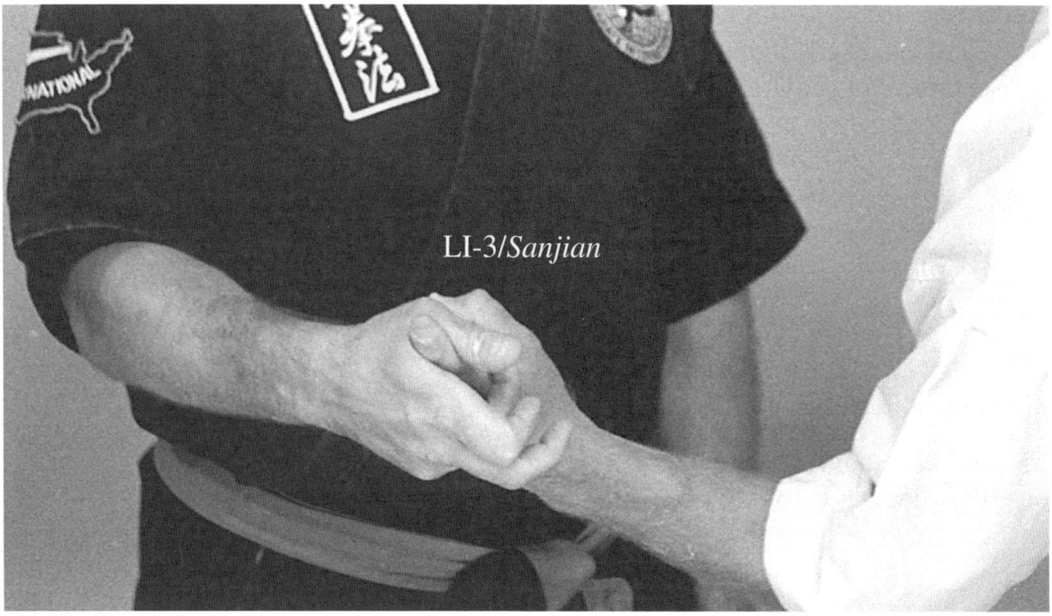
LI-3/*Sanjian*

POINTS ON THE UPPER EXTREMITIES (cont.)

Point Name: TW-3/*Zhongzhu*

Location: 1 AU proximal to the metacarpalphalangeal joints (knuckles) between the 4th and 5th metacarpals on the dorsal aspect of the hand in the fourth interosseous muscle. It is on the back of the hand, one third the distance from knuckles to wrist, between the bones of the fourth and fifth fingers.

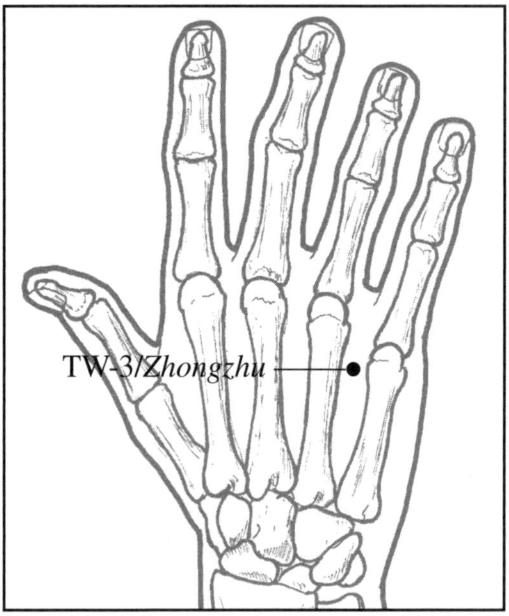

Anatomy: A dorsal branch of the ulnar nerve.

Method & Usage: Press this point with the thumb. It may also be struck to immobilize the hand.

Comments: Wood point of the Triple Warmer meridian.

Point Name: M-UE-24/*Luozhen*

Location: 1/2 AU proximal to the metacarpalphalangeal joints (knuckles) between the 2nd and 3rd metacarpals on the dorsal aspect of the hand in the interossei muscle of the second metacarpus. It is on the back of the hand, between the bones of the fourth and fifth fingers, in the hollow behind the knuckles.

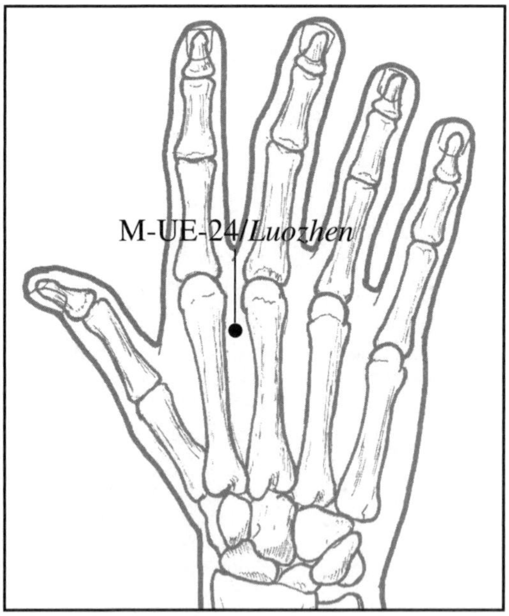

Anatomy: The deep terminal branch of the ulnar nerve.

Method & Usage: Press into the bone on either side when folding the wrist.

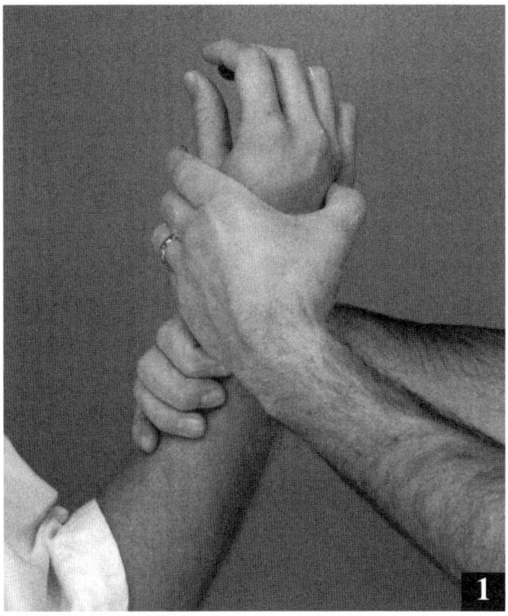
1

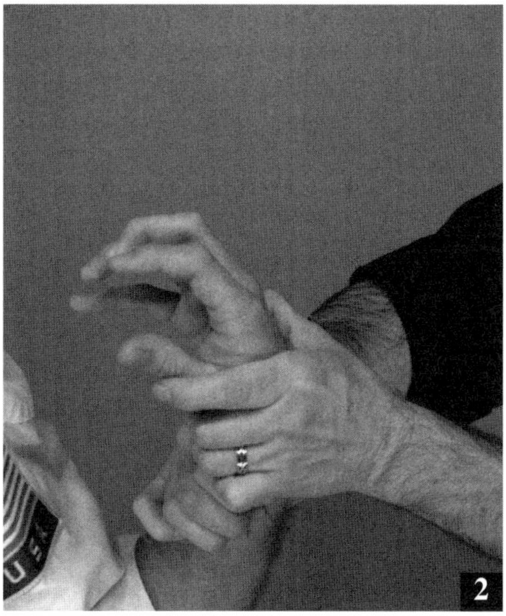
2

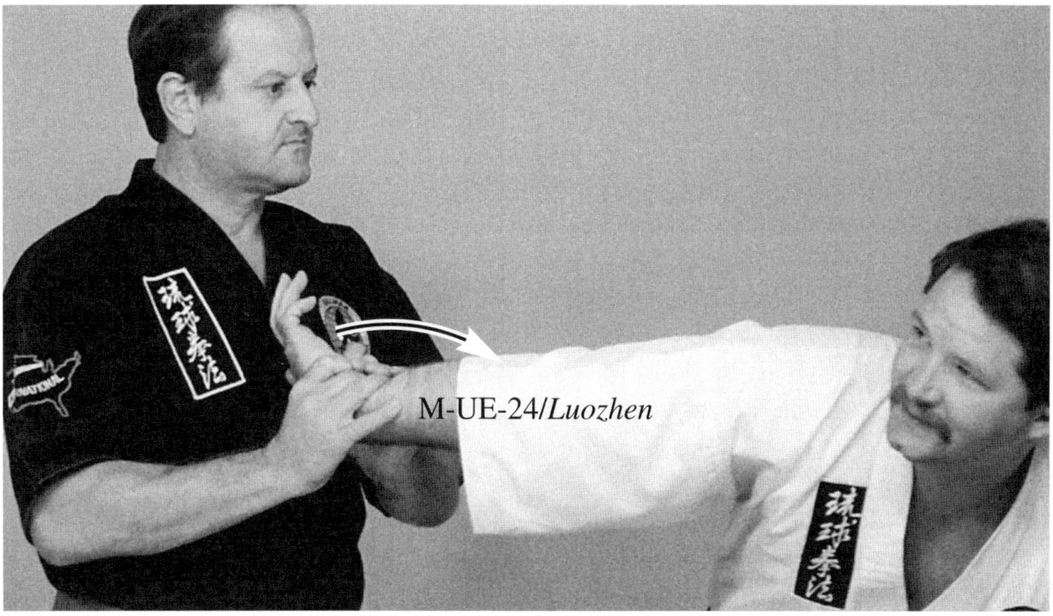
M-UE-24/*Luozhen*

POINTS ON THE UPPER EXTREMITIES (cont.)

Point Name: L-10/*Yuji*

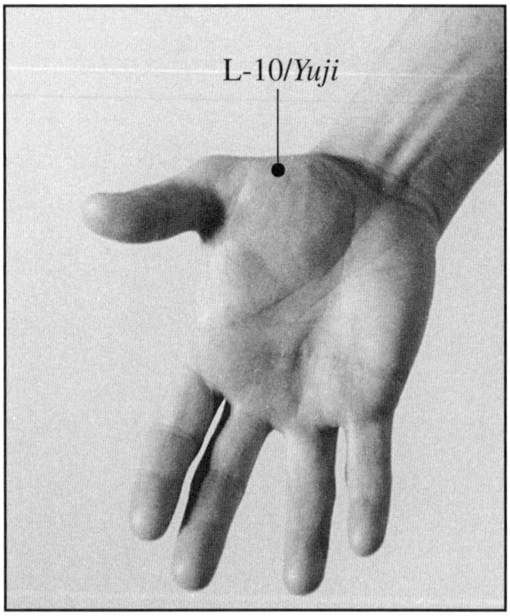

Location: Located at about the midpoint of the first metacarpal, on the thenar prominence in the lateral abductor pollicis brevis and opponens pollicis muscles. It is found in the "meat of the thumb" on the borderline between the (reddish) skin of the palm and the skin of the back of the hand.

Anatomy: A branch of the cephalic vein of the thumb. the lateral cutaneous nerve of the forearm and a superficial branch of the radial nerve.

Method & Usage: Press with the fingertips.

Comments: Fire point of the Lung meridian.

Point Name: H-8/*Shaofu*

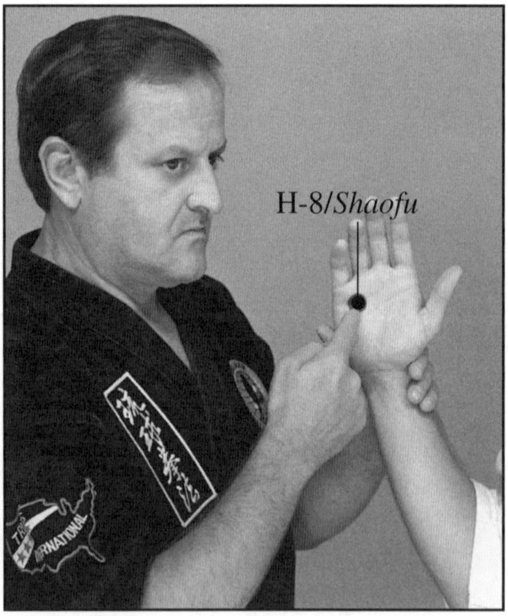

Location: On the palm of the hand between the 4th and 5th metacarpals, in the fourth lumbrical muscle and the tendon of the digitorum sublimis muscle. When the hand is closed into a (loose) fist, the tip of the little finger rests on this point.

Anatomy: The common palmar digital artery and vein, and the fourth common palmar digital branch of the ulnar nerve.

Method & Usage: Hook with the fingertips to release a grip.

Comments: Fire point of the Heart meridian.

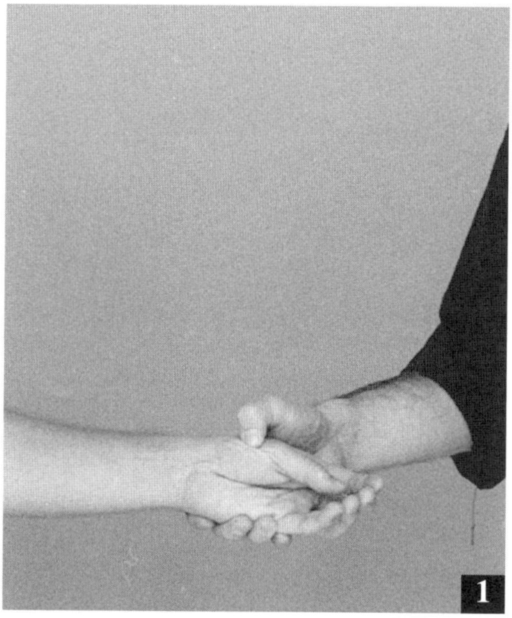
1

2

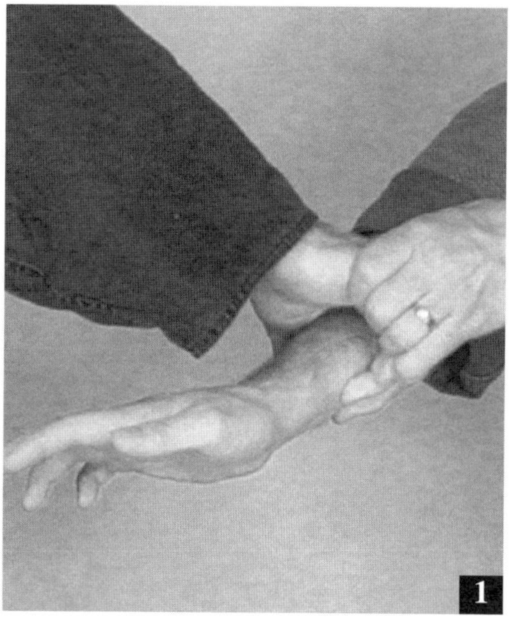
1

2

POINTS ON THE UPPER EXTREMITIES (cont.)

Point Name: LI-4/*Hegu*

Location: In the dorsal interosseus muscle between the 1st and 2nd metacarpals. It is in the "web of the thumb" slightly towards the bone of the index finger.

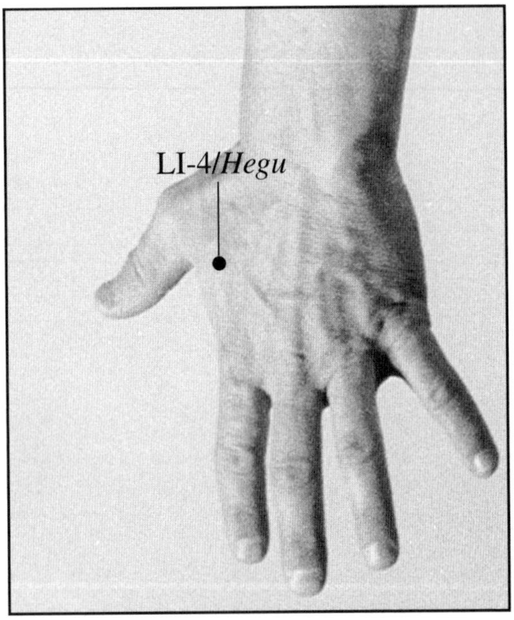

Anatomy: A superficial branch of the radial nerve.

Method & Usage: Press this point firmly into the edge of the index finger bone (2nd metacarpal).

Caution: Stimulation of this point can trigger labor in pregnant women.

Point Name: LI-5/*Yangxi*

Location: In the hollow between the extensor pollicis longus and the extensor pollicis brevis. It is found in the depression between the two tendons at the base of the thumb.

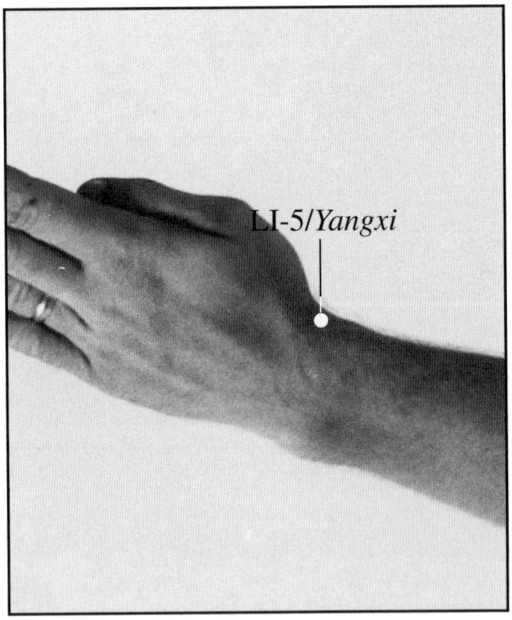

Anatomy: A superficial branch of the radial nerve.

Method & Usage: Press with the tip of the thumb between the tendons and towards the wrist. This point also responds well to a strike, but it is difficult to hit.

Comments: Fire point of the Large Intestine meridian.

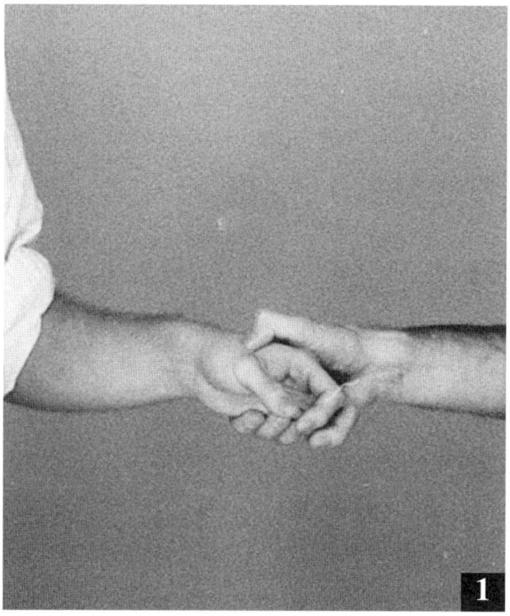
1

琉球拳法
2

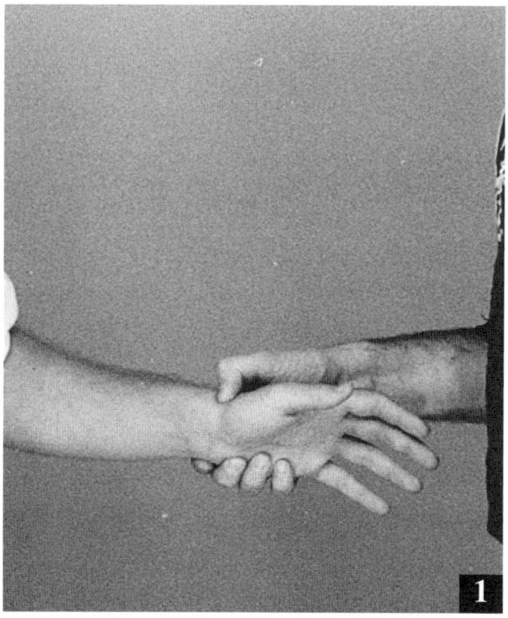
1

琉球拳法
2

POINTS ON THE UPPER EXTREMITIES (cont.)

Point Name: SI-6/*Yanglao*

Location: 1/2 AU up (proximal) from the crease of the wrist on the back (dorsal aspect) of the forearm, in the cleft of the bony nob (styloid process) of the ulna.

Anatomy: The dorsal branch of the ulnar nerve, and branches of the posterior antebrachial cutaneous nerve.

Method & Usage: Press this point against the bone and towards the hand to bend the wrist.

Comments: SI-6/*Yanglao* has a close relationship with the eyes.

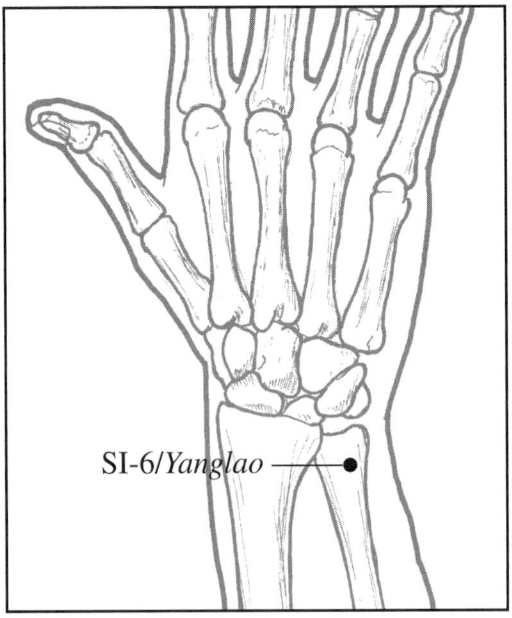

Point Name: LI-4/*Hegu*

Location: In the dorsal interosseus muscle between the 1st and 2nd metacarpals. It is in the "web of the thumb" slightly towards the bone of the index finger.

Anatomy: A superficial branch of the radial nerve.

Method & Usage: Press this point firmly against the side of the index finger bone (2nd metacarpal), when performing tuité techniques.

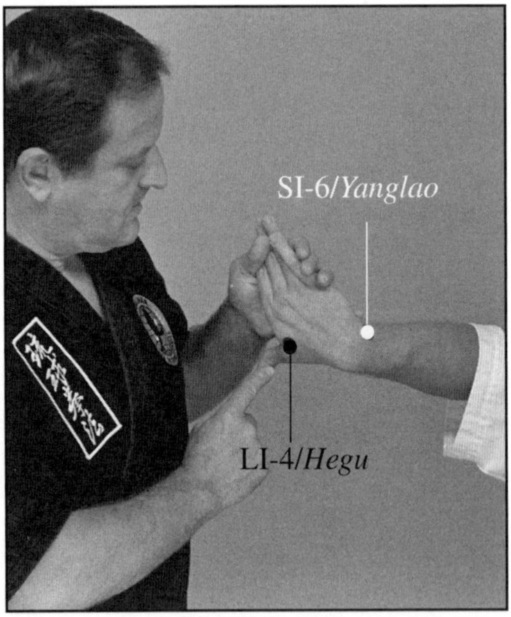

1

2

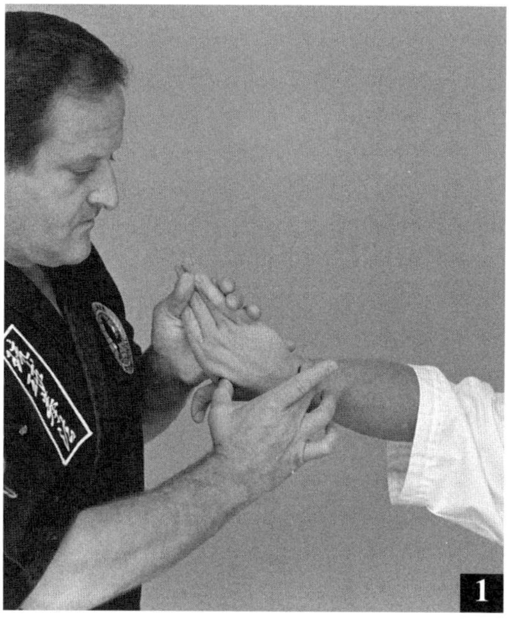
1

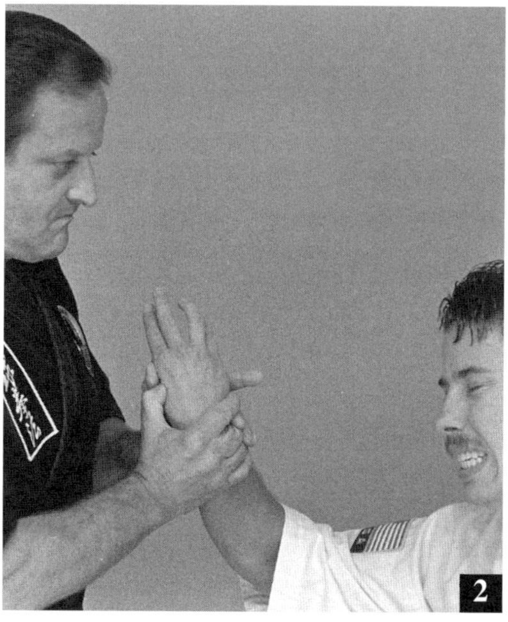
2

POINTS ON THE UPPER EXTREMITIES (cont.)

Point Name: L-7/*Lieque*

Location: 1.5 AU from the crease of the wrist, in the depression just behind the bony prominence (styloid process) of the radius, on the thumb side of the forearm.

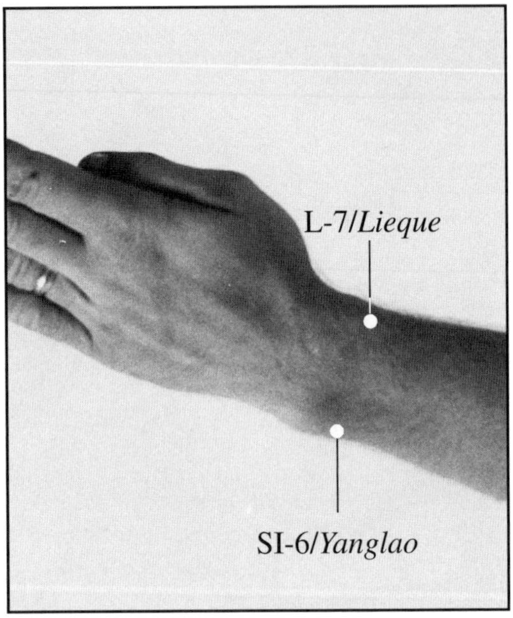

Anatomy: The lateral antebrachial cutaneous nerve, the superficial ramus of the radial nerve, and the cephalic vein.

Method & Usage: This point may be pressed, or struck towards the wrist to weaken the hand. When grabbing the wrist, roll the thumb across L-7/*Lieque*, while squeezing against SI-6/*Yanglao* with the fingertips.

Point Name: L-9/*Taiyuan*

Location: In the crease of the wrist, on the radial side of the radial flexor tendon of the wrist.

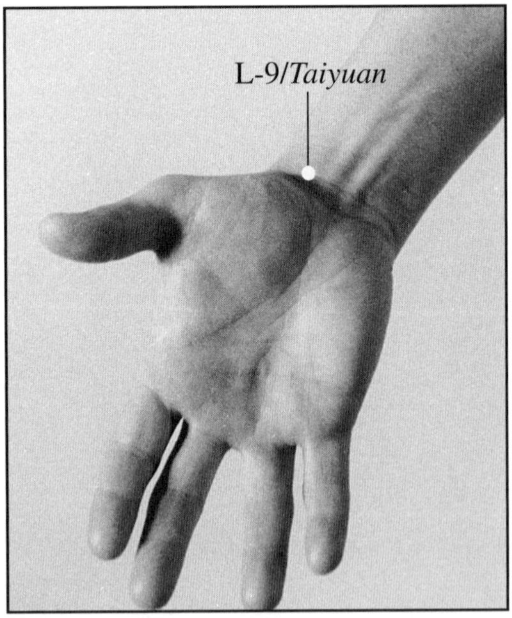

Anatomy: The lateral cutaneous nerve of the forearm, the superficial branches of the radial nerve.

Method & Usage: Press laterally to weaken the wrist. Pressure on L-9/*Taiyuan* is can be used to set-up L-8/*Jingqu* (next page).

Comments: L-9/*Taiyuan* is the Earth point of the Lung channel.

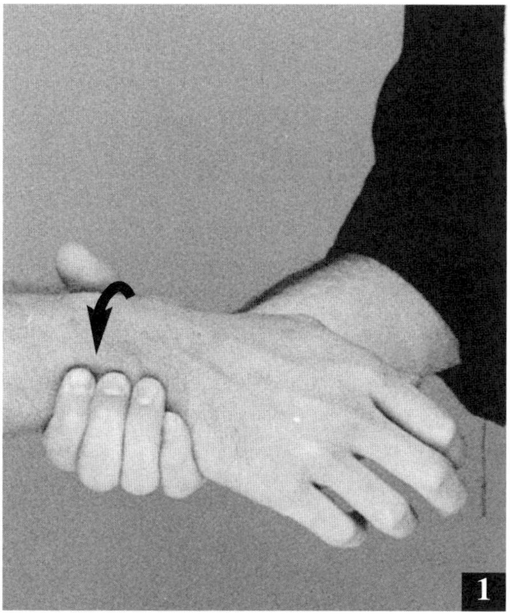
1

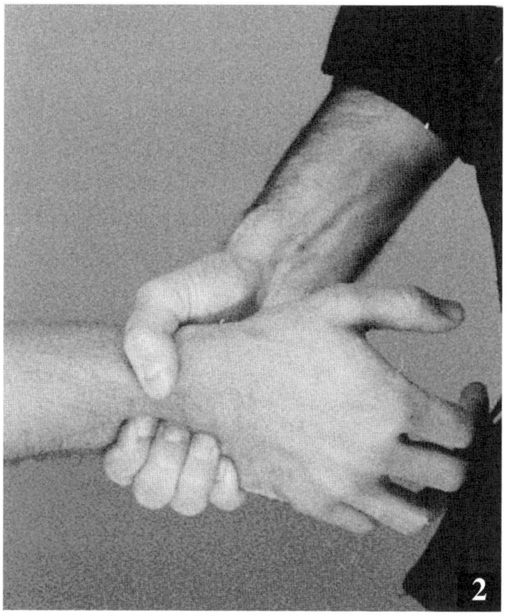
2

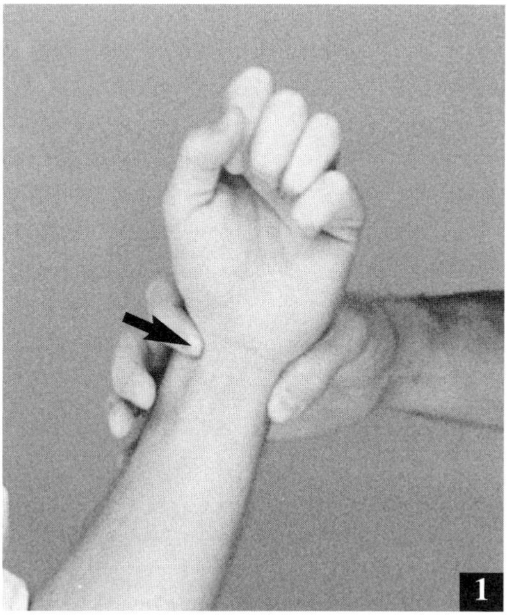
1

2

POINTS ON THE UPPER EXTREMITIES (cont.)

Point Name: L-8/*Jingqu*

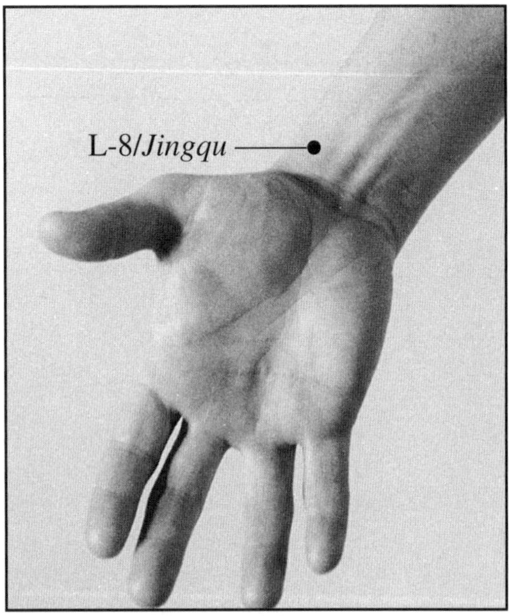

Location: One AU up (proximal) from the crease of the wrist in the depression by the radial artery (about the place a nurse takes a pulse).

Anatomy: The lateral antebrachial cutaneous nerve, the superficial ramus of the radial nerve.

Method & Usage: Press into the depression next to the radial bone, and up towards the wrist to weaken the hand. When grasping the wrist from the outside, squeeze the fingertips into this point, while pressing the thumb into H-6/*Yinxi* (next page).

Comments: L-8/*Jingqu* is the Metal point of the Lung channel.

Point Name: P-6/*Neiguan*

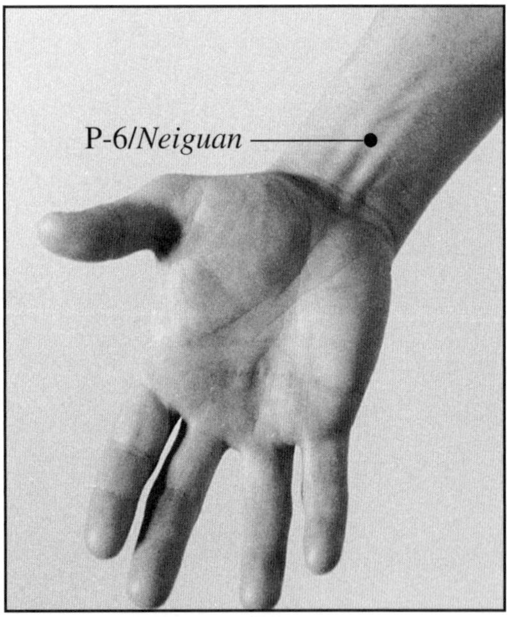

Location: Between the tendons of the flexor carpi radialis and the flexor digitorum sublimis muscle two AU above (proximal) from the center of the transverse crease in the wrist. This point can be found in the soft space between the tendons of the wrist.

Anatomy: The medial and lateral cutaneous nerves of the forearm. This point lies directly on the medial nerve.

Method & Usage: Press in and towards the fist to weaken the hand.

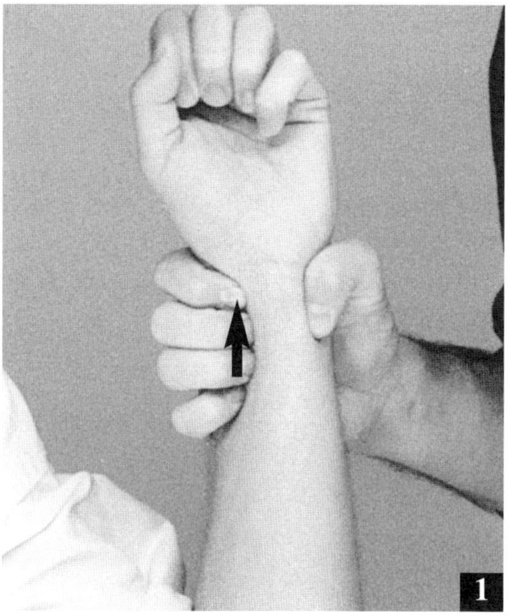
1

2

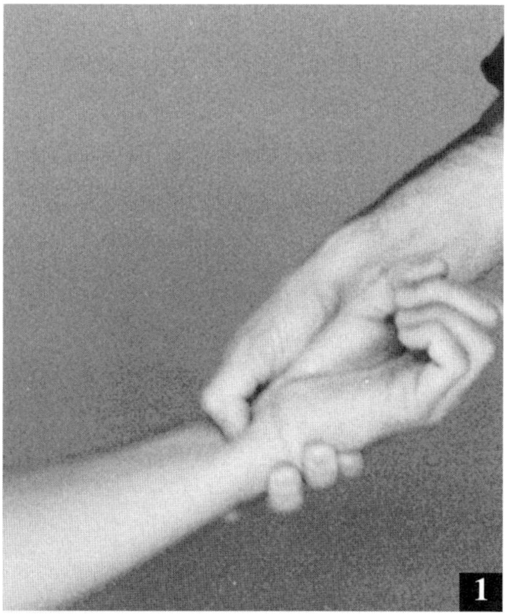
1

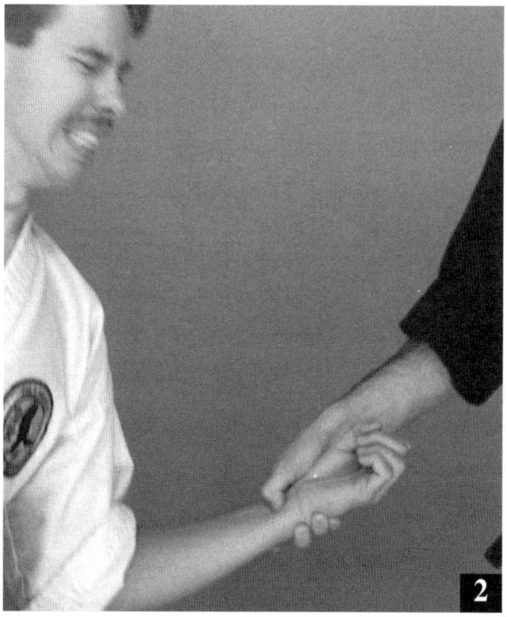
2

POINTS ON THE UPPER EXTREMITIES (cont.)

Point Name: H-6/*Yinxi*

Location: Proximal to the wrist crease, against the ulnar bone, next to the tendon of the flexor carpi ulnaris.

Anatomy: The ulnar nerve, and the medial antebrachial cutaneous nerve.

Method & Usage: Hook this point under the ulnar bone and towards the hand to weaken the grip and the wrist.

Comments: H-6/*Yinxi* is commonly used to release an attacker's grip and set up a tuité maneuver.

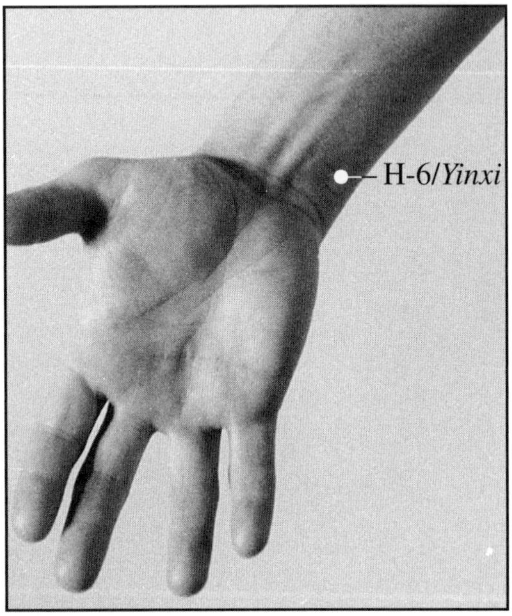

Point Name: H-7/*Shenmen*

Location: In the crease of the wrist, just outside the flexor carpi ulnaris tendon.

Anatomy: The ulnar nerve.

Method & Usage: With fingertip pressure, dig this point laterally toward the tendon to weaken the wrist. It is often used in tuité.

Comments: Earth point of the Heart meridian

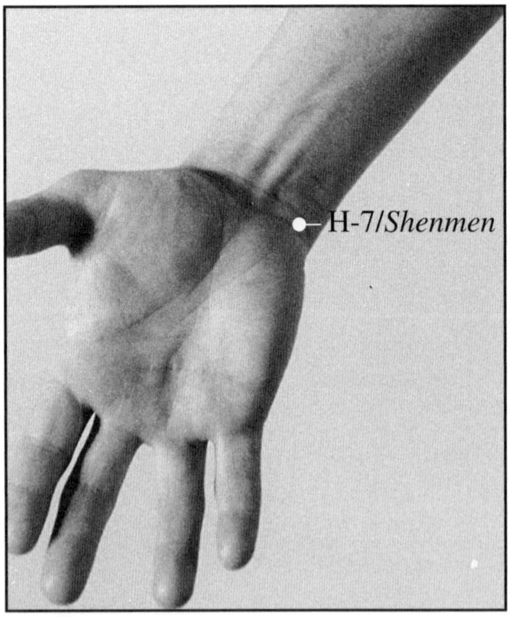

1

2

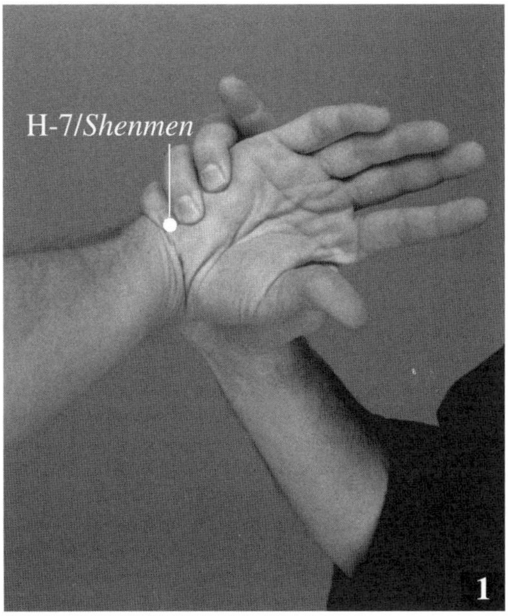
H-7/*Shenmen*
1

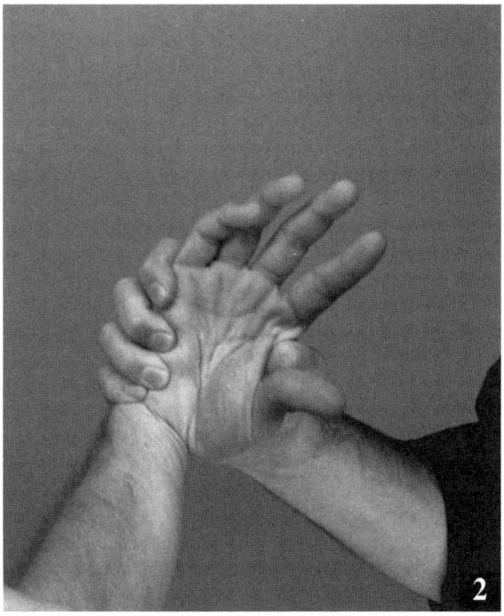
2

POINTS ON THE UPPER EXTREMITIES (cont.)

Point Cluster: Triple Warmer Triangle
TW-6/*Zhigou*

TW-7/*Huizong*

TW-8/*Sanyangluo*

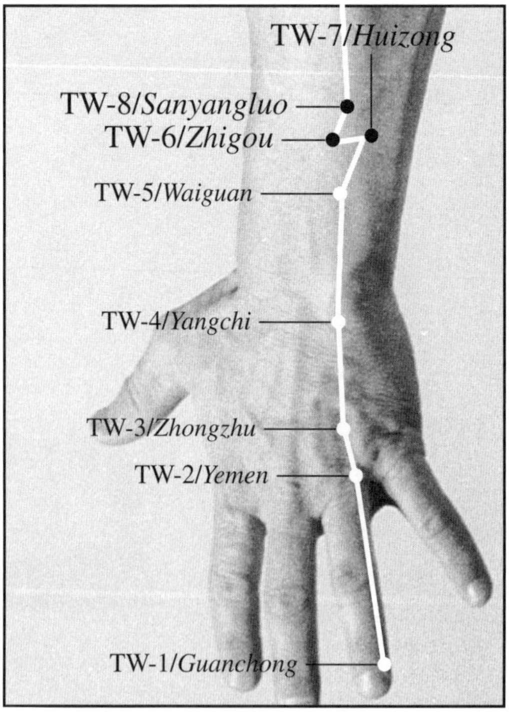

Location: TW-6/*Zhigou* is on the radial side of the extensor digitorum communis muscle, in the depression between the radius and ulna.

Anatomy: The posterior antebrachial cutaneous nerve, the posterior interosseus nerve of the radial nerve, and the anterior interosseus nerve of the median nerve.

Location: TW-7/*Huizong* in the depression between the ulna and the extensor digitorum communis muscle.

Anatomy: The posterior and medial antebrachial cutaneous nerves, the posterior and anterior interosseus nerves.

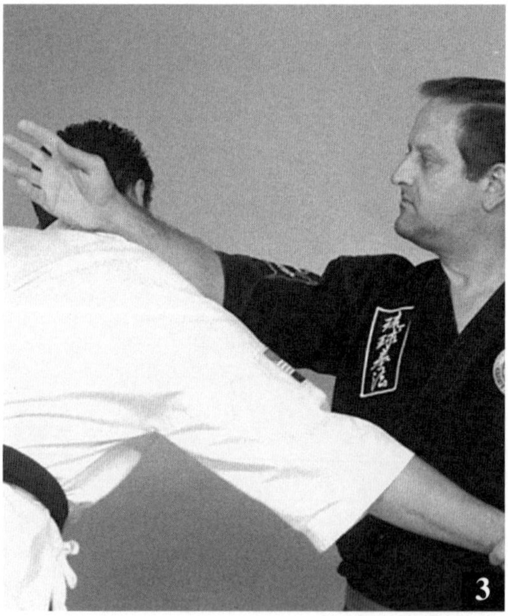

Location: TW-8/*Sanyangluo* is on the forearm, on the radial side of the extensor digitorum communis muscle.

Anatomy: The posterior and medial antebrachial cutaneous nerves, the posterior and anterior interosseus nerves.

Comment: These points form a zigzag on the Triple Warmer meridian where the flow of energy is "turbulent."

Mode and Usage: Grind across these points when performing tuité (1,2). Strike with these points to put energy (chi) into a target (3). Touch this cluster with an open palm while striking P-6/*Neiguan* (4).

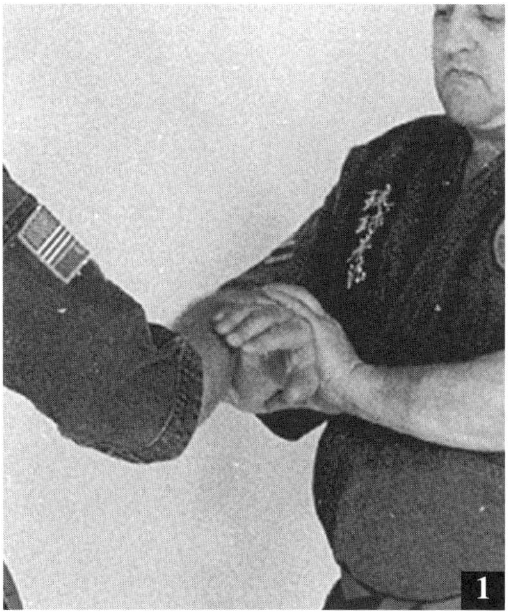
1

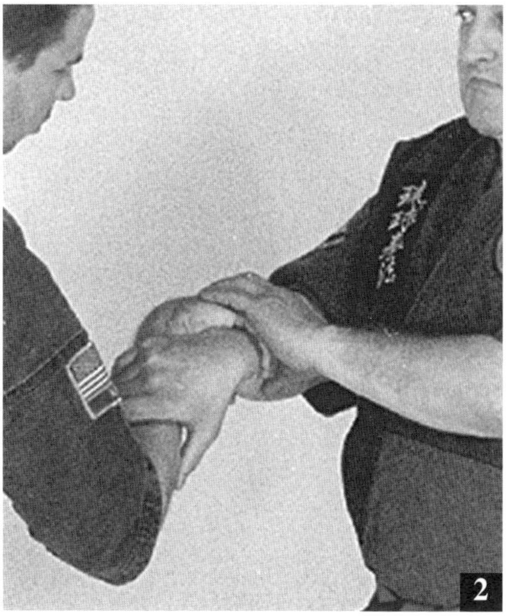
2

4

POINTS ON THE UPPER EXTREMITIES (cont.)

Point Name: L-6/*Kongzui*

Location: At about the middle of the radial bone, near the distal end of the brachioradialis.

Anatomy: It lies over the lateral cutaneous nerve of the forearm, and a superficial branch of the radial nerve.

Method & Usage: This point is struck as if driving it into the underlying bone to weaken the fist (in the case of a punch) or release the grip (in the case of a grab).

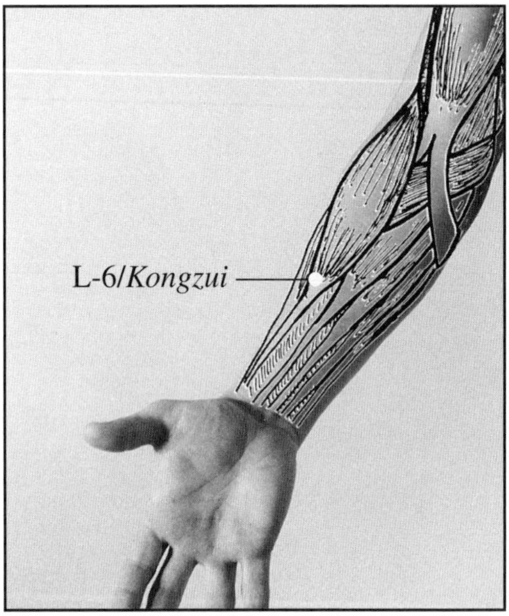

Point Name: M-UE-28/*Dingshu*

Location: In the flexor carpi ulnaris and the flexor digitorum profundus, 5 AU up (proximal) from the wrist, on the little finger side of the forearm.

Anatomy: The ulnar nerve and the palmar cutaneous branch of that nerve.

Method & Usage: Strike this point upwards against the ulna to weaken the wrist.

Comments: This is an excellent point to use when disarming an opponent.

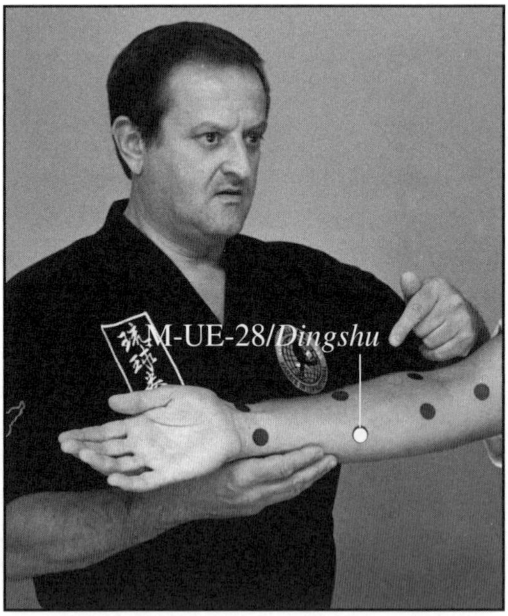

1

2

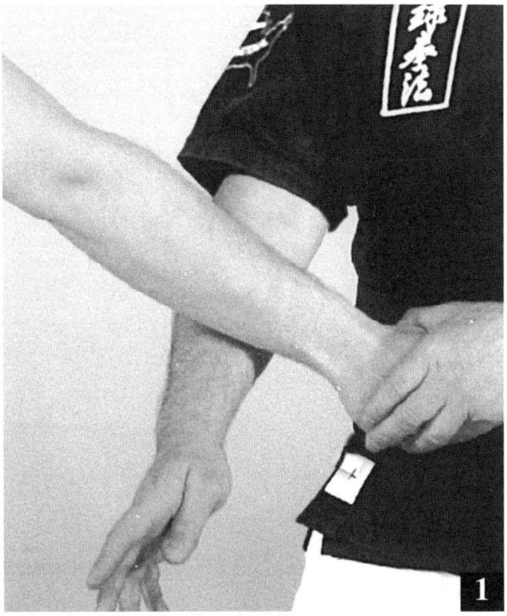
1

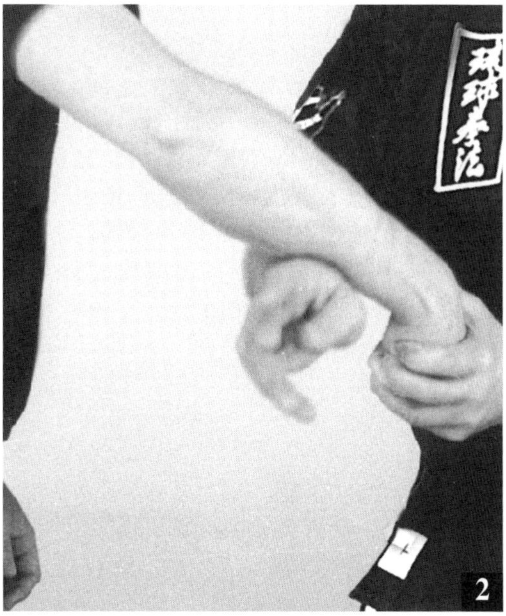
2

POINTS ON THE UPPER EXTREMITIES (cont.)

Point Name: L-5/*Chize*

Location: At the crease of the elbow, just outside (lateral) to the biceps tendon at the origin of the brachioradialis muscle.

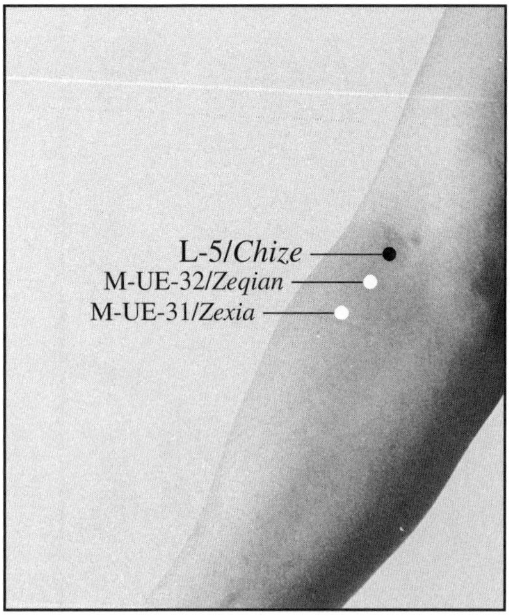

Anatomy: Branches of the radial recurrent artery and vein and the lateral cutaneous nerve of the forearm, directly above the main trunk of the radial nerve.

Method & Usage: This point may be manipulated with the tip of the thumb, though it is defined as a hit point. Strike in a manner that cuts back towards the hand (think of a C-shaped movement), which will cause the knees to buckle, and the head to come forward. On some individuals, striking this target while pulling on the wrist points can send them to the ground, or even knock them unconscious.

Comments: There are actually three points in this area, L-5/*Chize*, M-UE-32/*Zeqian,* and M-UE-31/*Zexia*. The extraordinary points lie on branchings of the lateral cutaneous nerve of the forearm. References to L-5/*Chize* should be understood as meaning any or all three of these points.

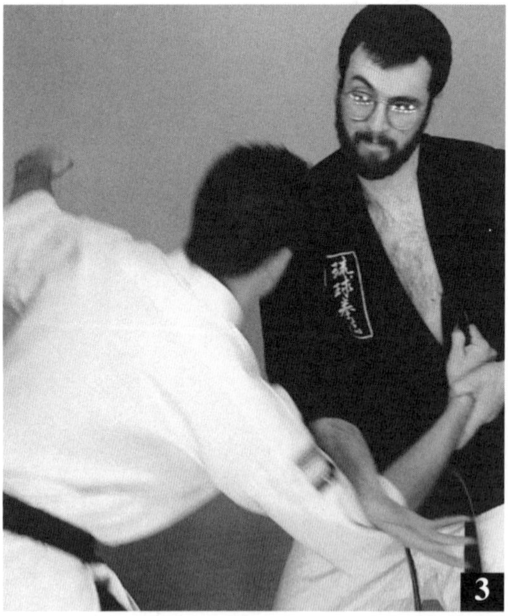

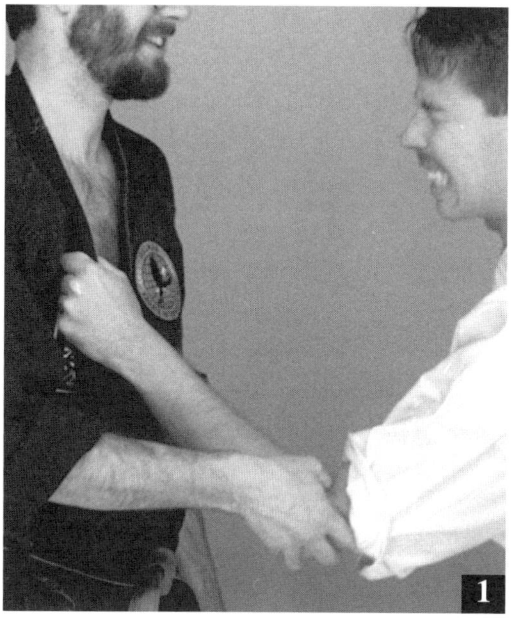
1

2

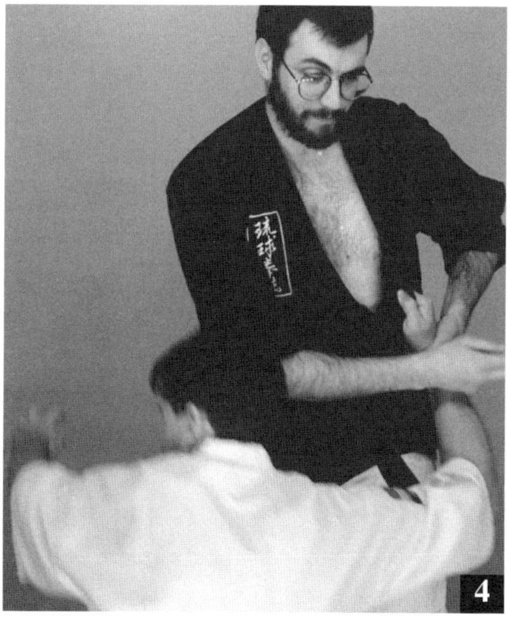
4

5

POINTS ON THE UPPER EXTREMITIES (cont.)

Point Name: LI-10/*Shousanli*

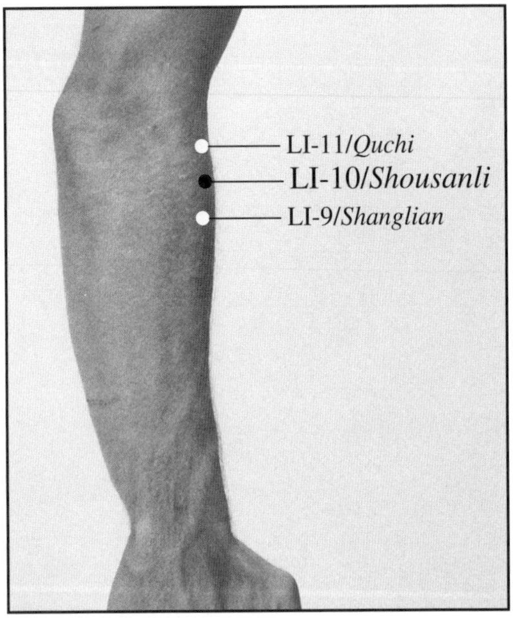

Location: 2 AU distal from the outside end of the crease of the elbow (the lateral end of the transverse cubital crease), between the supinator longus muscle (also called the brachioradialus) and the extensor carpi radialis longus. It is approximately one AU down (distal) from the elbow joint on the outside of the forearm.

Anatomy: The muscular branch of the musculo-spiral nerve, the antebrachial cutaneous nerve; a deep branch of the radial nerve.

Method & Usage: This point may be manipulated with the thumb, but it is designated a hit point (1,2). Strike to produce numbness in the arm, and turn an opponent's head to expose head and neck points to follow-up attack (3-5).

Comments: LI-10/*Shousanli* is flanked by LI-9/*Shanglian* & LI-11/*Quchi.* LI-10/*Shousanli* is the motor-nerve point (the location where the nerve enters the muscle) of the extensor carpi radialis longus. LI-11/*Quchi* is the motor nerve point for the brachioradialis (supinator longus) muscle. Because of the close proximity and similar function, these points are essentially interchangeable in kyusho-jitsu.

1

2

4

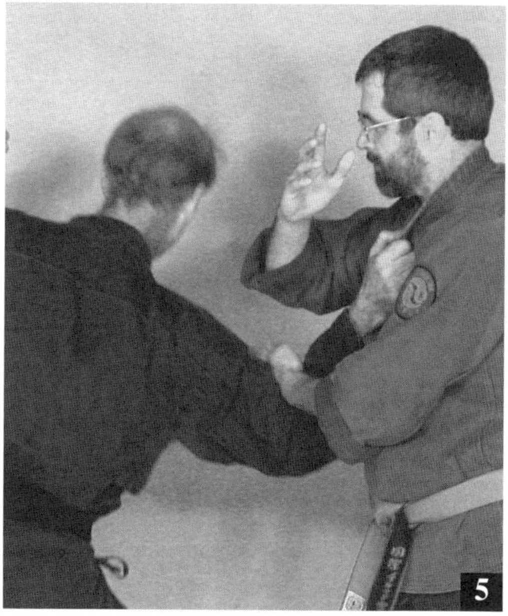

5

POINTS ON THE UPPER EXTREMITIES (cont.)

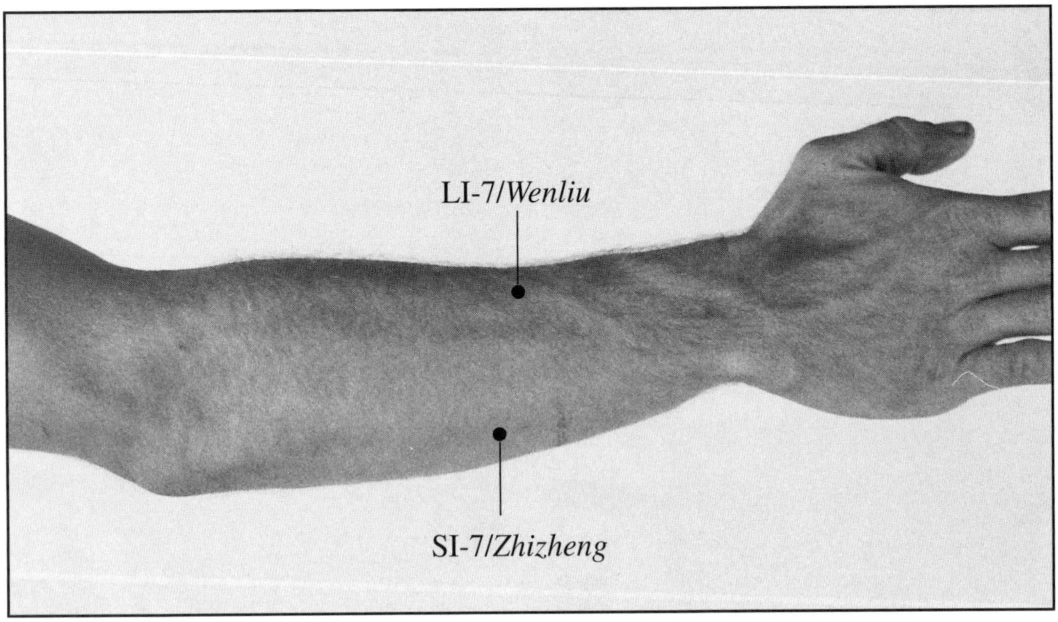

Point Name: SI-7/*Zhizheng*

Location: In the middle of the forearm, 5 AU up (proximal) from the wrist along the ulna at the end of the extensor carpi ulnaris muscle.

Anatomy: The branch of the medial antebrachial cutaneous nerve; more deeply, the posterior interosseous nerve.

Method & Usage: Strike this point against the bone to release the hand.

Point Name: LI-7/*Wenliu*

Location: About 5 AU up (proximal) from the wrist on the thumb side of the forearm.

Anatomy: The posterior antebrachial cutaneous nerve and the deep ramus of the radial nerve.

Method & Usage: Strike as if driving the point into the bone to cramp up the forearm.

Point Name: H-3/*Shaohai*

Location: In pronator teres and the brachialis muscles, on the ulnar side of the elbow, just below (distal) to the inner knob of the elbow (the medial condyle of the humerus).

Anatomy: The medial cutaneous nerve of the forearm.

Method & Usage: Strike or press this point to bend the elbow and to numb the arm.

Comments: H-3/*Shaohai* is often used in conjunction with tuité maneuvers.

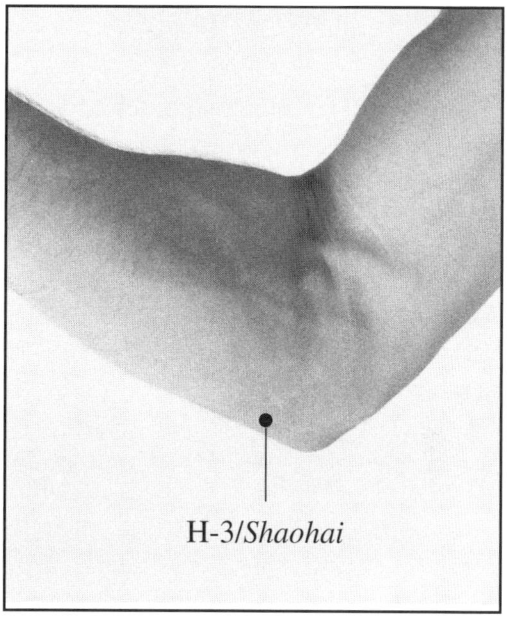

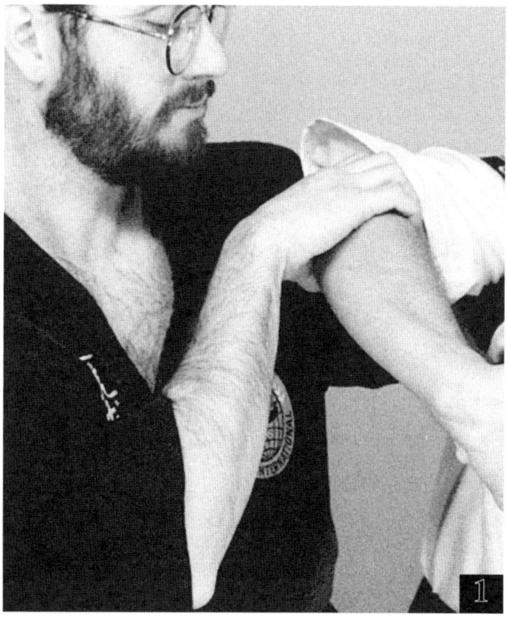

POINTS ON THE UPPER EXTREMITIES (cont.)

Point Name: H-1/*Jiquan*

Location: In the center of the axilla (armpit).

Anatomy: The intercostobrachial nerve, radial nerve, the ulnar nerve, the median nerve, medial cutaneous nerve of forearm, the medial cutaneous nerve of the arm.

Method & Usage: When the opponent's arm is raised, this point is vulnerable to a strike.

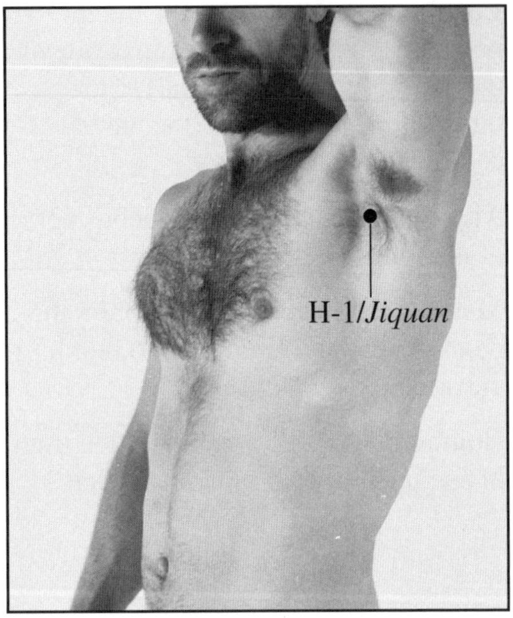

Point Name: P-2/*Tianquan*

Location: Two AU below (distal) the level of the fold of the armpit (axillary crease) along the mid-line of the biceps.

Anatomy: The muscular branches of the brachial artery, the medial brachial cutaneous nerve and the musculocutaneous nerve.

Method & Usage: This point can be struck straight-on to numb the biceps.

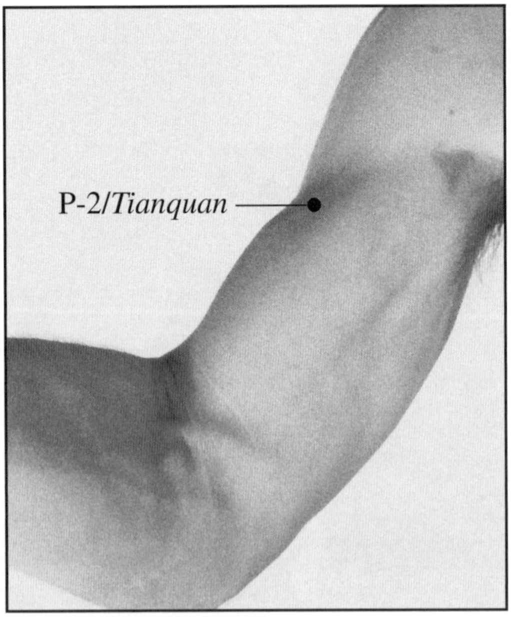

Point Name: N-UE-9/*Gongzhong*

Location: In the center of the biceps.

Anatomy: The medial cutaneous nerve and the musculocutaneous nerve.

Method & Usage: This point can be struck straight-on to numb the biceps.

Comments: Because N-UE-9/ *Gongzhong*, lies along the Pericardium meridian it may be used interchangeably with P-2/*Tianquan*.

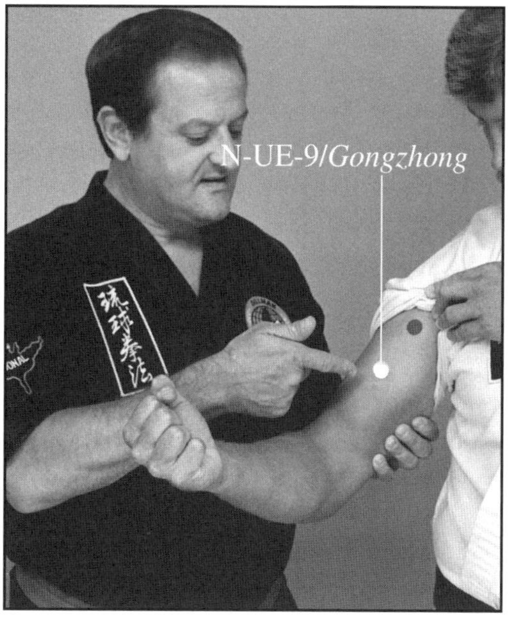

POINTS ON THE UPPER EXTREMITIES (cont.)

Point Name: TW-11/*Qinglengyuan*

Location: Two AU above the tip of the elbow on the tendon of the triceps.

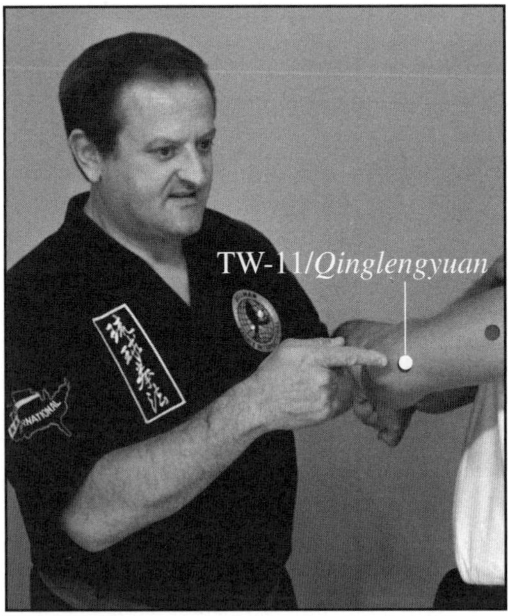

Anatomy: The posterior brachial nerve, the muscular branch of the radial nerve, and the Golgi tendon organ.

Method & Usage: Rub this point in and up and down motion to hyper-extend the elbow and lock the shoulder.

Comments: This is a rub-point which lies over a tendon-nerve spindle called a Golgi tendon organ. The function of the Golgi tendon organ is to monitor the condition of the tendon. Rubbing this point tricks the mind into thinking that the tendon is tearing, which causes an immediate relaxation of the shoulder and the elbow.

From the perspective of acupuncture, this point works because the rubbing action manipulates the internal energy of the meridian (ki/chi) from TW-11/*Qinglengyuan* to TW-10/*Tianjing* and back again.

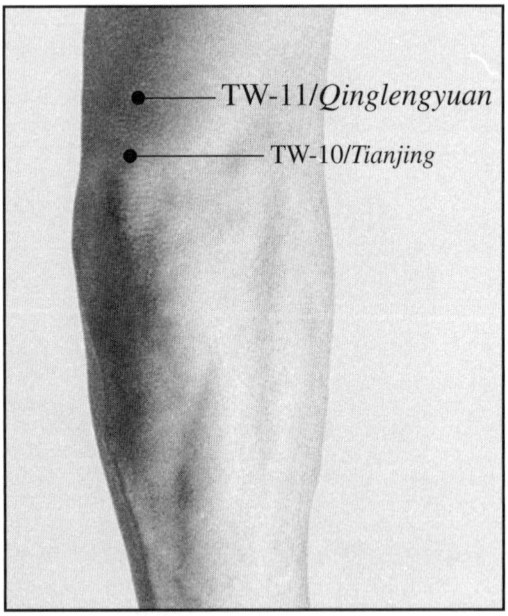

1

2

1

2

POINTS ON THE UPPER EXTREMITIES (cont.)

Point Name: TW-12/*Xiaolou*

Location: In the middle of the triceps.

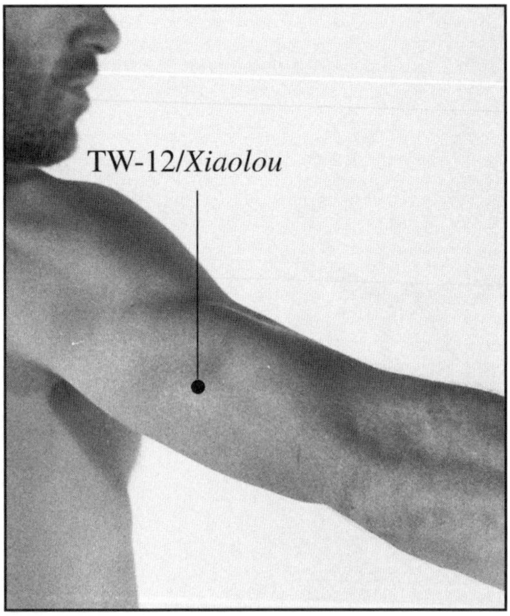

Anatomy: The median collateral artery, the posterior brachial cutaneous nerve, and the muscular branch of the radial nerve.

Method & Usage: Strike this point against the bone to release the shoulder and lock the elbow.

Comments: In the center of the humerus is a nerve receptor which monitors the condition of the bone. A strike is interpreted as a signal that the humerus being in danger of breaking. As a result, the shoulder immediately releases, thereby enabling the elbow to be locked.

Point Name: LI-13/*Shouwuli*

Location: In the hollow depression near the (distal) end of the biceps, about three AU above (proximal) the lateral epicondyle of the humerus (the outer knob of the elbow).

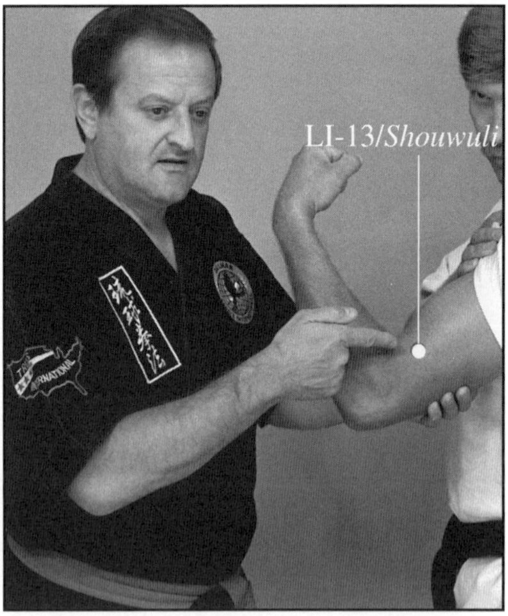

Anatomy: The radial collateral artery, the posterior antebrachial cutaneous nerve and the radial nerve.

Method & Usage: Hit this point against the underlying bone (humerus) to bend the arm inward and cause numbing and pain down the arm to the end of the thumb.

1

2

1

2

POINTS ON THE UPPER EXTREMITIES (cont.)

Point Name: H-2/*Qingling*

Location: Three AU above (proximal) the inside end of the crease of the elbow, in the space between the biceps and the triceps.

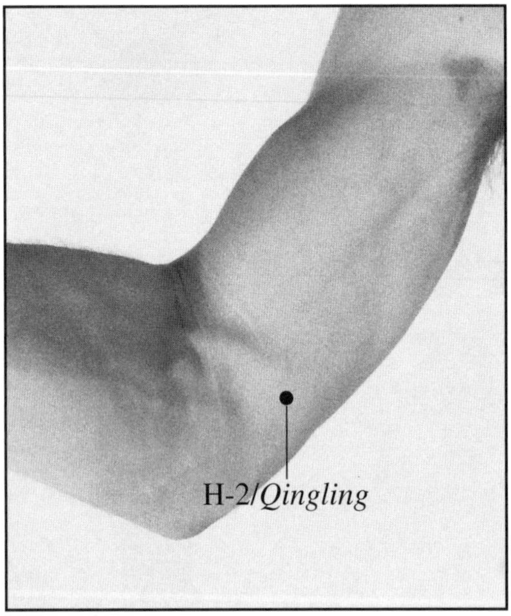

Anatomy: The superior ulnar collateral artery, the medial antebrachial cutaneous nerve and the ulnar nerve.

Method & Usage: This point may be may be struck or grabbed causing the elbow to bend and pain to shoot down to the little finger (and sometimes up to the armpit).

Comments: When grabbing this point, it is important to roll the fingers over the underlying nerves and tendons to cause greater pain.

POINTS ON THE HEAD AND NECK

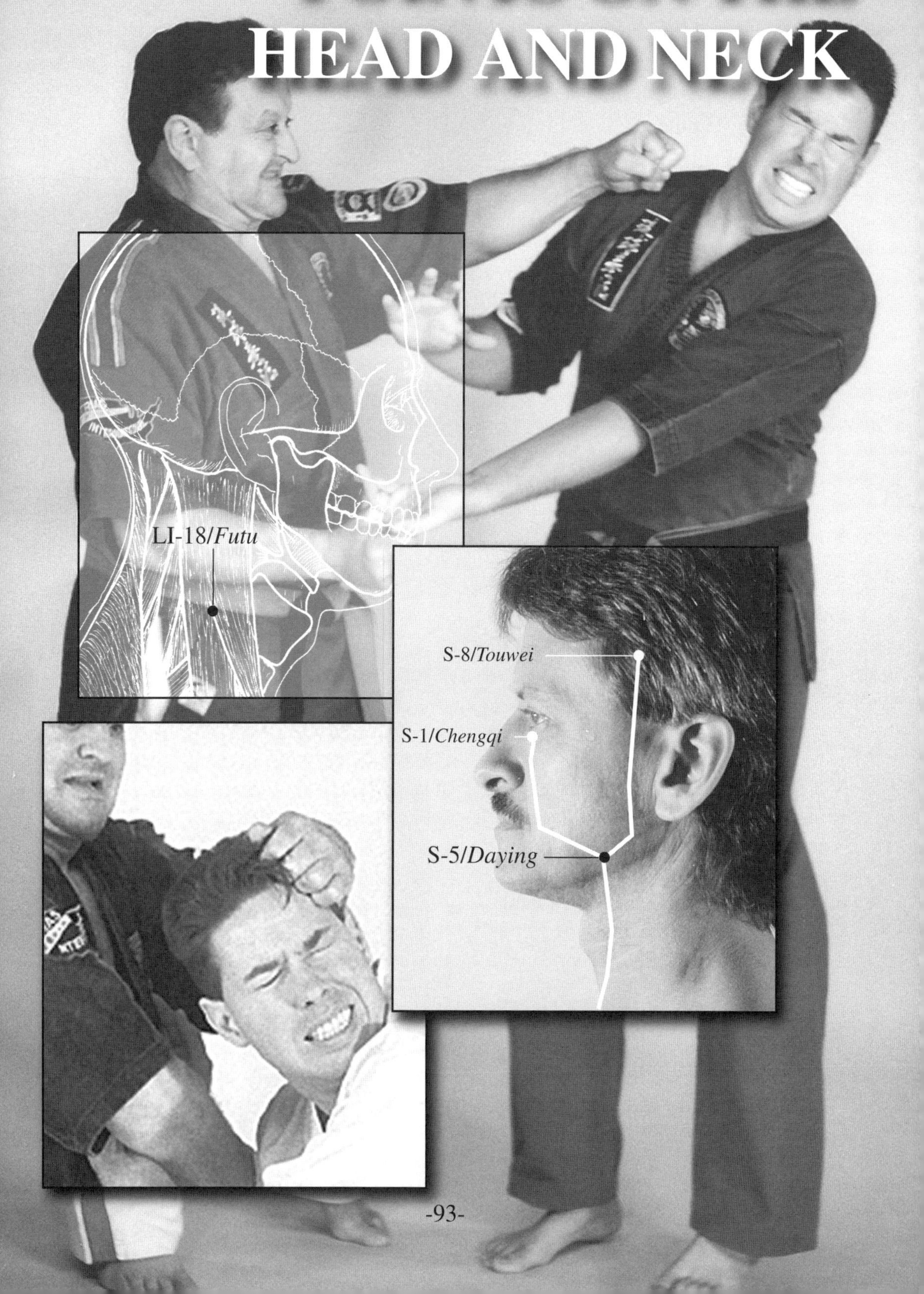

POINTS ON THE HEAD AND NECK

Point Name: S-10/*Shuitu*

Location: At the anterior margin of the sternocleidomastoid, midway between S-9/*Renying* and the clavicle.

Anatomy: A branch of the Herring's nerve and the superior cardiac nerve.

Method & Usage: May be pressed with the thumb to control and immobilize an attacker.

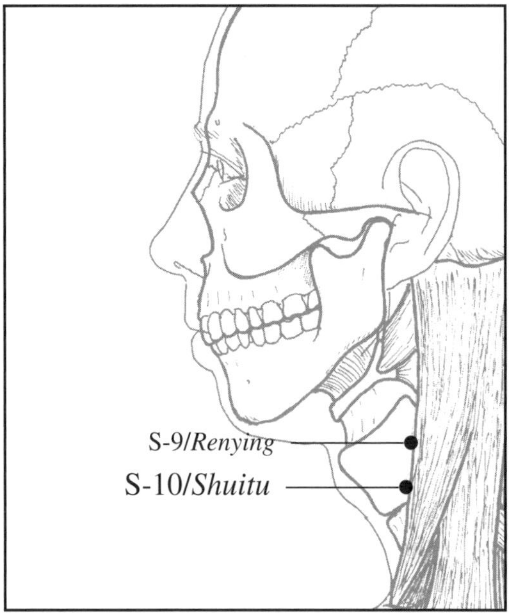

Point Name: S-9/*Renying*

Location: At the meeting of the anterior border of the sternocleidomastoid and the thyroid cartilage, level with the laryngeal prominence. It is level with the Adam's apple, at the crease of the neck muscle.

Anatomy: The bifurcation of the carotid arteries, the cutaneous colli nerve, a cervical branch of the facial (7th cranial) nerve, the vagus nerve, and a branch of the Herring nerve.

Method & Usage: Strike with a penetrating blow on a 45° angle into the neck to produce unconsciousness.

Comments: Strike in combination with S-10/*Shuitu* (above).

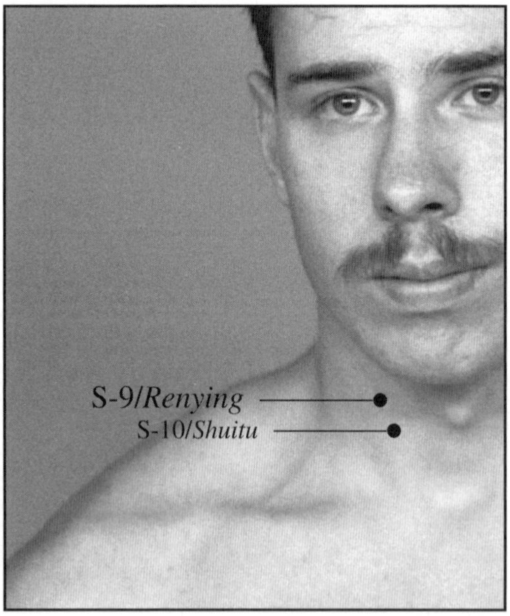

1

2

POINTS ON THE HEAD AND NECK (cont.)

Point Name: LI-18/*Futu*

Location: 3 AU lateral to the laryngeal prominence, in the posterior margin of the sternocleidomastoid. It can be found on the side of the neck, level with the Adam's apple and directly below the ear.

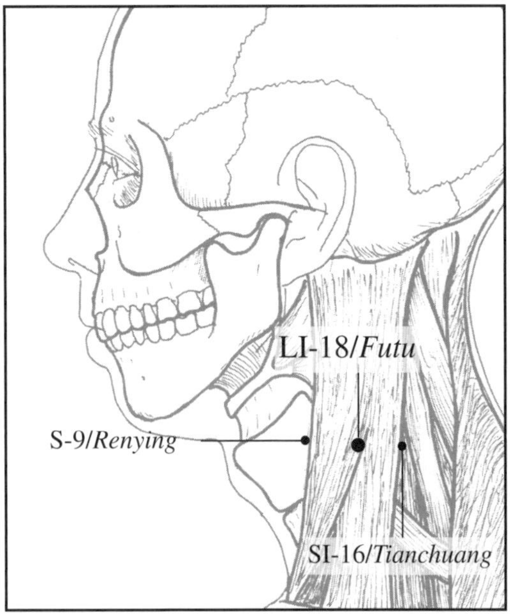

Anatomy: The ascending cervical artery, the great auricular nerve, the cutaneous colli nerve, the lesser occipital nerve and the accessory nerve.

Method & Usage: Touch LI-18/*Futu* on one side of the neck while striking matching LI-18/*Futu* on the opposite side. The direction of force is on a line connecting the points through the neck.

Comments: Practice with caution.

Point Name: SI-16/*Tianchuang*

Location: On the posterior border of the sternocleidomastoid, 1 AU posterior to LI-18/*Futu*. This point lies on the side of the neck, level with the Adam's apple, and just behind the muscle.

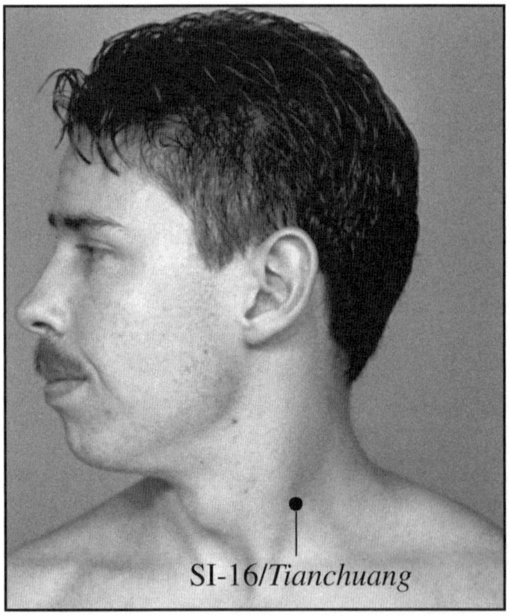

Anatomy: The ascending cervical artery, the cutaneous cervical nerve, and the emerging portion of the great auricular nerve.

Method & Usage: With the opponent's head turned slightly, strike this point at about a 30 degree angle from back to front.

POINTS ON THE HEAD AND NECK (cont.)

Point Name: TW-17/*Yifeng*

Location: Behind the jaw, in the depression under the ear.

Anatomy: The posterior auricular artery, the superficial jugular vein, the great auricular nerve and the facial (7th cranial) nerve at its point of emergence from the stylomastoid foramen.

Method & Usage: Strike diagonally back to front, hitting the point against the back of the jaw-bone, resulting in unconsciousness.

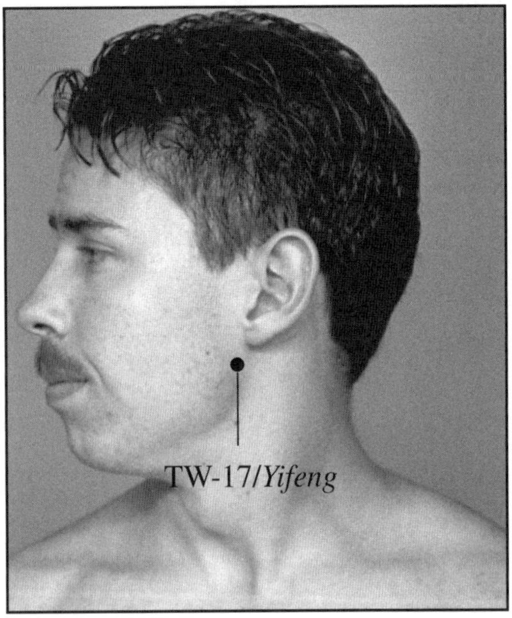

Point Name: SI-17/*Tianrong*

Location: Posterior to the angle of the mandible in the anterior margin at the insertion of the sternocleidomastoid muscle. It is located in the depression behind the corner of the jaw.

Anatomy: The internal carotid artery, a branch of the great auricular nerve, a cervical branch of the facial (7th cranial) nerve, and a superior cervical ganglion of the sympathetic trunk.

Method & Usage: This point is poked or struck on an upward 45° angle toward the center of the head.

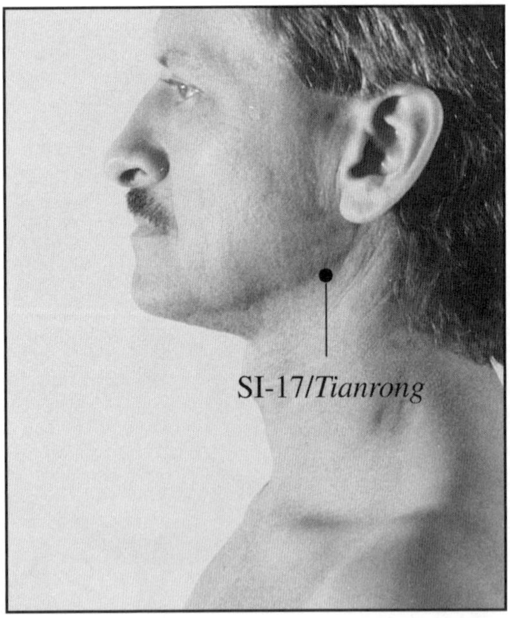

1

2

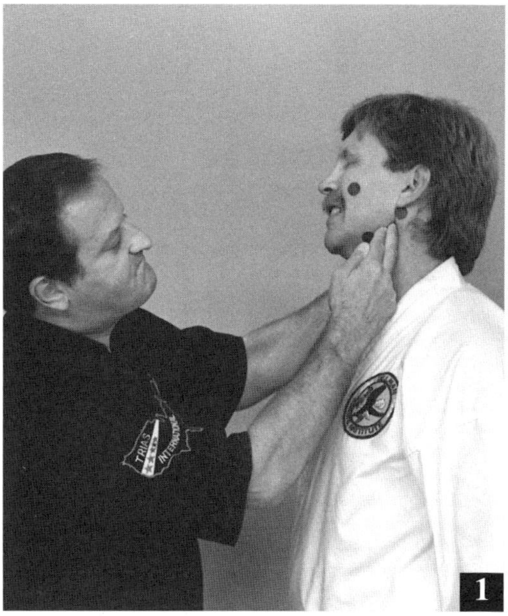
1

2

POINTS ON THE HEAD AND NECK (cont.)

Point Name: S-5/*Daying*

Location: Anterior to the angle of the mandible, on the anterior border of the masseter muscle, at the groove of the jaw. It is found at the notch along the bottom of the jaw.

Anatomy: The lower mandibular branch of the facial (7th cranial) nerve and the facial artery.

Method & Usage: Hit this point on a line 45 degrees towards the center of the head. Single knuckle or finger-tip strikes should roll into the inside of the bone. Palm strikes hit on the grove of the jaw with a slight twisting motion.

Comments: The Stomach meridian forks at this point. As a result, S-5/*Daying* is a site of energetic "turbulence," making it a vulnerable target. From an anatomical perspective, striking this point slams the lower mandibular branch of the facial (7th cranial) nerve against the underlying jaw bone.

Because of the splitting of the meridian, this point carries an exaggerated yin/yang quality. When a man is using a palm strike to hit S-5/*Daying* on another man, he should have both feet firmly planted on the floor. When a women palm strikes S-5/*Daying* on a man, she should lift the heel on her striking side (1,2).

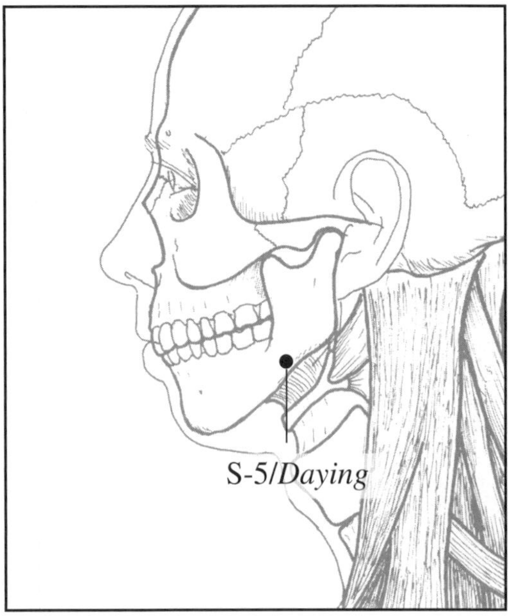

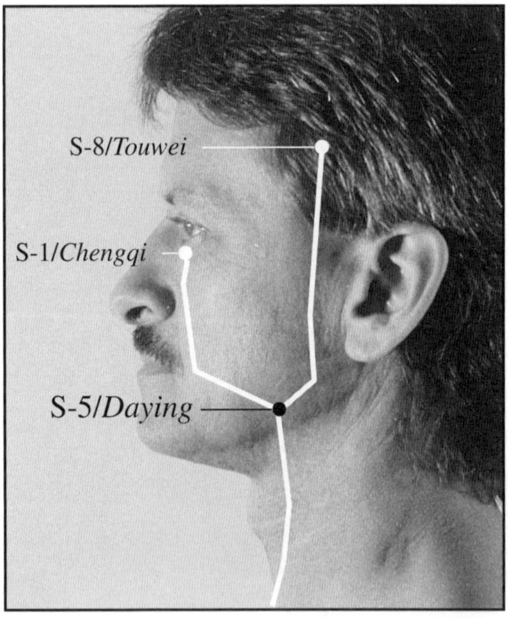

琉球拳法

1

2

POINTS ON THE HEAD AND NECK (cont.)

Point Name: S-6/*Jiache*

Location: About 1 AU from the corner of the jaw, in the masseter muscle.

Anatomy: Branches of the auricular nerve, the marginal mandibular branches of the facial nerve.

Method & Usage: Hit this point directly to stun.

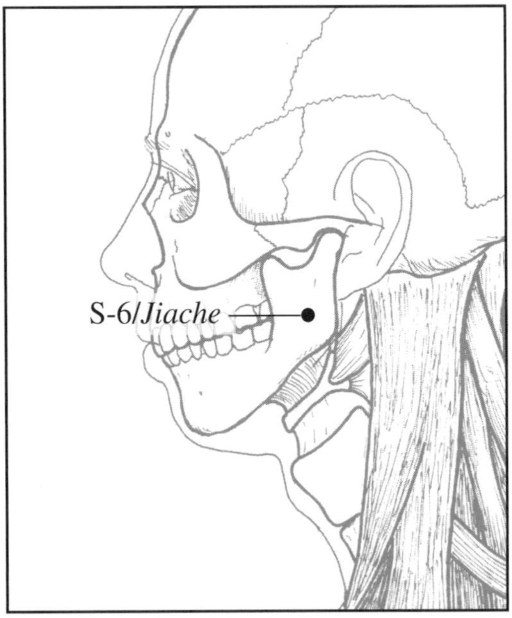

Point Name: Gv-26/*Rhenzhong*

Location: The philtrum, in the orbicularis oris muscle. It is located in the depression between the nose and the upper lip.

Anatomy: A buccal branch of the facial (seventh cranial) nerve and a branch of the infraorbital nerve.

Method & Usage: Contrary to popular teaching, this is not a hit-point. Rather, rub with the knuckles to control the opponent's head.

Comments: The Large Intestine meridian crosses the centerline of the body at Gv-26/*Rhenzhong*.

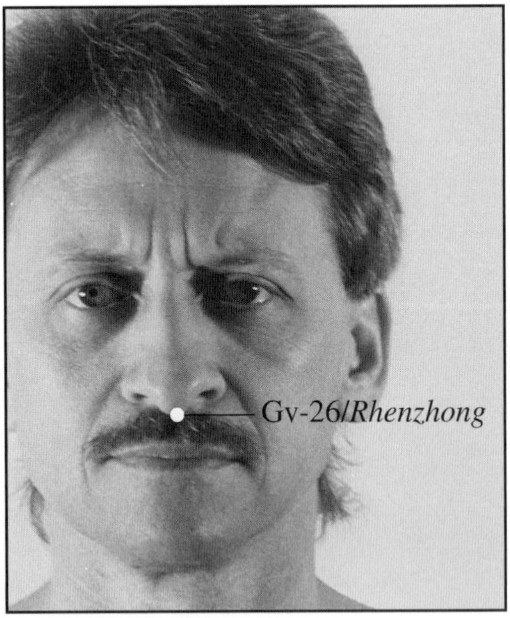

Point Name: LI-20/*Yingxiang*

Location: In the nasolabial groove. It is in the crease just outside the nostril.

Anatomy: Branches of the infraorbital nerve from the maxillary nerve, and the buccal branches of the facial nerve.

Method & Usage: Strike or grind with a single-knuckle fist.

Comments: This point on the left side of the face connects to the right side of the body, and vice versa. The Large Intestine meridian is the only organ related meridians to cross the center line.

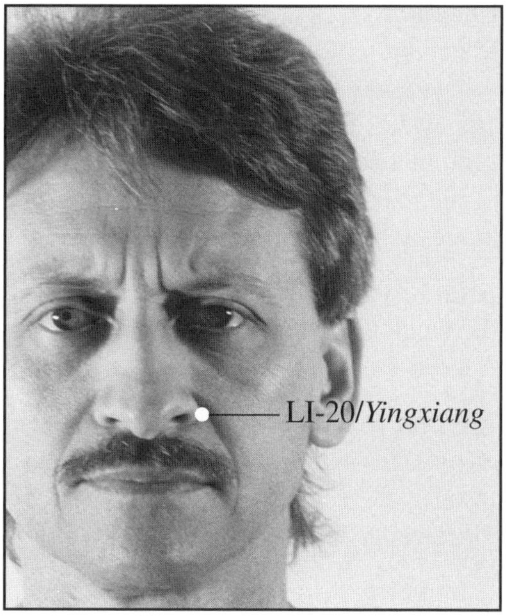

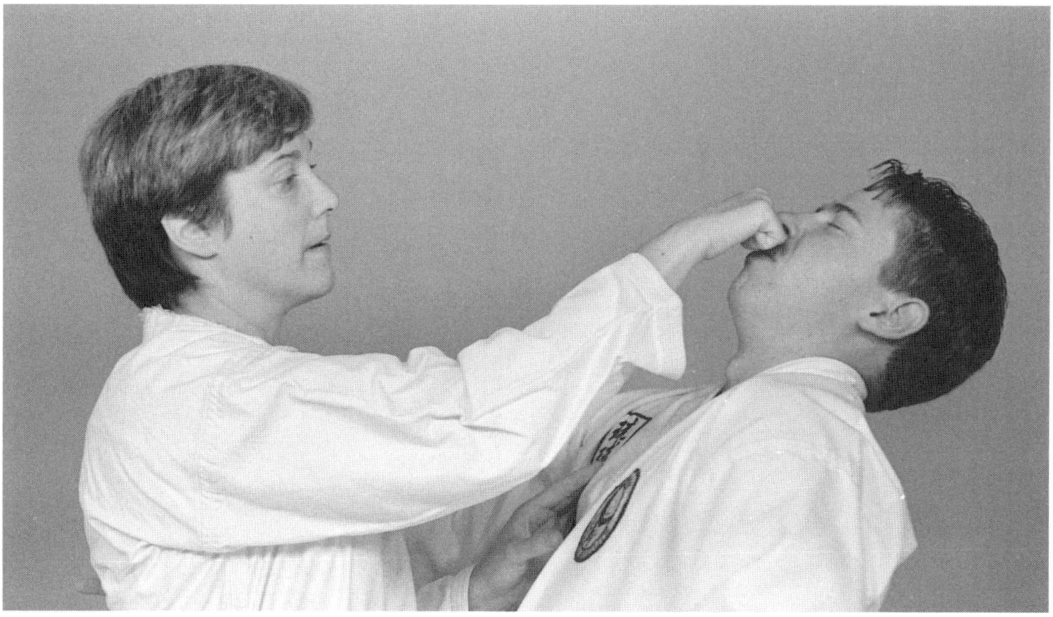

POINTS ON THE HEAD AND NECK (cont.)

Point Name: SI-18/*Quanliao*

Location: At the mid-point of the inferior margin of the zygomatic bone, directly below the outer canthus of the eye. It lies in the depression below the prominence of the cheekbone, in front of the masseter (the muscle which bulges when clenching the jaw).

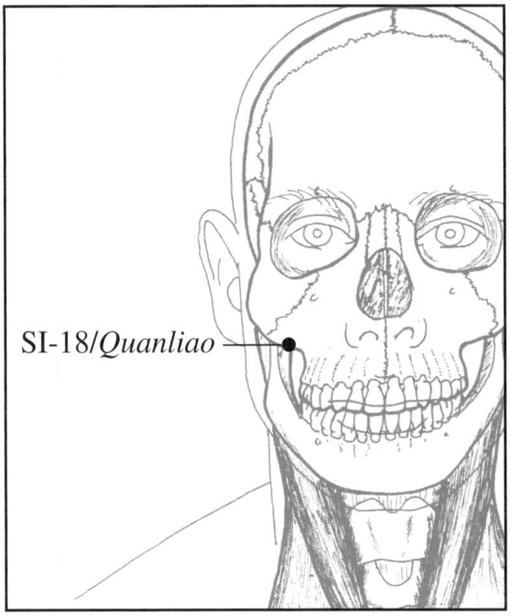

Anatomy: The transverse facial artery, the facial (7th cranial) nerve and the infraorbital nerve.

Method & Usage: This point is struck or pressed on an upward diagonal line towards the center of the head causing the neck to release.

Comments: A preferred method of attacking this point is with middle knuckle fist (nakadaka ken), which is formed by allowing the second joint of the middle finger to protrude like a spear-head. This particular fist is suited for delivering upward energy.

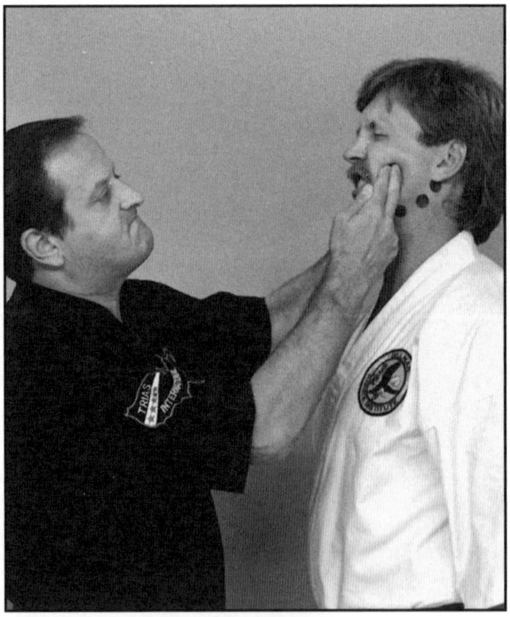

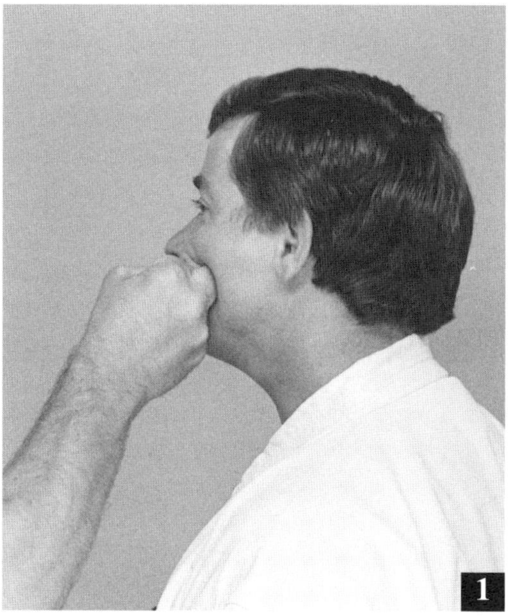

1

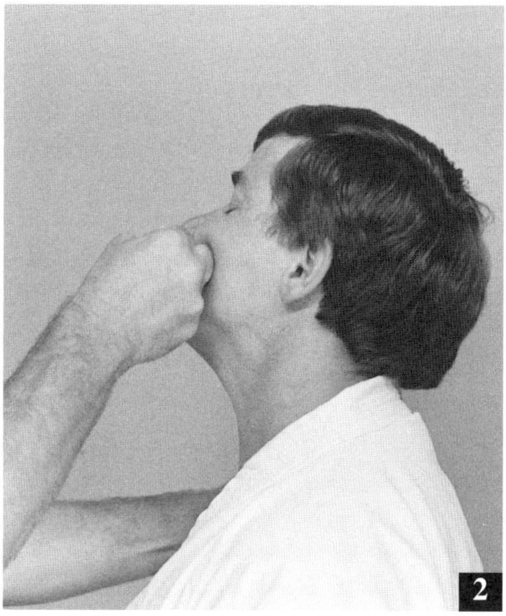

2

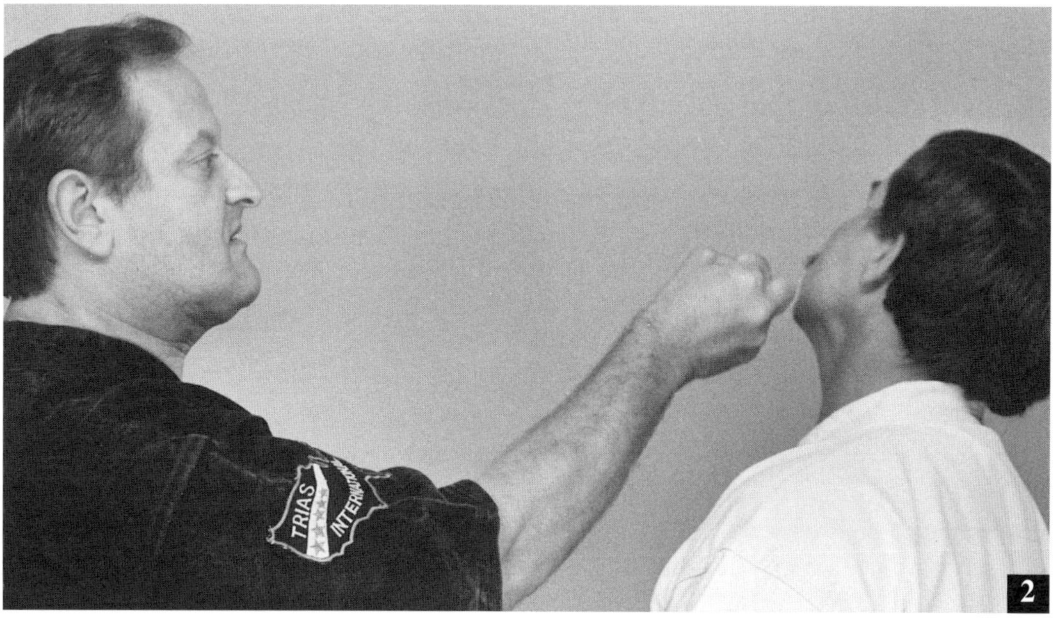

2

POINTS ON THE HEAD AND NECK (cont.)

Point Name: S-1/*Chengqi*

Location: Directly below the pupil (when the eye looks straight ahead) at the infraorbital ridge.

Anatomy: The inferior branch of the oculomotor nerve and the muscular branch of the facial (7th cranial) nerve.

Method & Usage: Responds to pressure or a light tap on a downward angle.

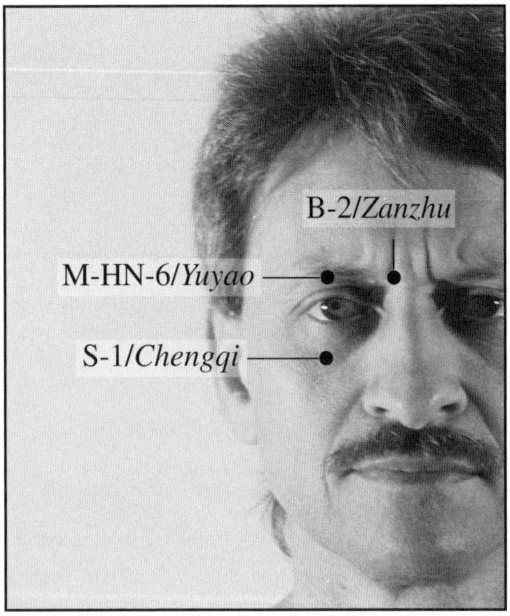

Point Name: B-2/*Zanzhu*

Location: At the inner end of the eyebrow, in the supraorbital notch.

Anatomy: A medial branch of the frontal nerve.

Method & Usage: Press to control the head and disrupt the vision.

Point Name: M-HN-6/*Yuyao*

Location: In the depression above the pupil on the eyebrow ridge.

Anatomy: Situated on the supraorbital foramen.

Method & Usage: Tap up against the orbit. *(Use extreme caution.)*

Special Comment: S-1/*Chengqi*, B-2/*Zanzhu*, and M-HN-6/*Yuyao*, ring the eye. They can be used together by placing the back of one hand over the eye, touching these points, then striking into the palm with the other hand (1,2).

1

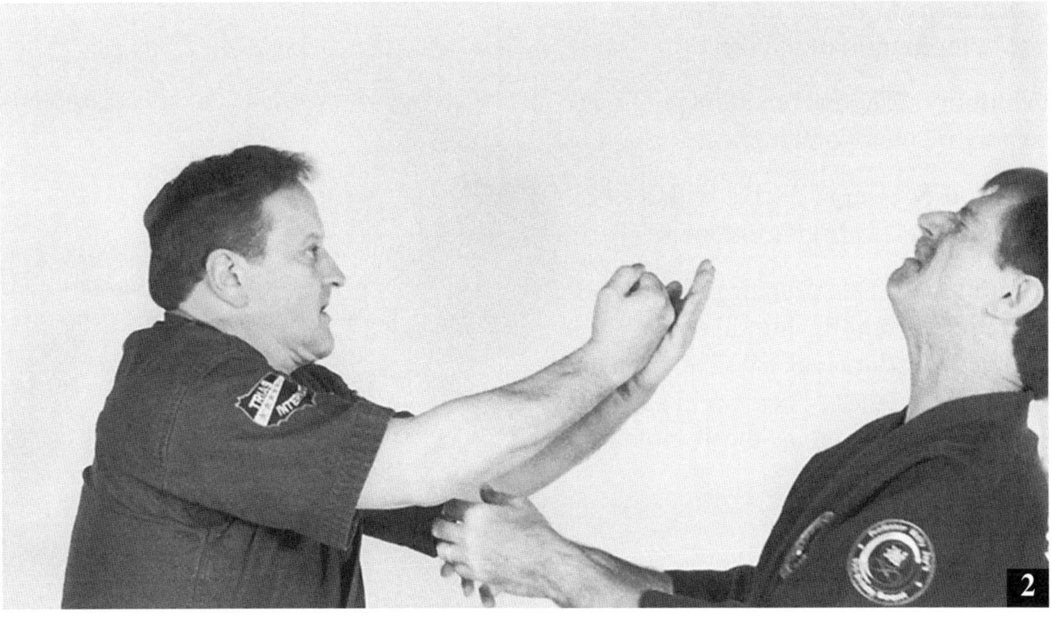

2

POINTS ON THE HEAD AND NECK (cont.)

Point Name: TW-23/*Sizhukong*

Location: In the oricularis oculi muscle, on the lateral border of the zygomatic process of the frontal bone. It is at the end of the eyebrow in the depression of the temple.

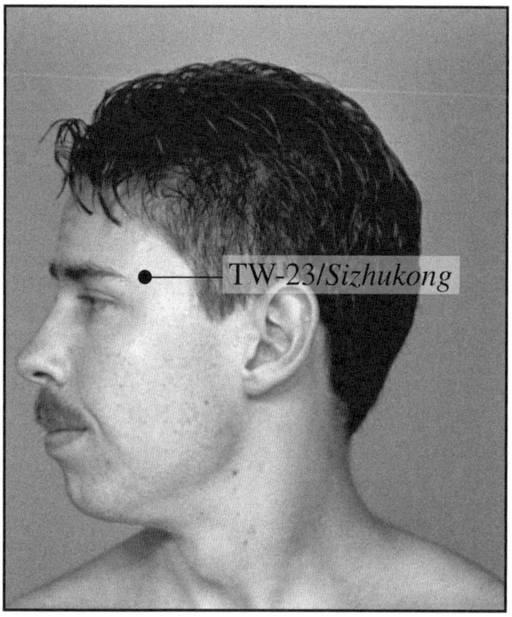

Anatomy: The zygomaticotemporalis nerve.

Method & Usage: Strike with a small surface, such as a middle- knuckle fist, from the side, and slightly forward.

Comments: TW-23/*Sizhukong* is the terminus point of the Triple Warmer meridian. A blow can break the bone and injure the eye.

Point Name: GB-1/*Tongziliao*

Location: At the corner of the eye, at the outer margin of the orbit.

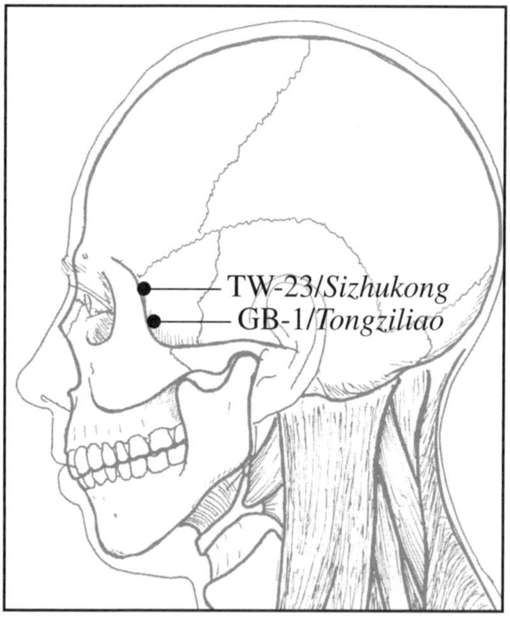

Anatomy: The zygomaticofacial and zygomaticotemporal nerves.

Method & Usage: Strike with a slightly back to front motion.

Comments: Due to their proximity, and relationship by diurnal cycle, GB-1/*Tongziliao* and TW-23/*Sizhukong* are used together. They could accurately be referred to as the Temple Point Cluster.

琉球拳法

POINTS ON THE HEAD AND NECK (cont.)

Point Name: M-HN-5/*Taiyang*

Location: Center of the temple.

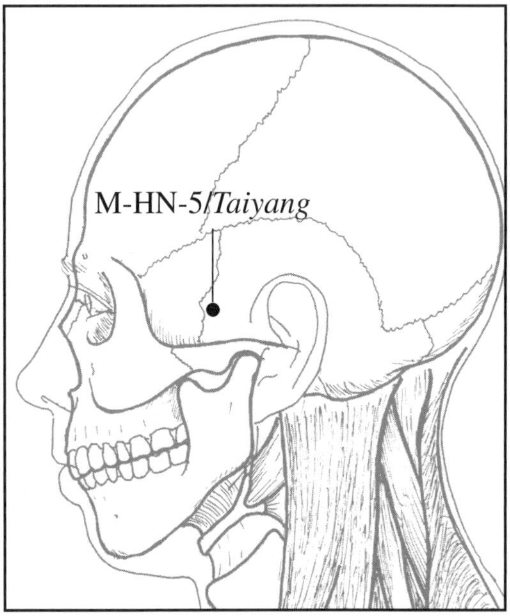

Anatomy: The zygomaticofacial branch of the zygomatic nerve, the temporal and zygomatic branches of the facial nerve, the temporal branch of the mandibular nerve and the branches of the superficial temporal artery and vein in this area.

Method & Usage: Strike from the side, typically with a single-knuckle fist (ippon-ken).

Comments: The skull is fragile at this point, so that a blow here is generally regarded as lethal.

Point Name: M-HN-14/*Bitong*

Location: At the lateral, inferior side of the nasal bone, at the superior end of the nasolabial sulcus. It is on the side of the nose, just at the juncture of the nose and the cheek.

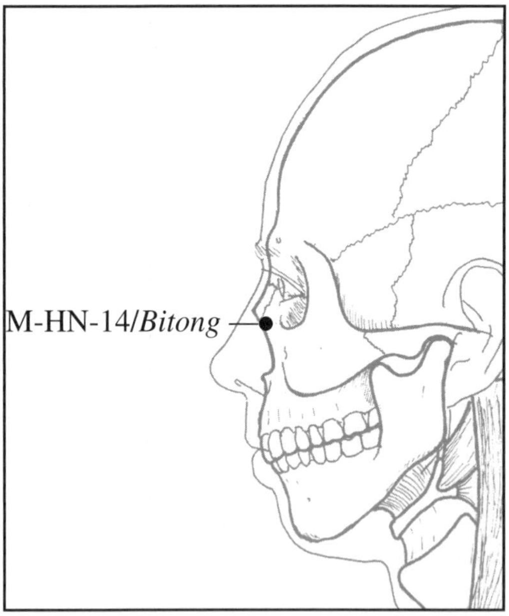

Anatomy: The infratrochlearis nerve, and a branch of the infraorbital nerve.

Method & Usage: Strike this point from the side to cause the eyes to close tightly and immediately tear up. A substantial blow will break the nose.

Comments: The nose is structurally strongest straight on. But a blow from the side against this pressure point can cause damage with minimal effort.

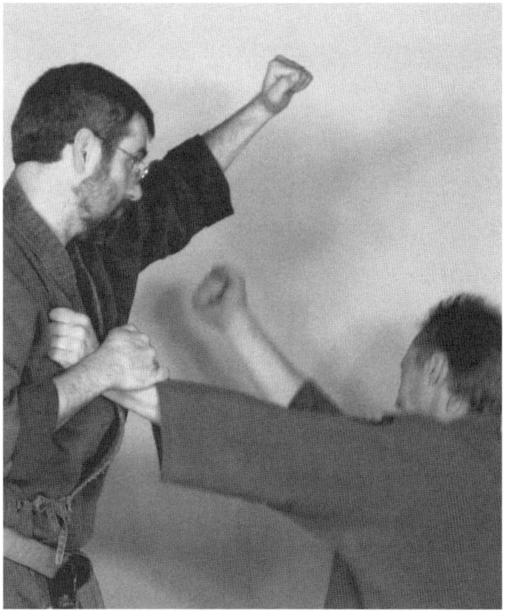

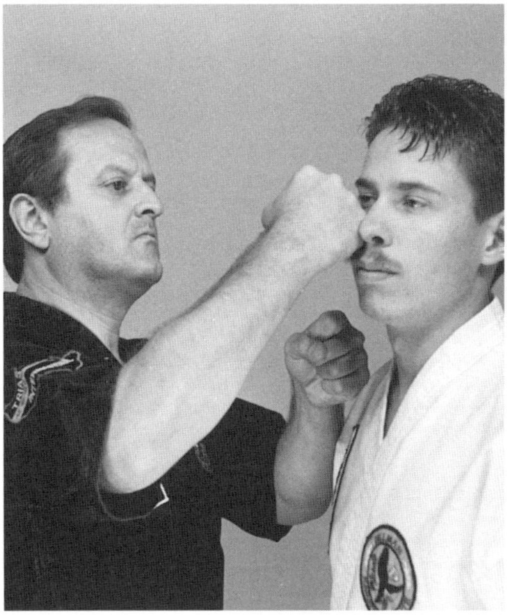

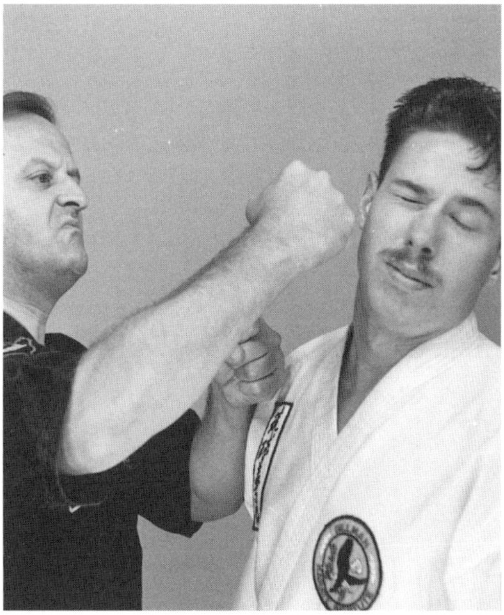

POINTS ON THE HEAD AND NECK (cont.)

Point Name: Anterior Nose Point/*Ganbi*

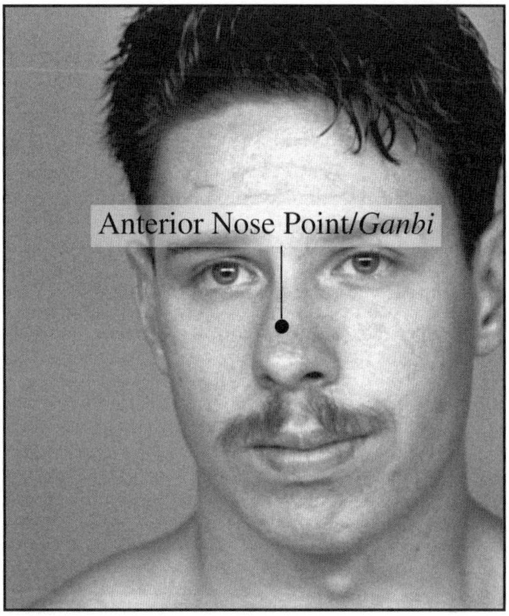

Location: Centered in the nasal cartilage, at the end of the nasal bone.

Anatomy: The anterior ethmoidal nerve.

Method & Usage: Strike 45° downward to stretch the nerve and disrupt vision. This point produces a significant kinesthetic response, and is very useful in self-defense.

Comments: This point is associated with the liver. It has no formal name or designation in acupuncture, so we use the name *Ganbi* (*gan* =liver + *bi* = nose) which would no doubt raise a smile from a native speaker of Chinese.

Point Name: M-HN-18/*Jiachengjiang*

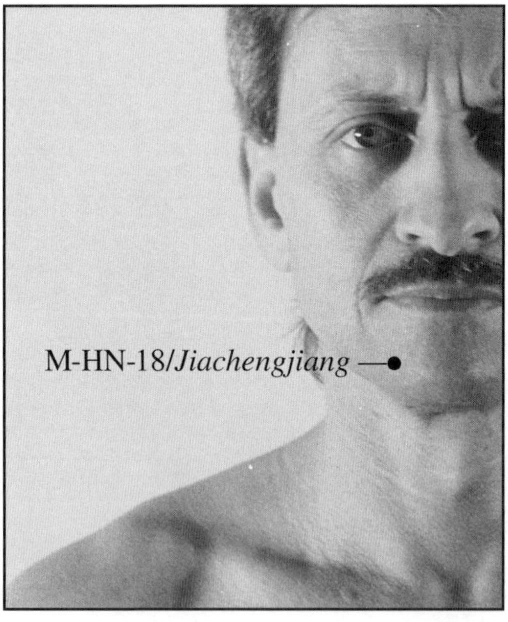

Location: Situated on the mental foramen.

Mode and Usage: Strike in and down to control the head, and stagger the assailant.

Comments: This point easily produces unconsciousness when struck. It is also used to release the neck for head control techniques.

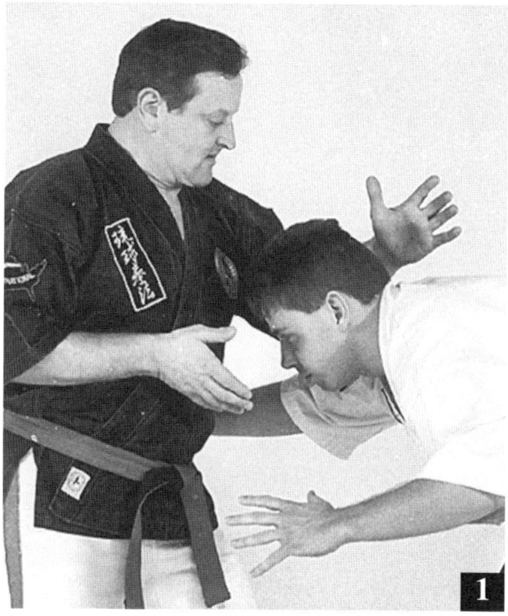
1

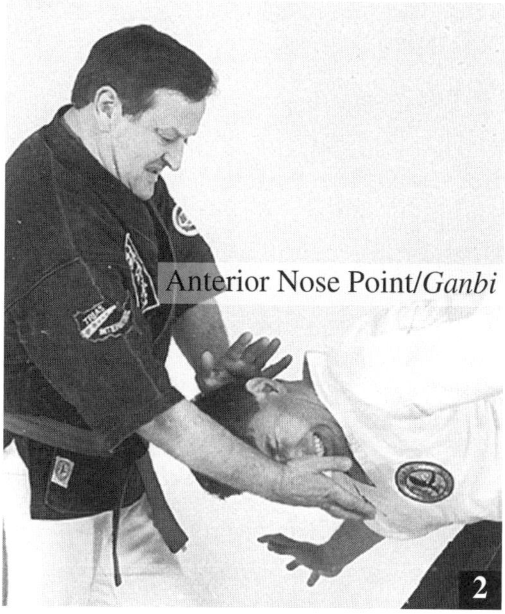
Anterior Nose Point/Ganbi
2

M-HN-18/Jiachengjiang
1

2

POINTS ON THE HEAD AND NECK (cont.)

Point Cluster: Forehead Cluster
GB-13/*Benshen*

GB-14/*Yangbai*

GB-15/*Toulinq*

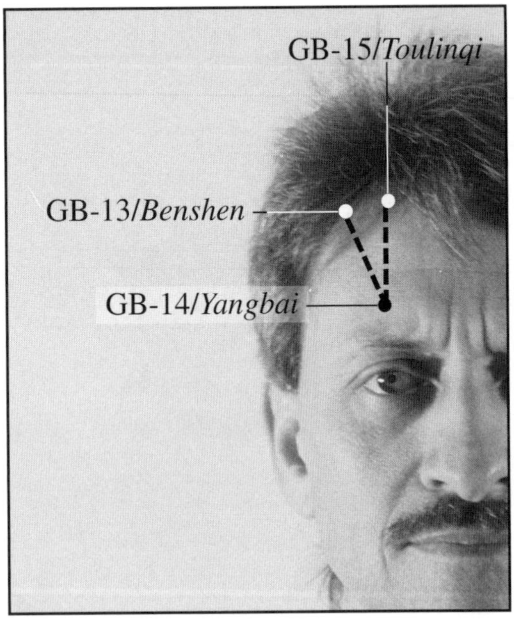

Location: GB-14/*Yangbai* is above the mid-point of the eyebrow, in the depression of the superciliary arch, about one third of the distance from the eyebrow to the top of the forehead.

Anatomy: Directly on a lateral branch of the frontal nerve.

Location: GB-13/*Benshen is located* in the hairline, to the side of GB-15/*Toulinqi*, in the lateral aspect of the forehead.

Anatomy: The lateral branch of the frontal nerve.

Location: GB-15/*Toulinqi* is in the hairline, directly above GB-14/*Yangbai*.

Anatomy: The anastomotic branch of the medial nerve and lateral branches of the frontal nerve.

Mode and Usage: Strike these points with a palm technique to cause motor impairment and disorientation leading to unconsciousness.

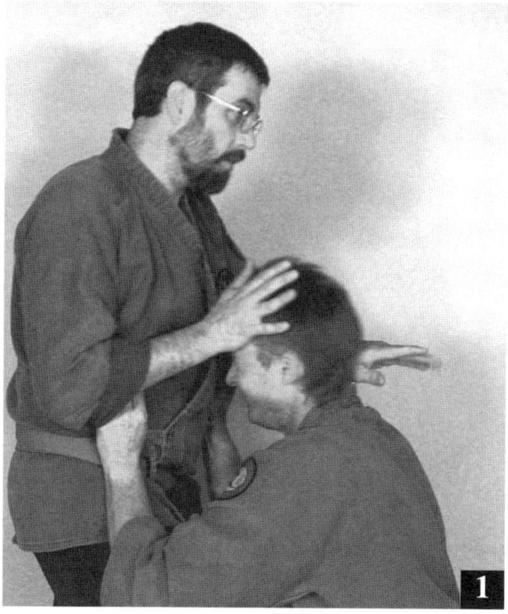

1

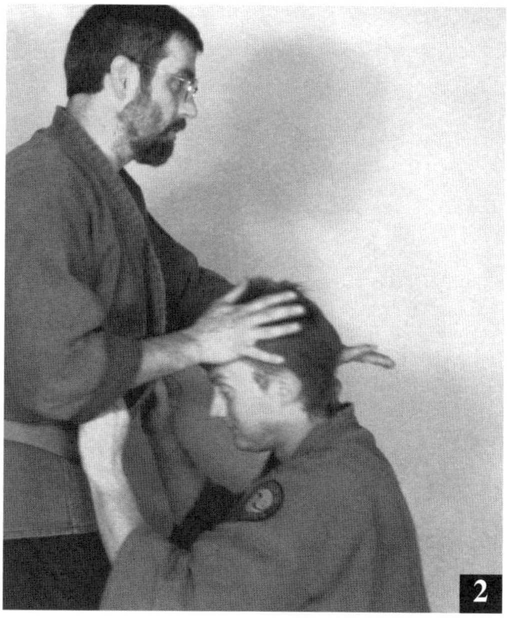

2

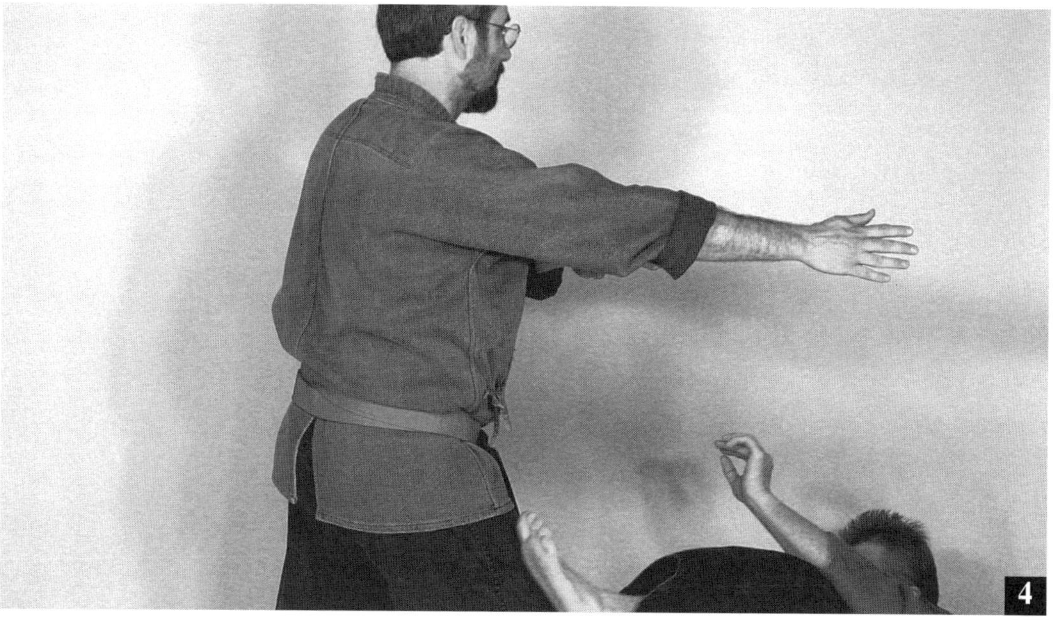

4

POINTS ON THE HEAD AND NECK (cont.)

Point Cluster: Scalp Points
GB-9/*Tianchong*

GB-10/*Fubai*

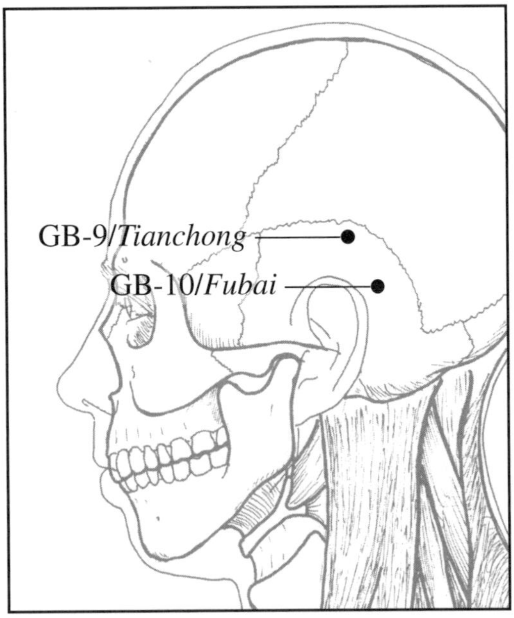

Location: GB-9/*Tianchong* is on the side of the head, just superior, and slightly posterior, to the apex of the ear.

Location: GB-10/*Fubai* is on the side of the head, just behind the ear, inferior and posterior to GB-9/*Tianchong*.

Anatomy: GB-9/*Tianchong* and GB-10/*Fubai* are supplied by a branch of the great occipital nerve.

Comments: GB-9/*Tianchong* and GB-10/*Fubai* are meeting points of the Gall Bladder and Bladder meridians.

Mode and Usage: Dig the knuckles into these points to release the neck.

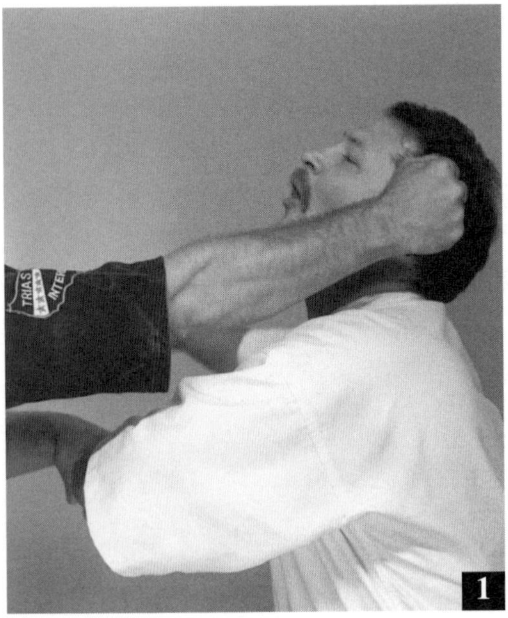
1

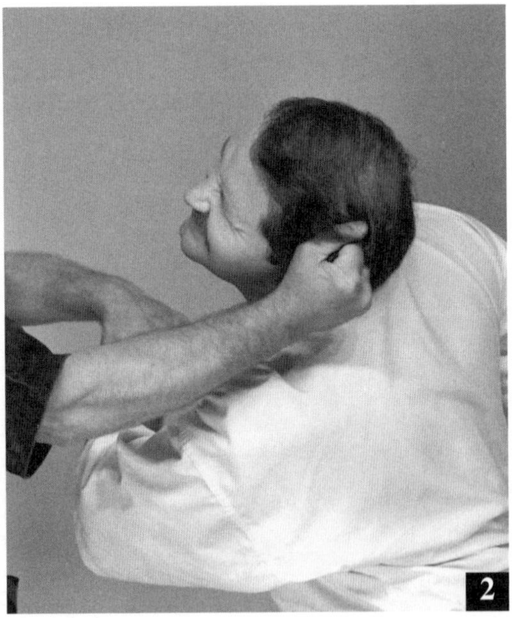
2

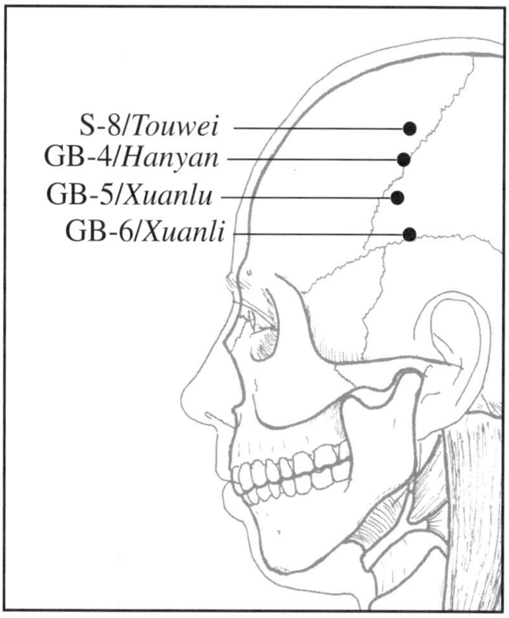

Point Cluster: Scalp Points
S-8/*Touwei*

GB-4/*Hanyan*

GB-5/*Xuanlu*

GB-6/*Xuanli*

Location: S-8/*Touwei* is on the side of the head in the hairline.

Anatomy: A branch of the auriculotemporal nerve and the temporal branch of the facial nerve.

Location: GB-4/*Hanyan* is on the side of the head, just below S-8/*Touwei*.

Anatomy: The temporal branch of the auriculotemporal nerve.

Location: GB-5/*Xuanlu* is on the side of the head, just below GB-4/*Hanyan*.

Anatomy: The temporal branch of the auriculotemporal nerve.

Location: GB-6/*Xuanli* is on the side of the head, just below GB-5/*Xuanlu*.

Anatomy: The temporal branch of the auriculotemporal nerve.

Mode and Usage: When grabbing the hair, dig the knuckles into these points to control the head.

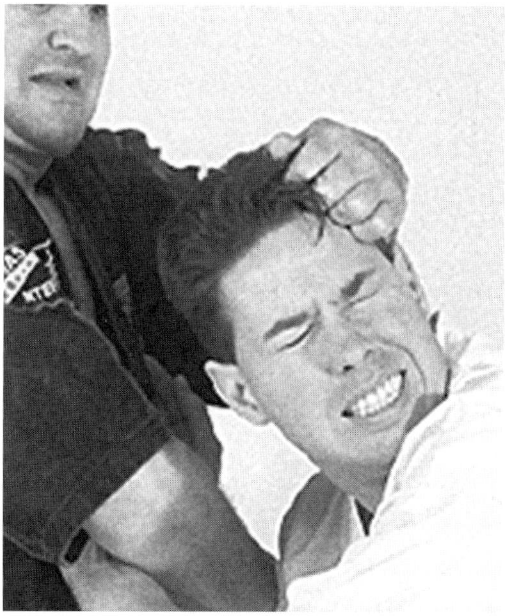

POINTS ON THE HEAD AND NECK (cont.)

Point Cluster: Scalp Points

B-7/*Tongtian*

B-8/*Luoque*

GB-17/*Zhengying*

GB-18/*Chengling*

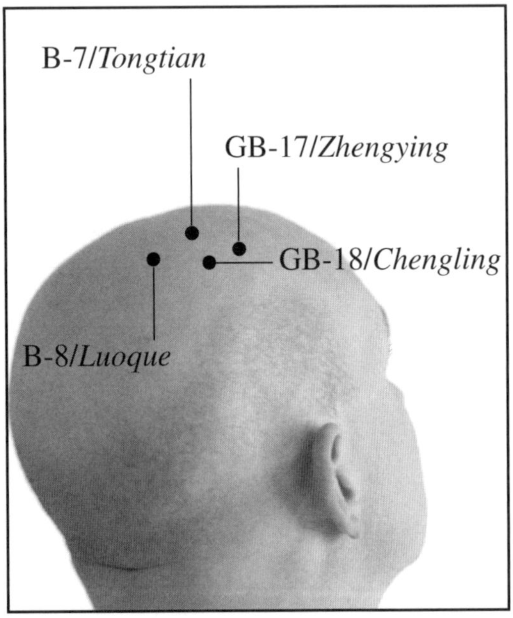

Location: B-7/*Tongtian* is on the top of the head, 1 AU lateral to the midline.

Anatomy: Branches of the frontal and the great occipital nerves.

Location: B-8/*Luoque* is on the top of the head, 1 AU lateral to the midline, and 1.5 AU posterior to B-7/*Tongtian*.

Anatomy: Branches of the frontal and the great occipital nerves.

Location: GB-17/*Zhengying* is on the top of the head, 2 AU lateral to the midline.

Anatomy: Branches of the frontal and the great occipital nerves.

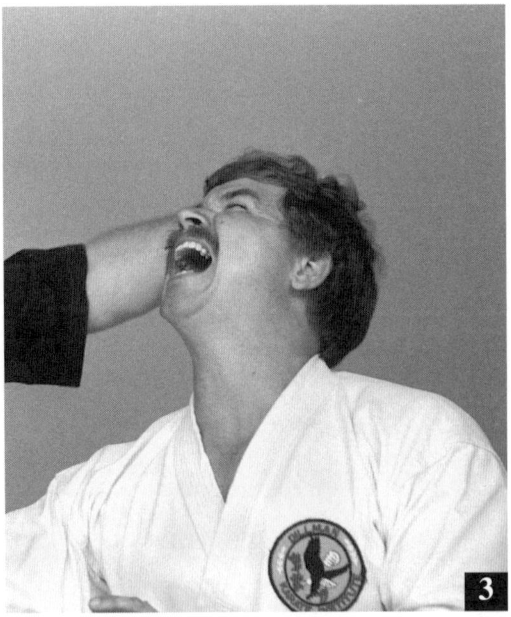
3

Location: GB-18/*Chengling* is on the top of the head, 2 AU lateral to the midline, and 1.5 AU posterior to GB-17/*Zhengying*.

Anatomy: Branches of the frontal and the great occipital nerves.

Comments: GB-17/*Zhengying* and GB-18/*Chengling* are meeting points of the Gall Bladder and the Yang Linking (extraordinary)meridian.

Mode and Usage: When grabbing the hair, dig the knuckles

1

2

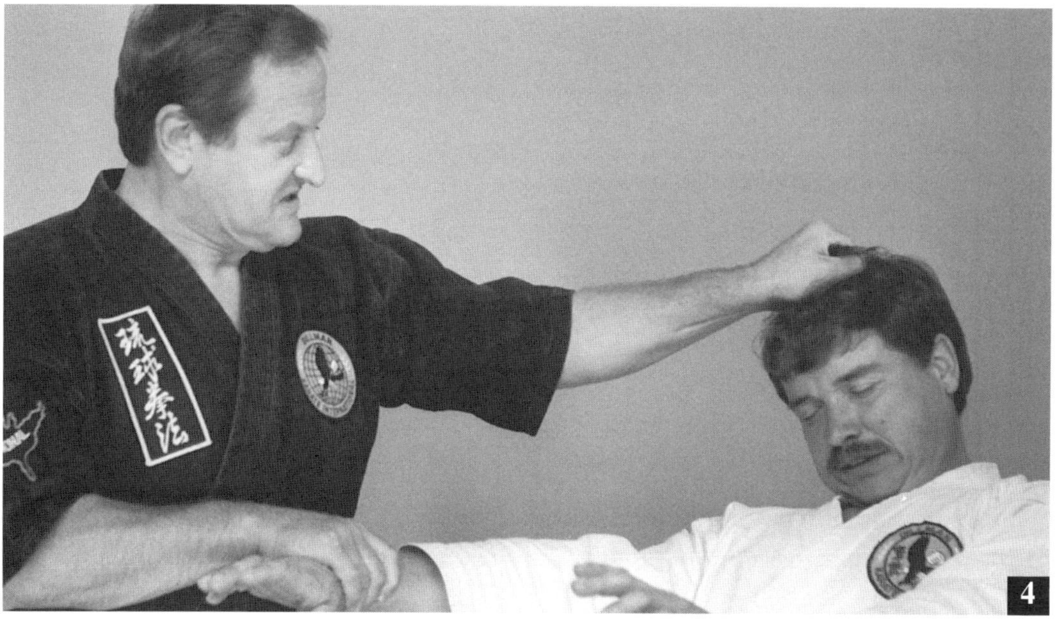

4

POINTS ON THE HEAD AND NECK (cont.)

Point Name: B-10/*Tianzhu*

Location: At the base of the skull, 1 AU lateral to the first cervical vertebrae, at the origin of the trapezius muscle.

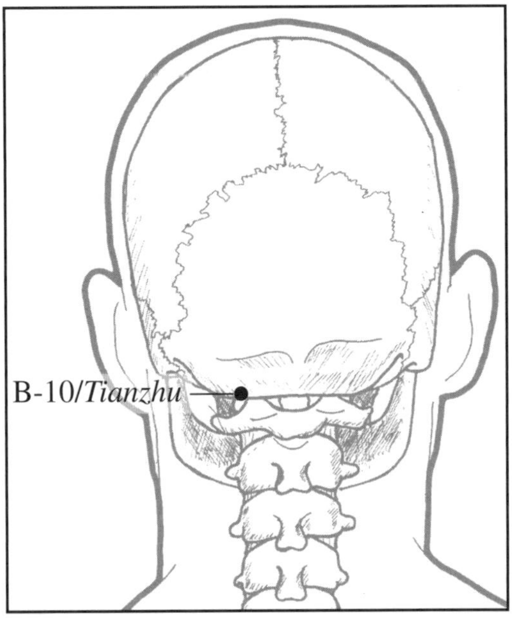

Anatomy: The trunk of the great occipital nerve.

Method & Usage: Strike this point on from back to front in a line toward the forehead to produce unconsciousness.

Comments: Use caution with this point because of the danger of accidentally disrupting the first cervical vertebrae.

Point Name: GB-20/*Fengchi*

Location: In the hollow at the back of neck (between the trapezius and sternocleidomastoid muscles), just below the occipital bone.

Anatomy: A branch of the lesser occipital nerve.

Method & Usage: Strike this point on a rising angle from back to front to produce unconsciousness. A light blow will cause a tingling sensation down the back of the body to the feet, typically causing the heels to pull off the ground.

Comments: Meeting point of the Gall Bladder and Triple Warmer meridians, and of the Yang Linking and Yang Heel Linking (extraordinary) meridians.

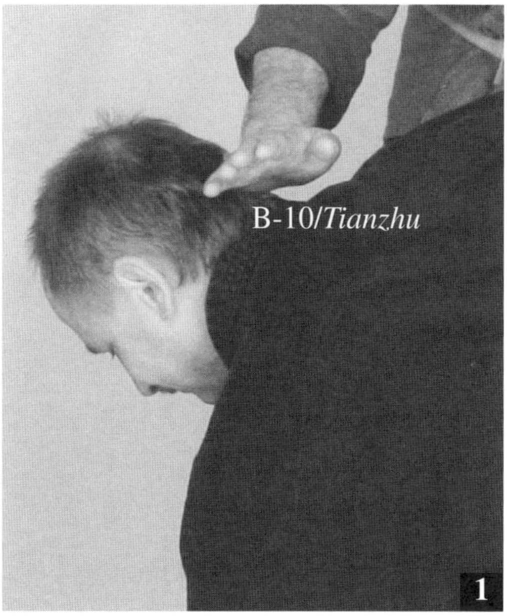
B-10/Tianzhu
1

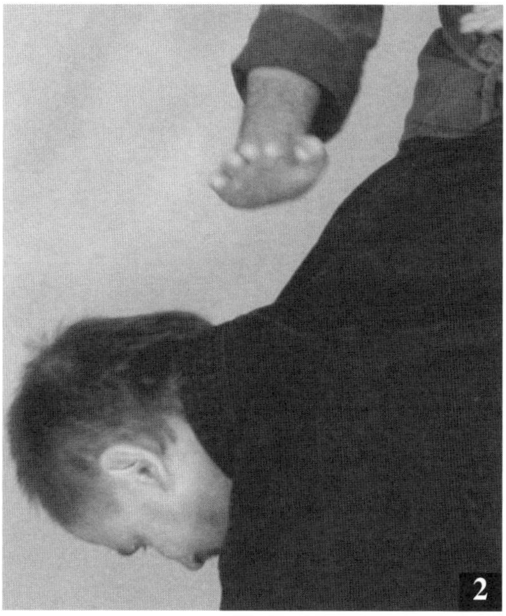
2

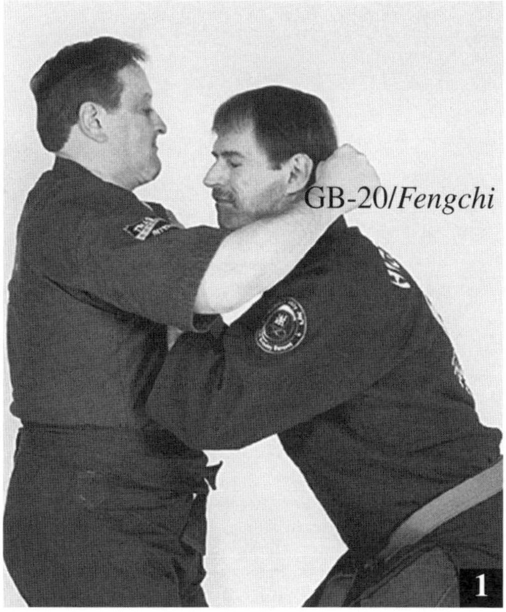
GB-20/Fengchi
1

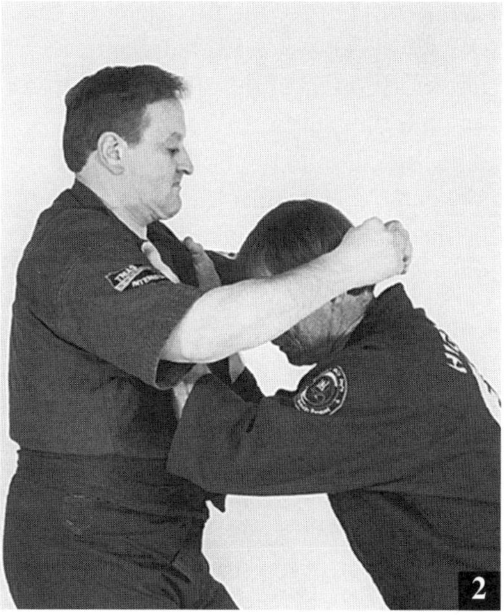
2

POINTS ON THE HEAD AND NECK (cont.)

Point Name: S-11/*Qishe*

Location: At the medial superior border of the clavicle, at the depression just lateral to the sternal head of the sternocleidomastoid muscle. It is in the hollow just behind the collar-bone, next to the sternal notch.

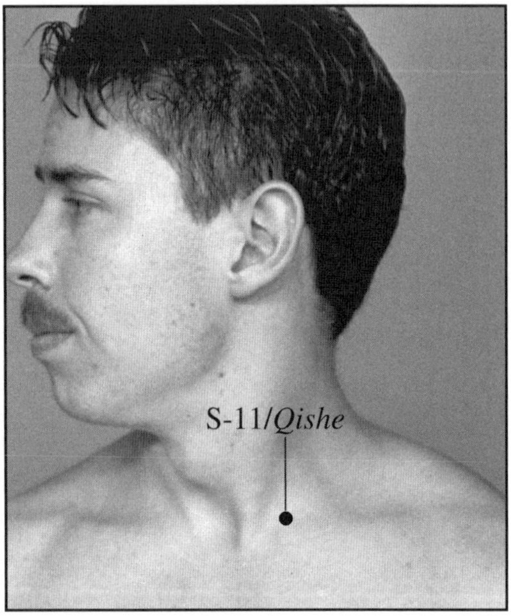

Anatomy: The anterior jugular vein, the common carotid artery, the medial supraclavicular nerve and the muscular branch of the ansa hypoglossi.

Method & Usage: Press with a fingertip in and down to drop an opponent.

Point Name: LI-17/*Tianding*

Location: On the lateral aspect of the neck, 2 AU above S-12, between the posterior border of the sternocleidomastoid and the anterior border of the trapezius. It is in the hollow triangle between the two muscles on the side of the neck, where the neck rises from the body.

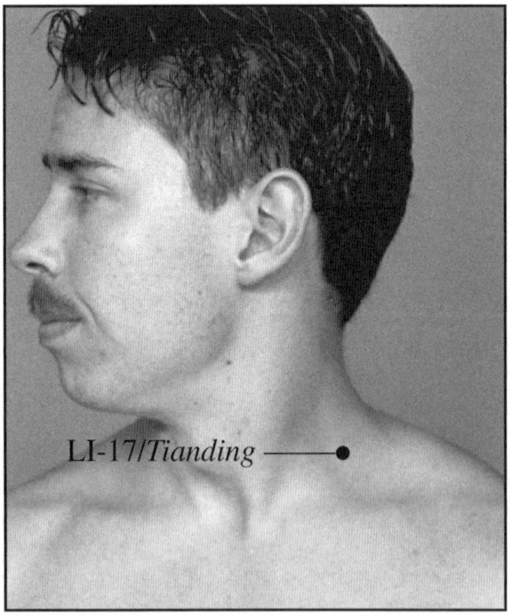

Anatomy: The external jugular vein, the cutaneous cervical nerve, and the phrenic nerve.

Method & Usage: Strike this point at a downward diagonal angle to disrupt the lungs. Even a moderate blow can cause an episode of uncontrollable coughing.

POINTS ON THE TORSO

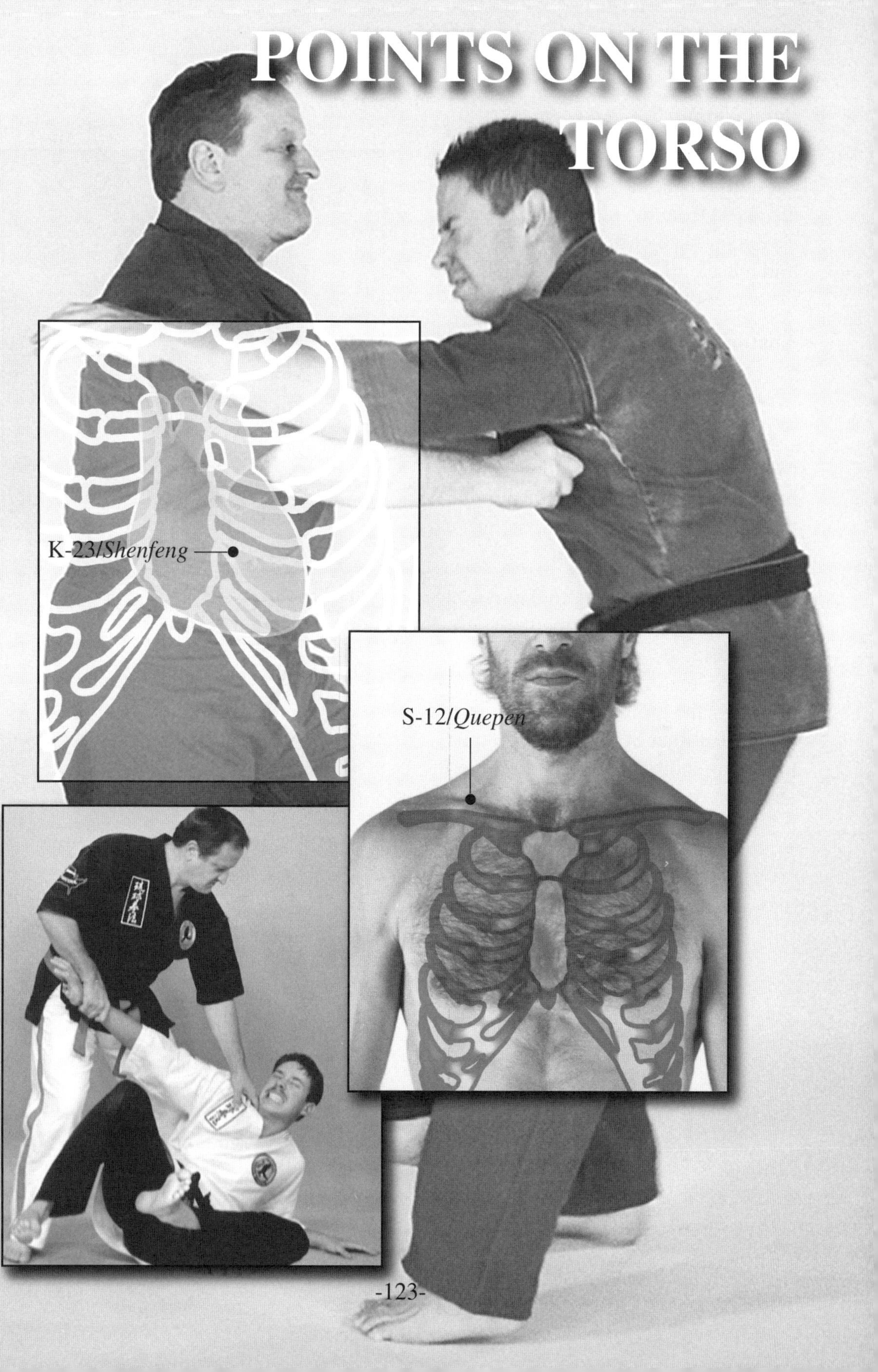

POINTS ON THE HEAD AND NECK (cont.)

Point Name: S-12/*Quepen*

Location: In the depression at the middle of the superior border of the clavicle, 4 AU from the median line, at the clavicular head of the sternocleidomastoid muscle. This point lies just behind the center of collar-bone.

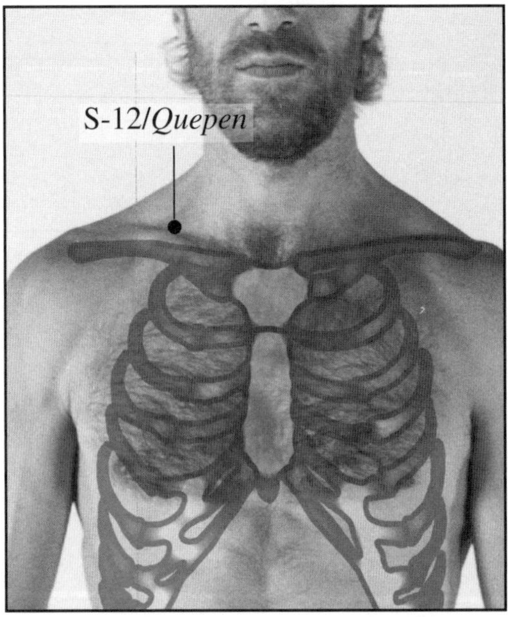

Anatomy: The transverse cervical artery, the intermediate, supraclavicular nerve, and the supraclavicular portion of the brachial plexus.

Method & Usage: Press downward behind the collar bone with the fingertips to drive the opponent to the ground (1-4).

Comments: According to the most ancient acupuncture texts, the three arm yang meridians – Small Intestine, Triple Warmer, Large Intestine – actually cross the Stomach meridian here. This means that S-12/ *Quepen* can be treated as another point on those meridians.

3

1

2

4

POINTS ON THE TORSO

Point Name: L-1/*Zhongfu*

Location: In the upper portion of the pectoralis muscle, about 1 AU below the lateral end of the clavicle in the first intercostal space. It is on the curve of the upper chest near the meeting of the chest and shoulder.

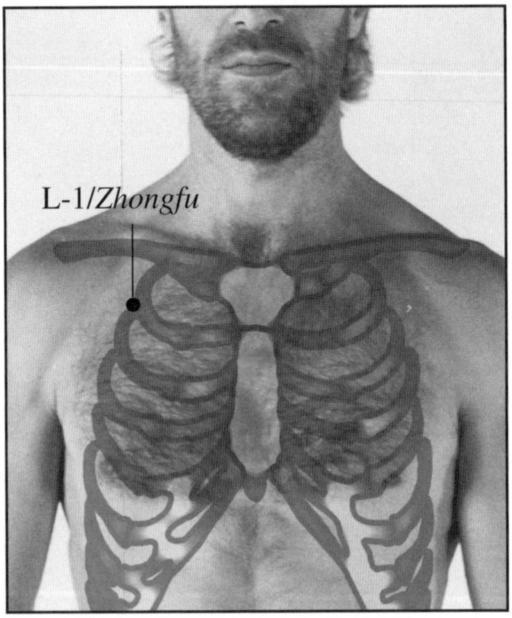

Anatomy: An intermediate branch of the supraclavicular nerve, a branch of the anterior thoracic nerve and the first intercostal nerve.

Method & Usage: Strike this point in a downward and inward direction to disrupt the respiratory system.

Comments: L-1/*Zhongfu* is the alarm point for the lung meridian, which makes it a particularly vulnerable point.

Point Name: GB-23/*Zhejin*

Location: In the fifth intercostal space, behind the pectoral muscle.

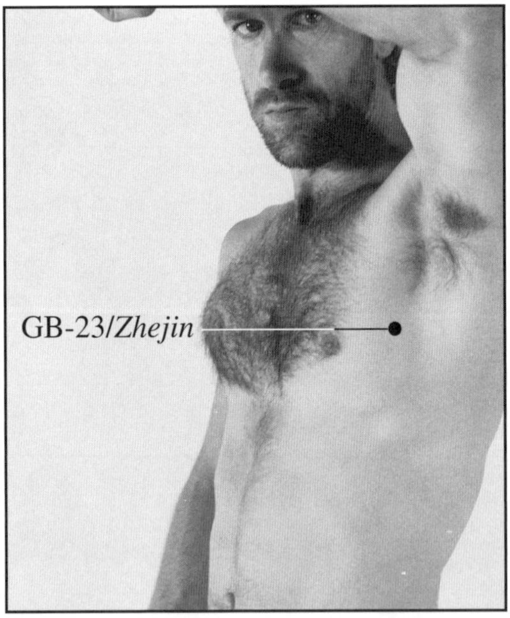

Anatomy: The lateral cutaneous branch of the fifth intercostal nerve.

Method & Usage: Strike in the direction of the spine.

Comments: A blow at this point can also cause pain at B-15/*Xinshu*.

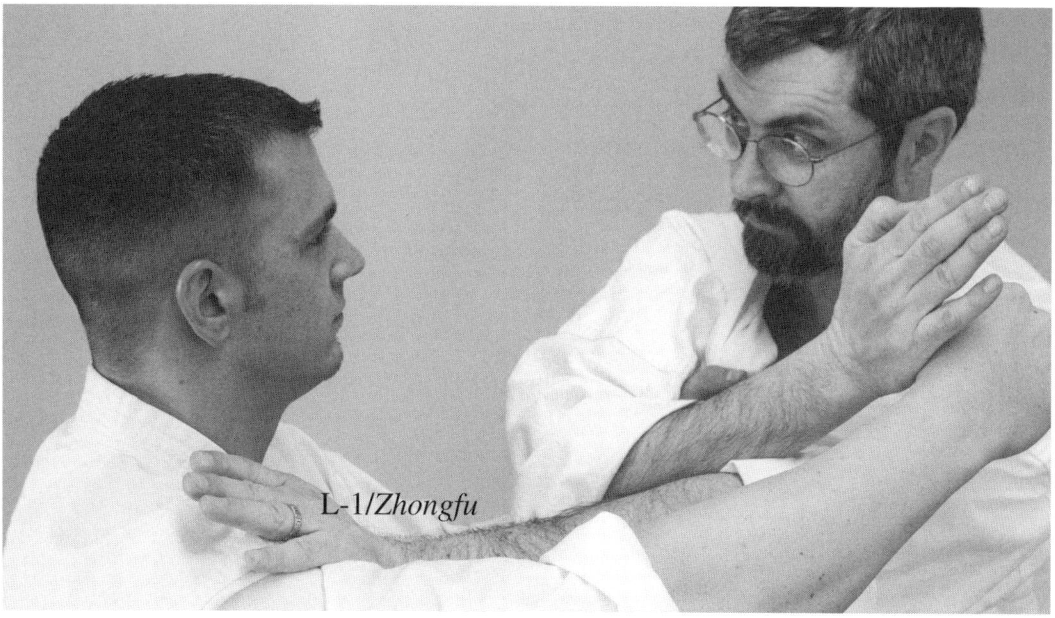

Point Name: Sp-21/*Dabao*

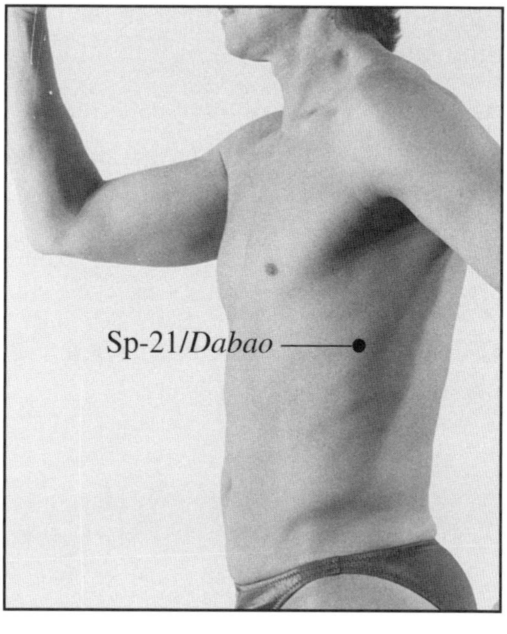

Location: On the mid-axillary line, in the seventh intercostal space. This point can be found on the side of the body, midway between the center of the armpit and the free end of the eleventh (floating) rib.

Anatomy: The seventh intercostal nerve and the terminal branch of the long thoracic nerve.

Method & Usage: Strike this point from the side towards the body-center.

POINTS ON THE TORSO (cont.)

Point Name: Sp-17/*Shidou*

Location: In the fifth intercostal space, just outside the curve of the pectoral muscle.

Anatomy: The fifth intercostal nerve.

Method & Usage: With a rising and inward motion.

Comments: On the left side, this point affects the heart.

CAUTION: Do not strike this point in practice.

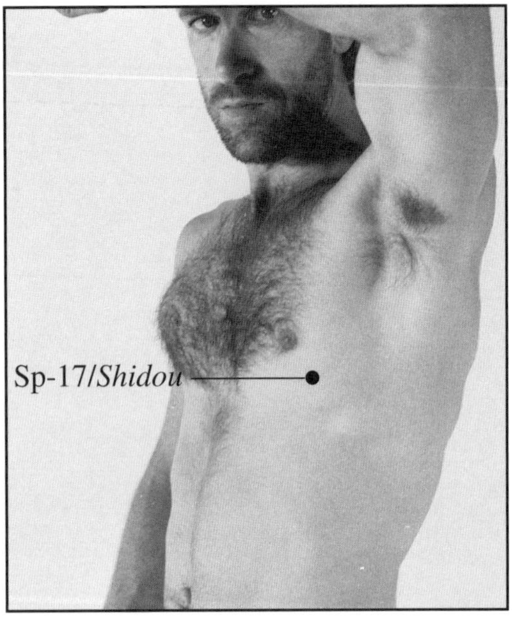

Point Name: S-16/*Yingchuan*

Location: Above the nipple in the third intercostal space.

Anatomy: The third intercostal nerve.

Method & Usage: Strike downward to collapse the structure.

Comments: On the left side this point affects the heart.

CAUTION: Do not strike this point in practice.

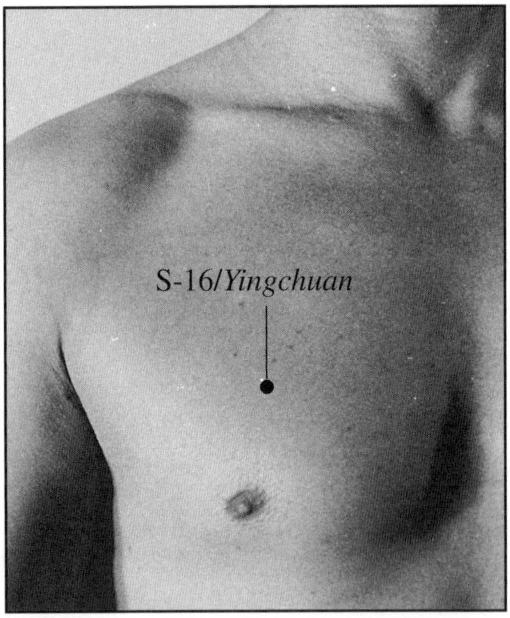

Point Name: S-18/*Rugen*

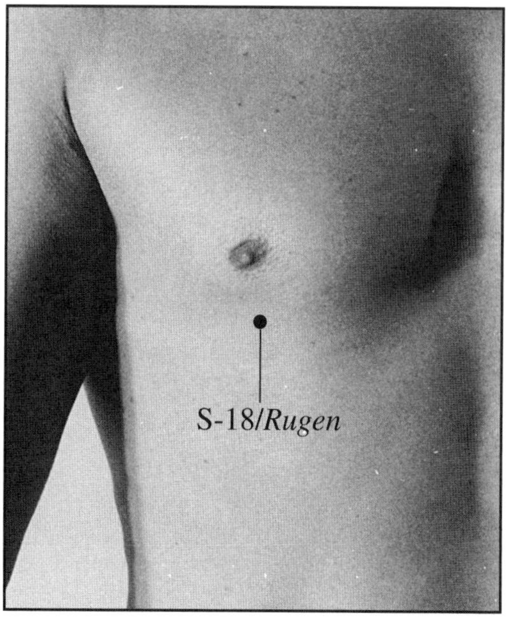

Location: Below the nipple in the fifth intercostal space, at the lower margin of the pectoralis muscle.

Anatomy: The branch fifth intercostal nerve.

Method & Usage: Punch this point on an upward angle.

Comments: The pectoralis muscle is a poor target because of its mass, particularly on body-builders. However, just below the muscle, at S-18/*Rugen*, the body is vulnerable, especially on those who have stretched and lifted the nerves by over-developing the muscle. On the left side, S-18/*Rugen* is a point where an electrode is attached during a twelve-lead EKG.

POINTS ON THE TORSO (cont.)

Point Name: P-1/*Tianchi*

Location: In the fourth intercostal space, 1 AU supralateral to the nipple. It is just to the outside and above the nipple in the space between the 4th and 5th ribs.

Anatomy: The muscular branch of the anterior thoracic nerve and the 4th intercostal nerve.

Method & Usage: Strike this point on a line towards the center of the back.

CAUTION: Do not strike this point in practice.

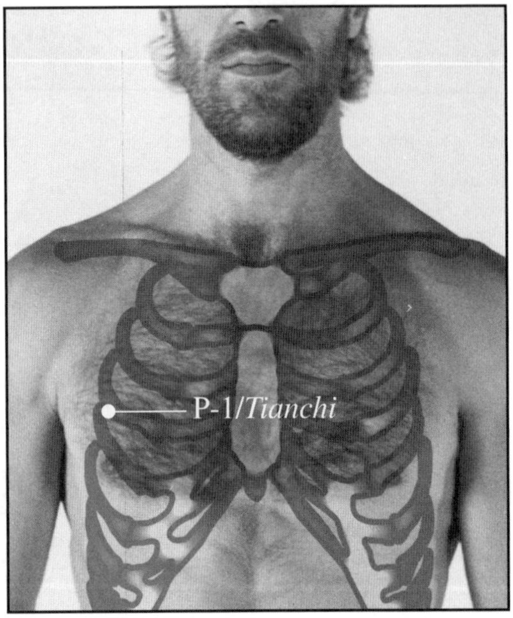

Point Name: K-23/*Shenfeng*

Location: In the fourth intercostal space, 2 AU lateral to the mid-line. This point is level with the nipples, just to either side of the sternum.

Anatomy: The fourth intercostal nerve, as well as an anterior cutaneous branch of the same.

Method & Usage: Strike this point directly, typically with a single-knuckle fist (ippon-ken).

Comments: On the left side this point lies directly over the heart.

CAUTION: Do not strike this point in practice.

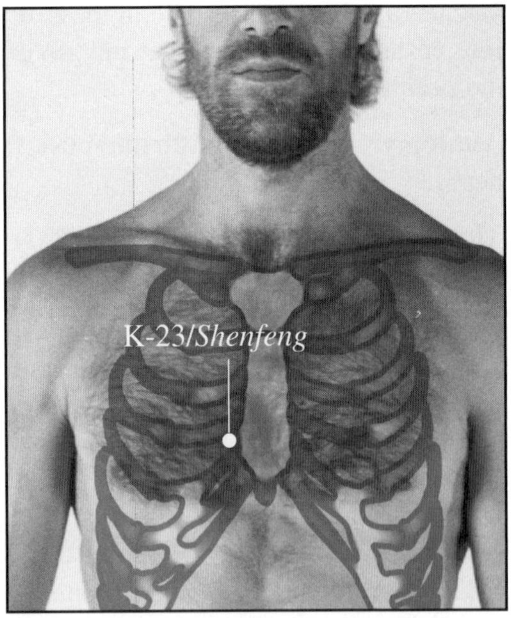

Point Name: K-24/*Lingxu*

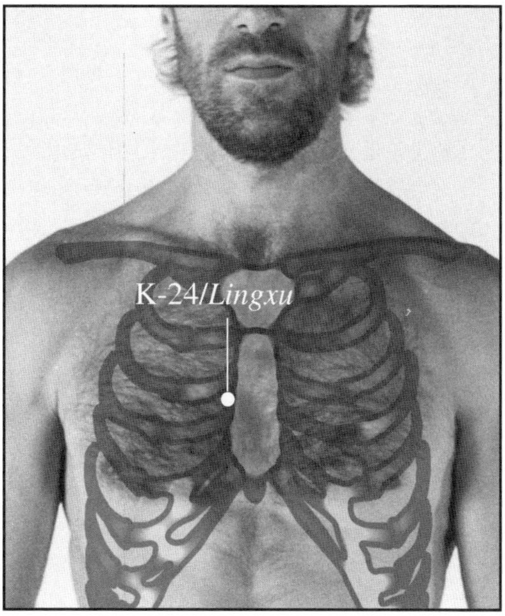

Location: In the third intercostal space, 2 AU lateral to the mid-line.

Anatomy: The third intercostal nerve, as well as an anterior cutaneous branch of the same.

Method & Usage: Strike this point directly, typically with a single-knuckle fist (ippon-ken).

Comments: On the left side this point lies directly over the heart.

CAUTION: Do not strike this point in practice.

Point Name: Co-17/*Shanzhong*

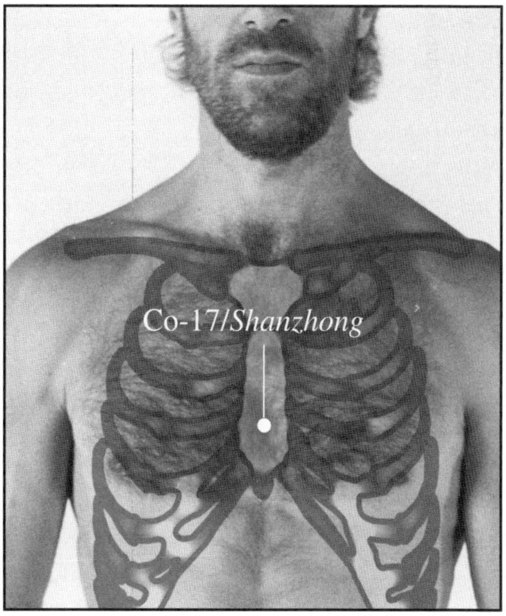

Location: On the sternum, level with the nipples, and just above the articulation of the right and left fifth rib.

Anatomy: A medial anterior cutaneous branch of the fourth intercostal nerve.

Method & Usage: Punch this point directly.

Comments: This is the alarm point of the Pericardium meridian, and the intersection point of the Spleen, Kidney, Small Intestine and Triple Warmer meridians on the Conception channel. It is considered one of eight influential points dominating ki. It also lies directly over the heart.

CAUTION: Do not strike this point in practice.

SPECIAL COMMENT[1]: Commotio Cordis is the medical term for sudden cardiac arrest following an impact to the chest wall. It is seen among athletes who are struck by baseballs or hockey pucks. Frequently, the ball is bouncing up into the chest. In an animal study (designed to examine the underlying mechanism of Commotio Cordis in the hopes of eventually developing protective equipment for young athletes[2]), swine were struck in the chest wall. The researchers reported 4 variables at work: 1) the force of the blow; 2) the hardness of striking object; 3) the location of the impact; 4) the timing of the blow in relation to the rhythm of the heart.

The research found that ventricular fibulation (VF) only occurred when the impact on the chest wall fell within a narrow (20 ms) window corresponding to the upslope of the T-wave. (The T-wave represents the period when the heart is relaxing after a contraction.) The study further found that only blows directly over the heart produced VF. Impacts with softer balls produced fewer VF, while harder baseballs produced more. (Interestingly, impact with a wooden object was 90% effective in producing VF when all other variables were maximized). Finally, when the swine were struck with velocities ranging from 20 to 60 mph, VF was not produced at 20 mph, was consistently (100%) produced at 40 mph, and was infrequently produced (20%) at 60 mph (again, when all other variables were maximized).

Kyusho-jitsu theory is in significant agreement with these empirical observations. Kyusho-jitsu teaches that precise strikes to select pressure points, of sufficient but not excessive force, delivered at the correct angle to the torso, will reliably stop the heart. This differs from the medical understanding primarily in that it specifies a handful of acupuncture points (which lie around the heart) as being the proper targets for attack. Further, these targets are struck at precise angles (rather than "perpendicular to the chest wall" as in the animal study) to produce cardiac arrest. Finally, kyusho-jitsu theory holds that cardiac arrest can be reliably reproduced without concern for the narrow 20 ms window. In other words, the kyusho-jitsu perspective is that, while accidental blows over the heart can produce death if they fall within the narrow upslope T-wave window, martial arts strikes can produce the effect regardless of cardiac phase.

However, how can the pressure point theory be verified? Certainly animal studies involving precise impacts on specific pressure points at specific angles could be performed, but they probably never will. So, are martial artists to practice this on each other to test the theory? Any volunteers? This is where the modern practice of kyusho-jitsu (pressure point fighting) becomes particularly valuable.

Rather than focusing on lethal techniques, the contemporary approach is to concentrate on methods of producing incapacitation (i.e. loss of consciousness, loss of motor control, cognitive impairment, etc.). Over the past 25 years of practice, it has been demonstrated that these techniques can be safely performed by expert practitioners. And this has led to a significant difference in traditional martial arts teaching and contemporary pressure point instruction.

The traditional martial artist conveys information passed across the generations, and says, "Hit here and death will result." But how do we know that is true? On the other hand, the contemporary kyusho-jitsu practitioner can say, "Hit here to produce loss of motor control," and then can proceed to demonstrate that outcome. So, we believe that specific points can be used to stop the heart. But, we caution against attempting to practice this for two important reasons: first, to reliably practice these techniques would be lethal to any training partners; second, to attempt an unpracticed technique in a life or death situation would be foolhardy. Our presentation of information about these matters here is only intended to set the practice of kyusho-jitsu into its full context.

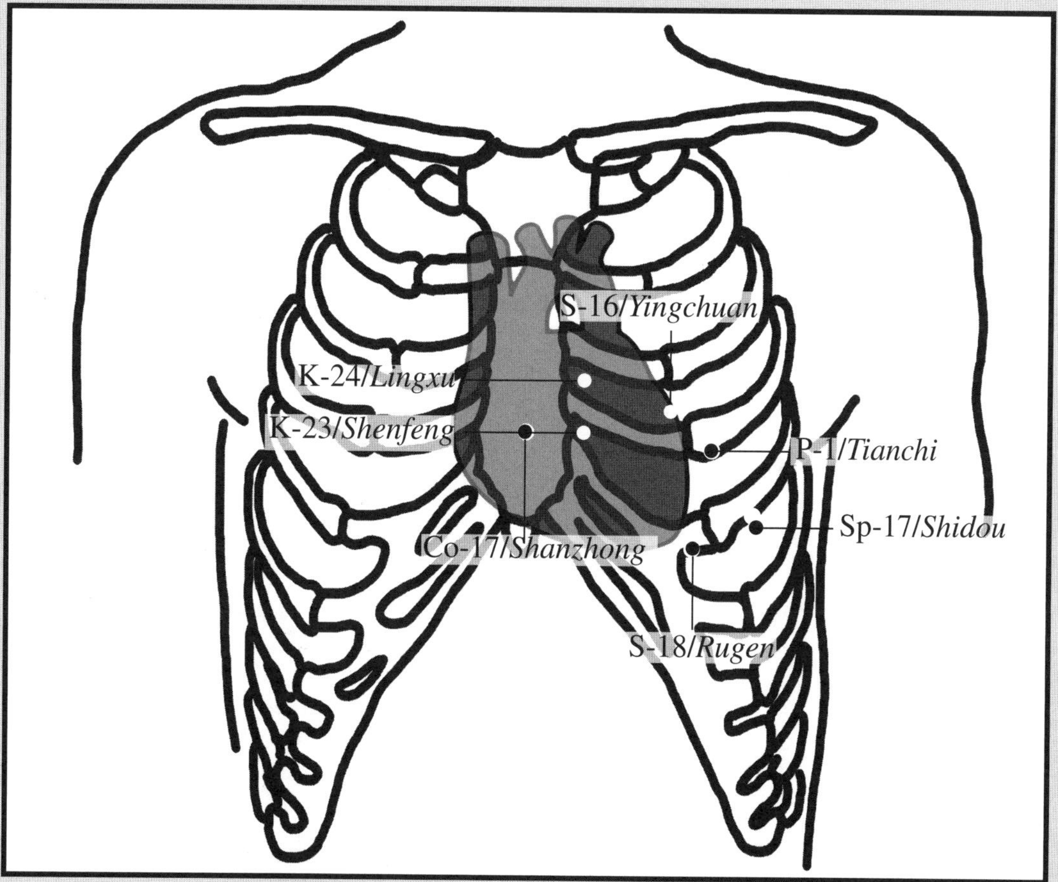

1. Portions of this discussion were previously published as part of the article "One Punch Kill: Understanding Okinawan Karate's Highest Ideal", by Chris Thomas, Black Belt Magazine, October, 2006

2. Kohl, Peter; Nesbitt, Alex D.; Cooper, Patricia J.; Lei, Ming
"Sudden cardiac death by *Commotio cordis*: role of mechano-electric feedback"
Cardiovascular Research 50 (2001) 280-289

POINTS ON THE TORSO (cont.)

Point Name: Rib cage Border Cluster
Li-14/*Chimen*

GB-24/*Riyue*

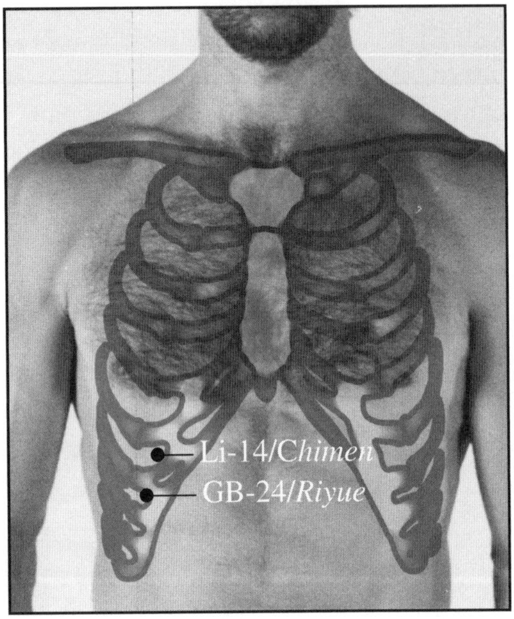

Location: Li-14/*Chimen* is below the nipple, in the sixth intercostal space

Anatomy: The sixth intercostal nerve.

Comments: L-14 is the alarm point for the Liver meridian as well as a linking point between the Liver and Spleen meridians.

Location: GB-24/*Riyue* is below the nipple, in the seventh intercostal space

Anatomy: The seventh intercostal nerve.

Comments: This is the alarm point for the Gallbladder meridian, as well as a linking point between the Gallbladder and Bladder meridians.

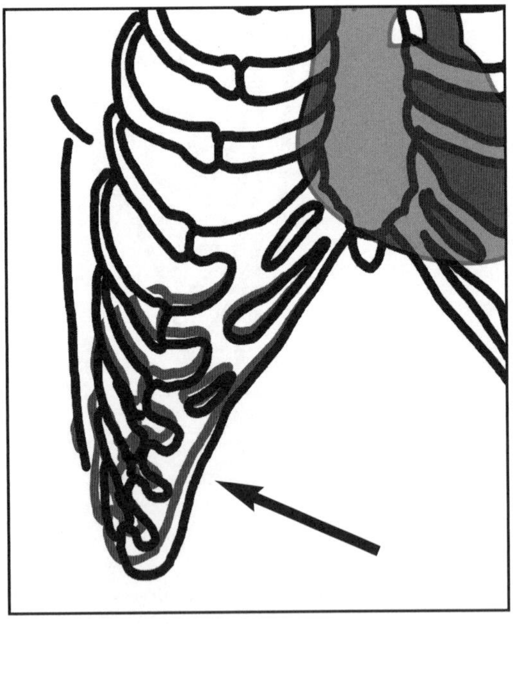

Mode and Usage: Because these points are in the intercostal space, they must be reached with a single knuckle punch (*ippon-ken*). However, a common method for attacking them is to strike the medial border of the costal angle with an outward movement which drives the cartilage into the points. Alternately, a fingertip strike is sometimes used as if trying to reach under the ribs. This point cluster is a particularly potent target because a strike here affects both yin (Liver and Spleen) and yang (Gallbladder and Bladder) simultaneously. It also contains a cycle of destruction (Wood >> Earth >> Water).

Point Name: Li-13/*Zhangmen*

Location: In the internal and external oblique muscles at the anterior end of the eleventh rib. This point can be located at the free end of the longer of the two floating ribs, at about the place the elbow touches the side of the body.

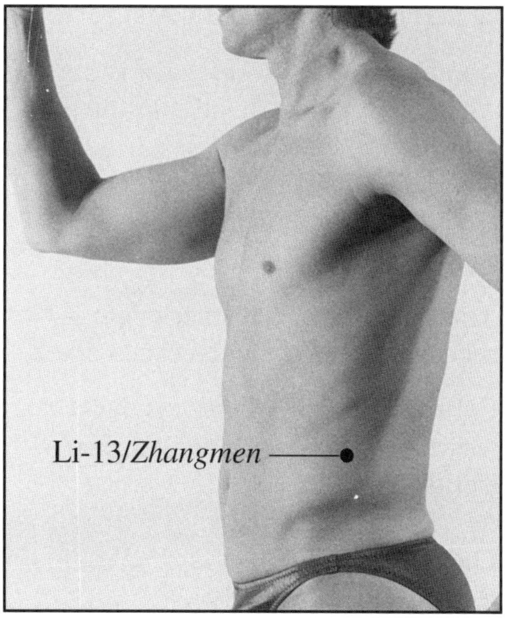

Anatomy: The tenth intercostal nerve.

Method & Usage: Strike this point diagonally upward.

Comments: Li-13/*Zhangmen* is the alarm point of the Spleen meridian. This point contains an internal cycle of destruction as it relates to the Liver (Wood) and Spleen (Earth) meridians.

CAUTION: Do not strike this point in practice.

POINTS ON THE TORSO (cont.)

Point Clusters: Tanden Points

Co-3/*Zhongji*

Co-4/*Guanyuan*

Co-5/*Shimen*

Co-6/*Qihai*

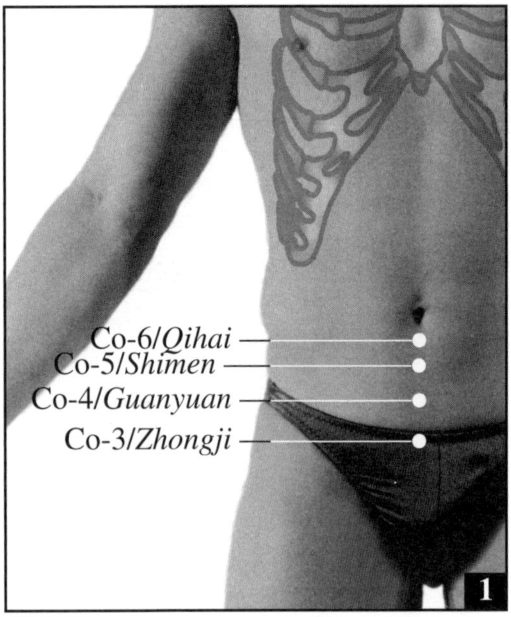

Location: Co-3/*Zhongji* is 4 AU directly below the navel.

Anatomy: A branch of the iliohypogastric nerve.

Comments: Co-3/*Zhongji* is the Alarm point of the Bladder meridian. It is also the point at which the three leg yin meridians (Kidney, Spleen and Liver) intersect on the Conception meridian.

Location: Co-4/*Guanyuan* is 3 AU directly below the navel.

Anatomy: A medial anterior cutaneous branch of the intercostal nerve.

Comments: Co-4/*Guanyuan* is the Alarm point of the Small Intestine meridian.

Location: Co-5/*Shimen* is 2 AU directly below the navel.

Anatomy: A medial anterior cutaneous branch of the intercostal nerve.

Comments: Co-5/*Shimen* is the Alarm-point for the Triple Warmer meridian.

Location: Co-6/*Qihai* is 1.5 AU directly below the navel.

Anatomy: A medial anterior branch of the eleventh intercostal nerve.

Comments: Th name *Qihai* means "Sea of Ki". This point is the energy center (tanden) of the body.

Mode and Usage: Strike these points either diagonally downward or diagonally upward to incapacitate an opponent.

CAUTION: Three classics of Chinese acupuncture -- "The Great Compendium", "Bronze Statue" and "The Glorious Anthology of Acupuncture" -- state the Co-5 should not be needled on women or they will be "rendered incapable of bearing children for life" (*Fundamentals of Chinese Acupuncture*, pg 350). We advise that techniques directed against the Tanden Points only be indicated in practice with women.

Point Name: TW-15/*Tianliao*

Location: Superior to the scapula, in the center of the supraclavicular fossa. This point can be found level with the tip of the shoulder and midway towards the spine.

Anatomy: The spinal accessory nerve and the supraclavicular nerve.

Method & Usage: Strike this point diagonally downward. It also will respond to thumb pressure.

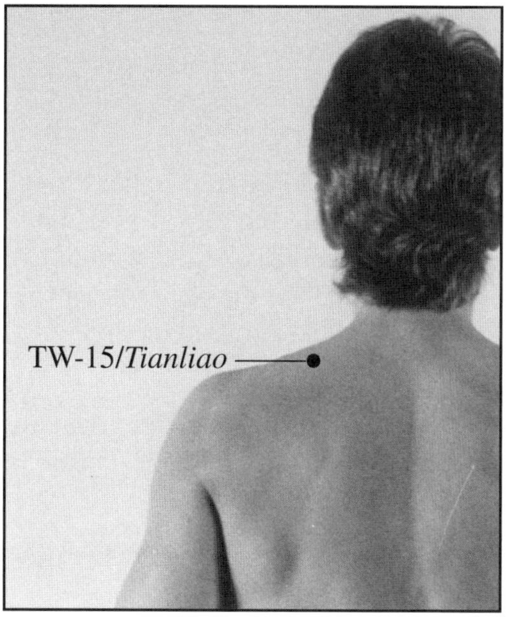

Point Name: GB-21/*Jianjing*

Location: On the bulge of the trapezius muscle, midway between the spine and the acromion process.

Anatomy: The supraclavicular nerve and the branches of the dorsal scapular nerve.

Method & Usage: Strike downward toward the center of the body

Comments: GB-21/*Jianjing* is the meeting point of the Gall Bladder, Triple Warmer and Stomach channels.

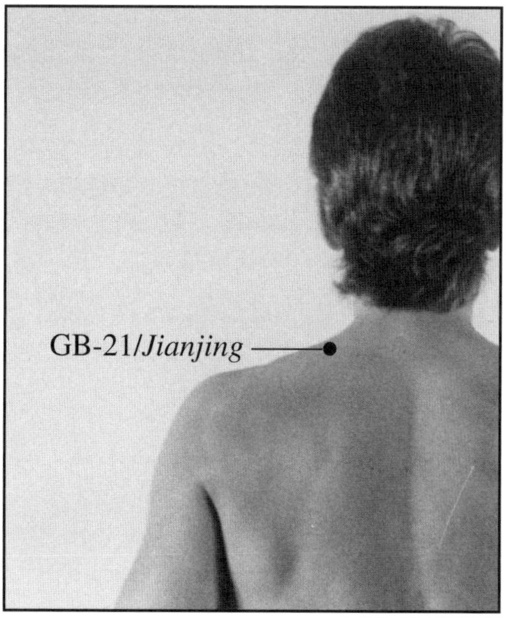

POINTS ON THE TORSO (cont.)

Point Clusters: Paraspinal Cluster

B-13/*Feishu*

B-14/*Jueyinshu*

B-15/*Xinshu*

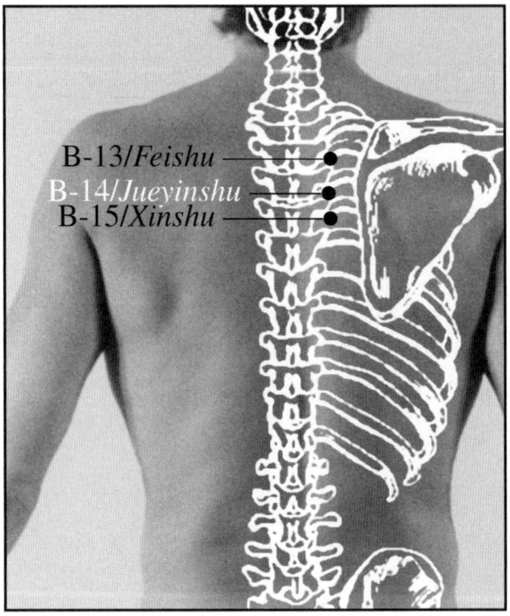

Location: B-13/*Feishu* is in the trapezius and rhomboid muscles, 1.5 AU lateral to the lower edge of the spinous process of the third thoracic vertebra (T-3). It is found between the shoulder-blade and the spine.

Anatomy: A medial branch of the dorsal ramus of the third thoracic spinal nerve.

Comments: B-13/*Feishu* is the associated point of the Lung Meridian.

Location: B-14/*Jueyinshu* is in the trapezius and rhomboid muscles, 1.5 AU lateral to the lower edge of the spinous process of the fourth thoracic vertebra (T-4). It is found between the shoulder-blade and the spine, 1 AU below B-13/*Feishu*.

Anatomy: Directly on a medial cutaneous branch of the dorsal ramus of the fourth thoracic spinal nerve.

Comments: B-14/*Jueyinshu* is the associated point of the Pericardium Meridian.

Location: B-15/*Xinshu* is in the trapezius and rhomboid muscles, 1.5 AU lateral to the lower edge of the spinous process of the fifth thoracic vertebra (T-5). It is found between the shoulder-blade and the spine, 1 AU below B-14/*Jueyinshu*.

Anatomy: A medial branch of the dorsal ramus of the fifth thoracic spinal nerve.

Comments: B-15/*Xinshu* is the associated point of the Heart Meridian.

Mode and Usage: Strike these points in the direction of the heart.

CAUTION: Because these points are related to the circulatory system, they should only be indicated during practice. It is particularly dangerous to strike the points on the left side of the spine.

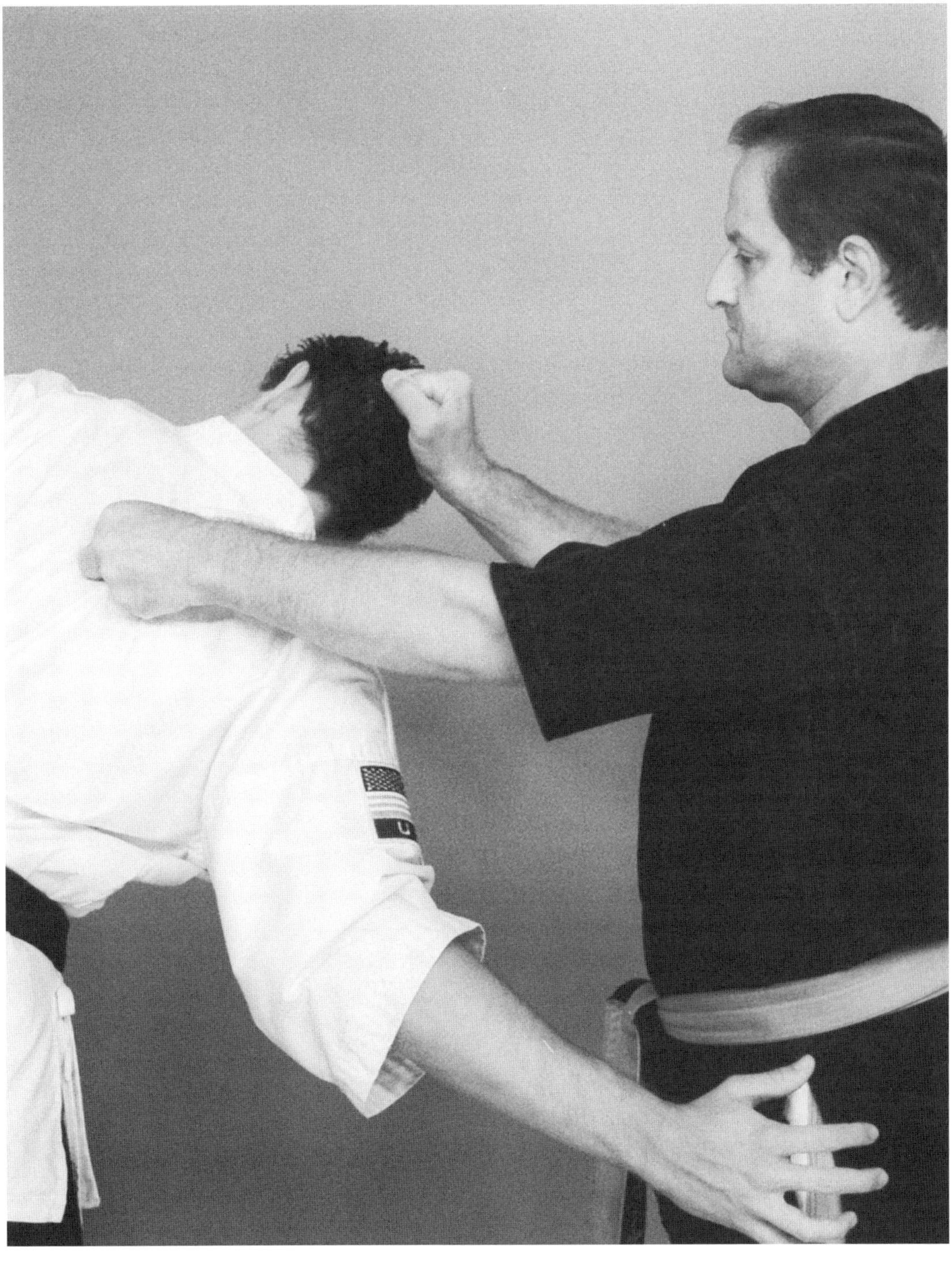

POINTS ON THE TORSO (cont.)

Point Clusters: Kidney Cluster
B-23/*Shenshu*

GB-25/*Jingmen*

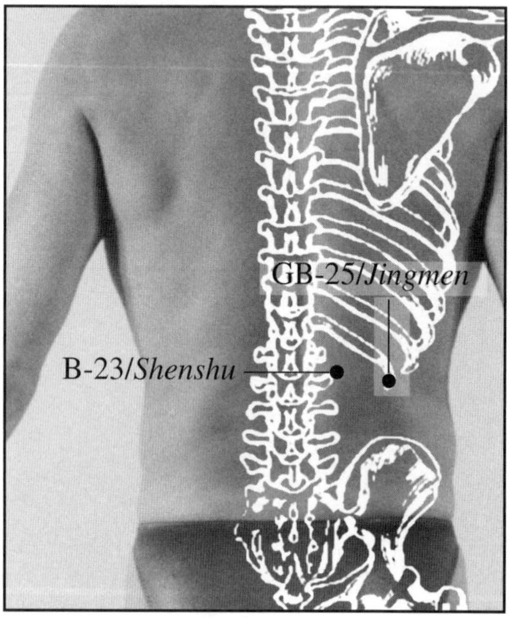

Location: B-23/*Shenshu* is in the lumbodorsal fascia, between the longissimus and iliocostalis muscles, 1.5 AU lateral to the lower end of the spinous process of the 2nd lumbar vertebra (L-2). This point is beside the spine, level with the free end of the twelfth (floating) rib.

Anatomy: Branches of the first lumbar spinal nerve.

Comments: B-23/*Shenshu* is the associated point of the Kidney meridian.

Location: GB-25/*Jingmen* is at the inferior border of the free end of the twelfth (floating) rib. This point is just at the tip of the smaller of the two floating ribs.

Anatomy: The 11th intercostal nerve.

Comments: GB-25/*Jingmen* is the alarm point of the Kidney meridian.

Mode and Usage: Strike to access the kidney (both organ and meridian). An open hand strike allows both points to be struck with one hand.

POINTS ON THE LOWER EXTREMITIES

POINTS ON THE LOWER EXTREMITIES

Point Name: GB-41/*Zulinqi*

Location: In the depression just in front of the merging of the fourth and fifth metatarsal bones. It is located just in front of the bulge on the top of the foot where the bones of the fourth and fifth toes connect.

Anatomy: The dorsal digital nerve of the fourth metatarsus.

Method & Usage: Stomp this point. If an opponent is shoe-less and kicking, GB-41/*Zulinqi* may also be struck with a single knuckle.

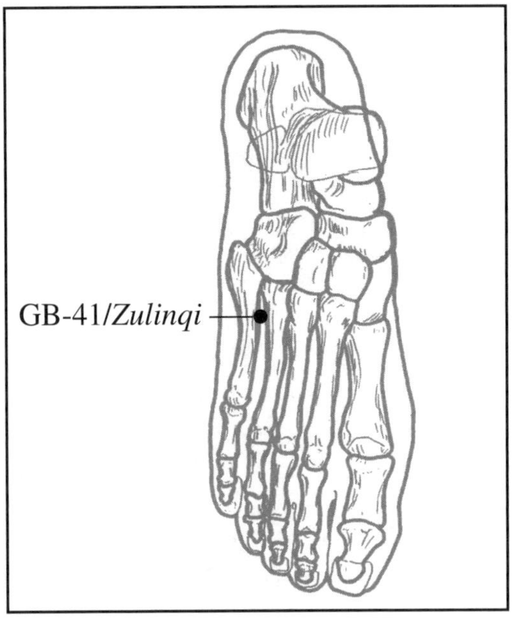

Point Name: Li-3/*Taichong*

Location: In the depression between the first and second metatarsals. This point can be found on the top of the foot, between the two bones leading to the first (big) and second toes.

Anatomy: The peroneal nerve.

Method & Usage: Press or strike this point diagonally downward.

Comments: Li-3/*Taichong* is best used when the opponent's feet are unshod, or in lightweight shoes.

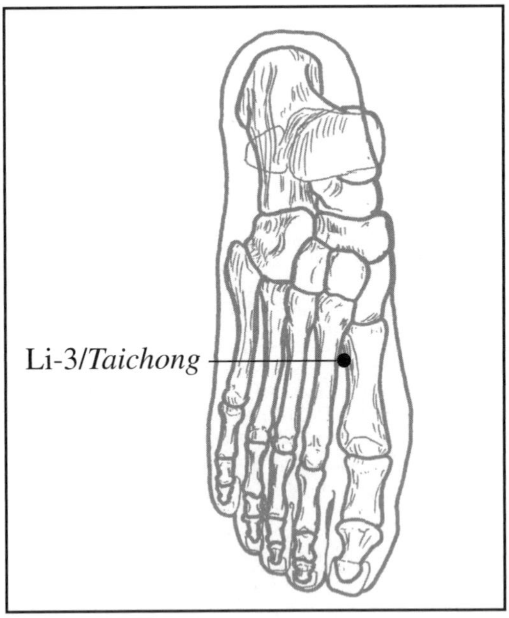

Point Name: B-50(36)/*Chengfu*

Location: At the inferior margin of the gluteus maximus muscle, at the midpoint of the transverse crease. This point can be found at the back of the thigh just below the buttocks.

Anatomy: The posterior cutaneous nerve of the thigh and the sciatic nerve.

Method & Usage: Kick this point to immobilize the leg.

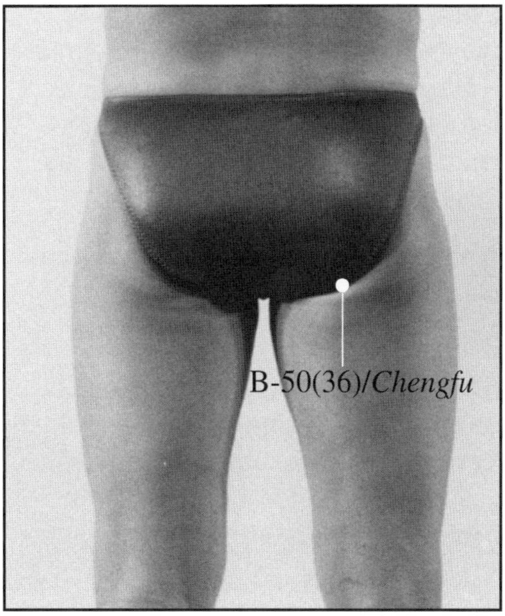

Point Name: B-55/*Heyang*

Location: 2 AU below the crease of the knee, between the medial and lateral heads of the gastrocnemius. It is found on the top of the calf muscle.

Anatomy: The posterior cutaneous nerve of the thigh, the medial cutaneous nerve of the calf, and the tibial nerve.

Method & Usage: Stomp this point as if aiming at the tip of the toes, to collapse the leg.

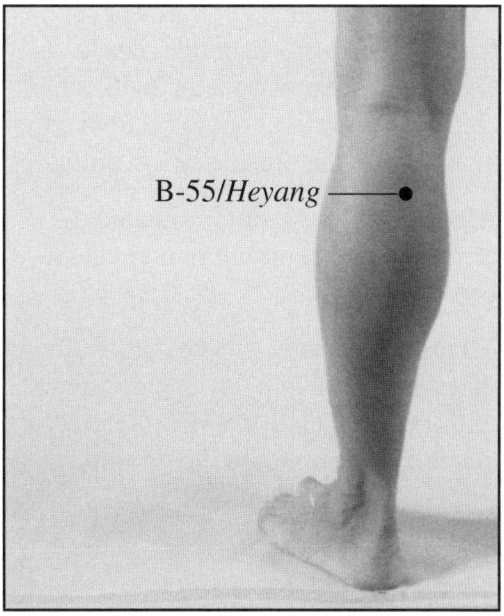

POINTS ON THE LOWER EXTREMITIES (cont.)

Point Name: Sp-10/*Xuehai*

Location: At the superior margin of the medial condyle of the femur, in the medial margin of the vastus medialis muscle. This point is on the inner aspect of the leg, about 3 AU above the level of the knee-cap.

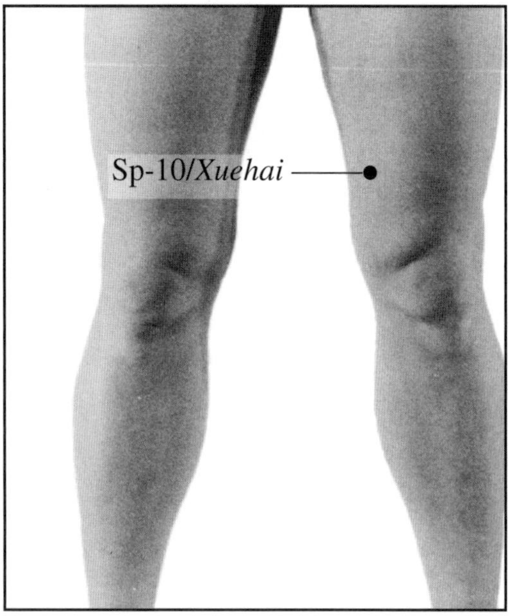

Anatomy: The anterior femoral cutaneous nerve, and a muscular branch of the femoral nerve.

Method & Usage: Strike diagonally downward following an imaginary line through the center of the knee to dislocate the joint and/or knock the opponent to the ground.

Point Name: S-34/*Liangqiu*

Location: On the lateral aspect of the thigh in the vastus lateralis muscle, at the border of the vastus medialis muscle. This point is about 3 AU above the knee-cap on the outside of the thigh.

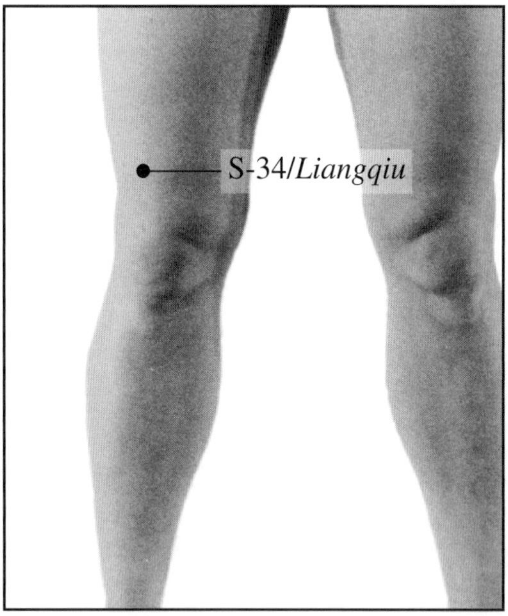

Anatomy: This point is situated directly on the lateral femoral cutaneous nerve.

Method & Usage: Strike diagonally downward on a line through the center of the knee to dislocate the joint and/or knock the opponent to the ground.

Point Name: Sp-9/*Yinglingquan*

Location: In the depression between the posterior margin of the tibia and the gastrocnemius muscle, at the origin of the soleus. This point is on the inner aspect of the knee about 2 AU below the knee-cap.

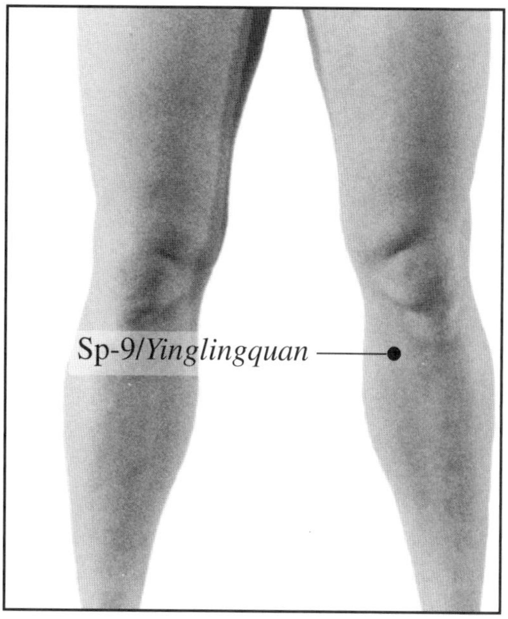

Anatomy: A cutaneous branch of the saphenous nerve, and the tibial nerve.

Method & Usage: Strike diagonally upward on a line through the center of the knee to dislocate the joint and/or knock the opponent to the ground.

Point Name: N-LE-7/*Liwai*

Location: About 3 AU below the knee lateral to the tibia in the tibialis anterior muscle.

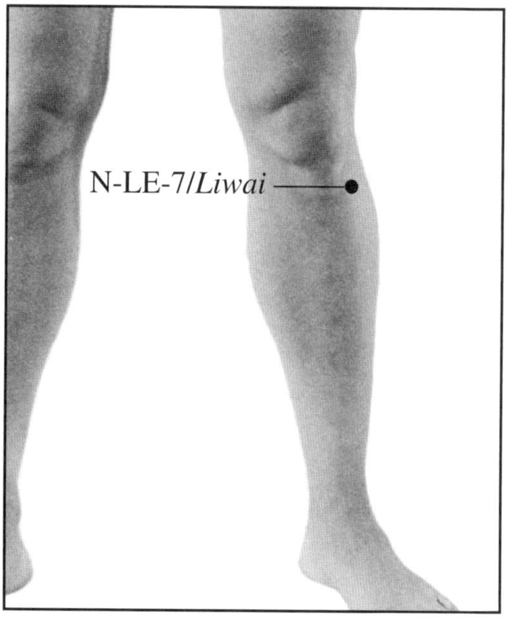

Anatomy: The lateral cutaneous nerve of the calf, a cutaneous branch of the saphenous nerve and the deep peroneal nerve.

Method & Usage: Strike this point diagonally upward through the center of the knee to dislocate the joint and/or knock the opponent to the ground.

POINTS ON THE LOWER EXTREMITIES (cont.)

NOTE ON KNEE POINTS: When striking one of the knee points (S-34/*Liangqiu*, N-LE-7/*Liwai*, Sp-10/*Xuehai*, Sp-9/*Yinglingquan*) with a very small surface (such as a knuckle) accurate placement is essential in order to effortlessly use these points to knock an opponent down. However, when kicking, a shorthand method can be used for locating them: Simply envision an "X" drawn across the knee, and attack the ends of the "X" on an imaginary line which passes through the center of the joint.

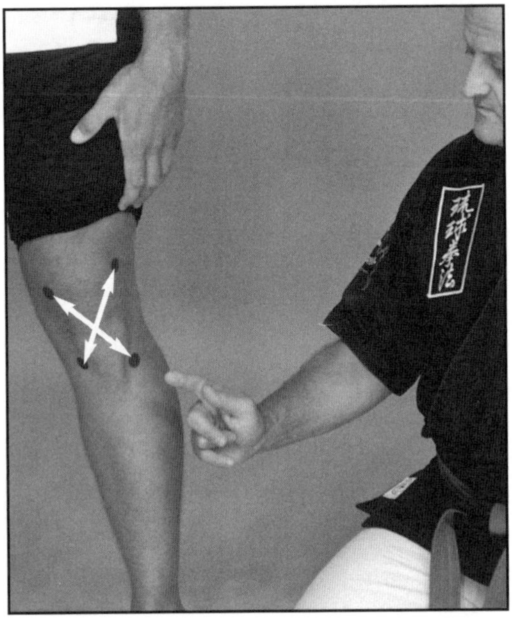

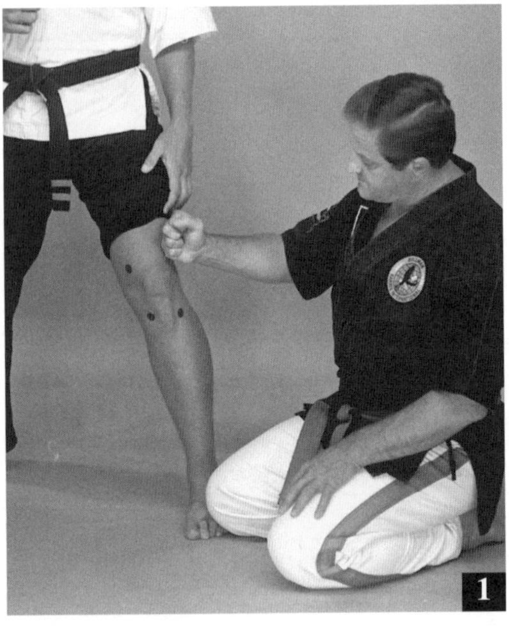

1

2

Point Name: GB-31/*Fengshi*

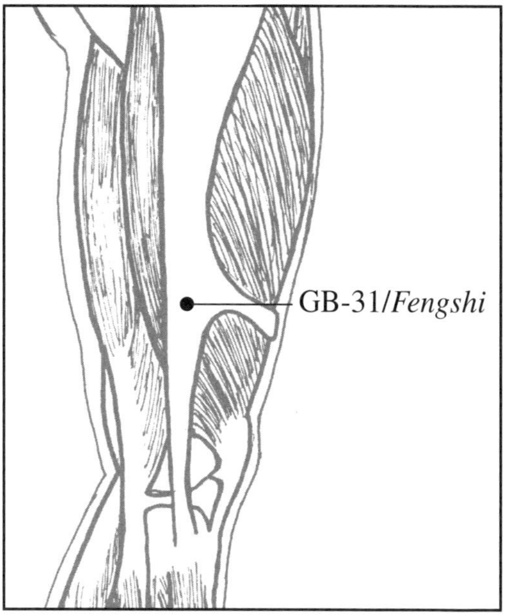

Location: Beneath the tensor fasciae latae, in the vastus lateralis muscle, at the median line of the lateral aspect of the thigh, 7 AU above the knee. This point can be found by standing upright with the arm extended along the side of the leg. GB-31 will be just at the tip of the middle finger.

Anatomy: The lateral cutaneous nerve of the thigh, and a muscular branch of the femoral nerve.

Method & Usage: Strike this point from the side.

Comments: This is a motor-nerve point, and the favorite target of the Muay Thai shin kick.

Point Name: Sp-6/*Sanyinjiao*

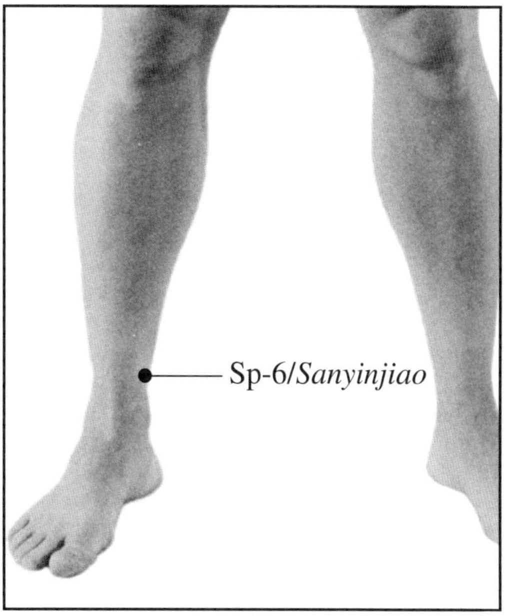

Location: Between the posterior margin of the tibia and the soleus muscle, 3 AU above the medial malleolus of the ankle. It is on the inside of the leg, just along the rear edge of the bone (tibia) about midway between the prominence of the ankle and the lower edge of the calf muscle.

Anatomy: A cutaneous branch of the saphenous nerve, and the tibial nerve.

Method & Usage: Kick this point from the inside to rob the leg of energy.

Comments: This point is the intersection of the Kidney, Liver and Spleen meridians. Sp-6/*Sanyinjiao* functions as a point of all three meridians.

POINTS ON THE LOWER EXTREMITIES (cont.)

Point Name: Li-9/*Yinbao*

Location: On the lateral aspect of the thigh in the vastus lateralis muscle, at the border of the vastus medialis muscle. This point is about 3 AU above the knee-cap on the outside of the thigh.

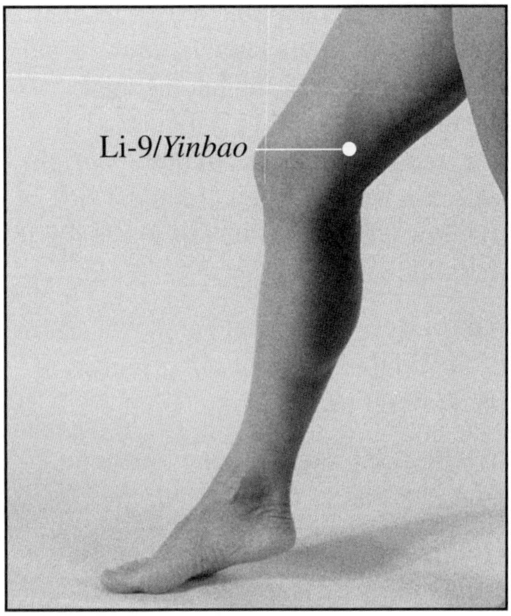

Anatomy: This point is situated directly on the lateral femoral cutaneous nerve.

Method & Usage: Strike diagonally downward on a line through the center of the knee to dislocate the joint and/or knock the opponent to the ground.

Point Name: Li-7/*Xiguan*

Location: In the upper portion of the gastrocnemius.

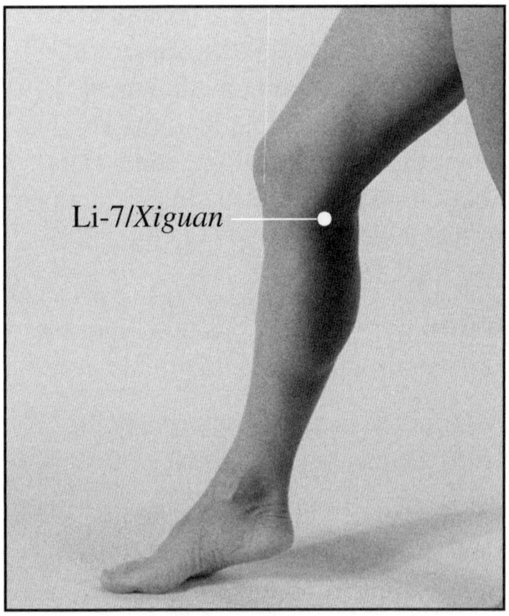

Anatomy: The medial sural cutaneous nerve.

Method & Usage: Strike with a downward angle, slightly back to front, to fold the knee and cramp the calf muscle.

Li-9/*Yinbao*
1

2

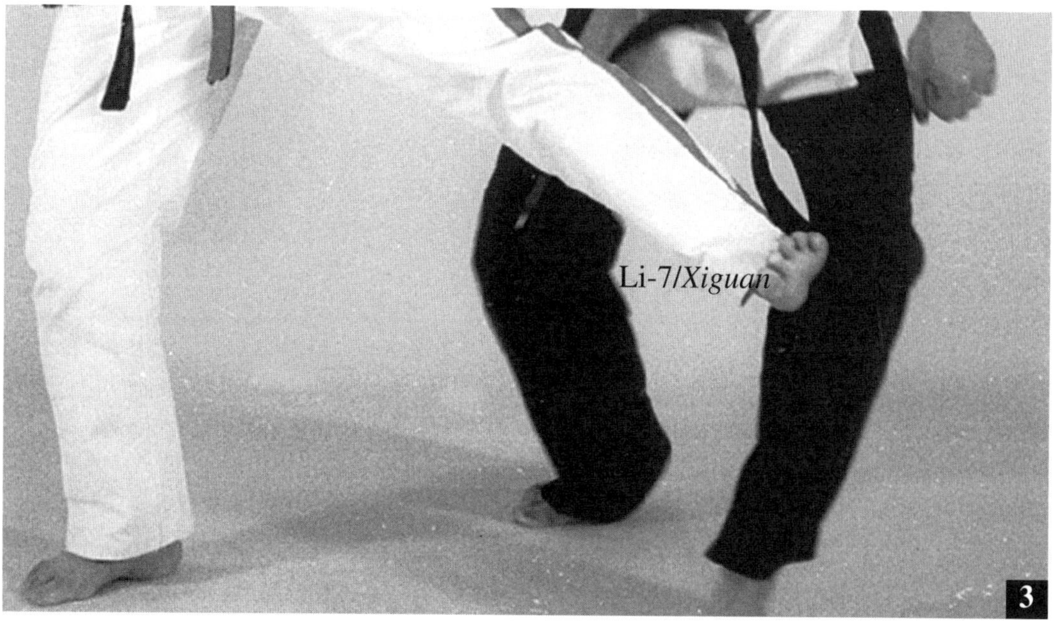
Li-7/*Xiguan*
3

POINTS ON THE LOWER EXTREMITIES (cont.)

Point Clusters: Inguinal Crease Cluster

Li-12/*Jimai*

Sp-12/*Chongmen*

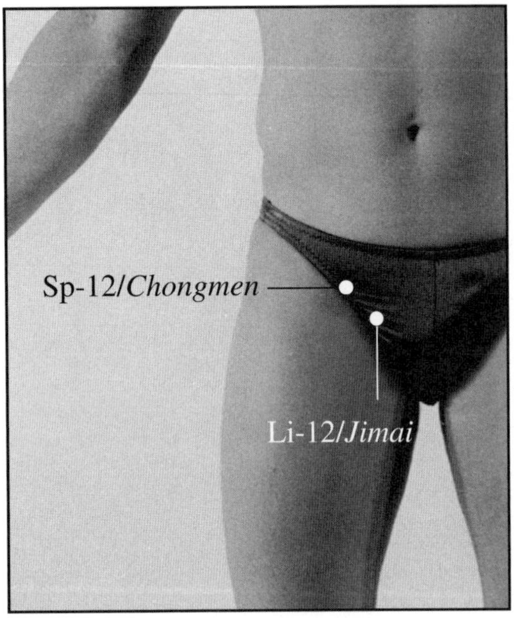

Location: Li-12/*Jimai* is level with the pubic symphysis, 2.5 AU either side of the centerline, in the inguinal groove. It is located in the crease found at the border of the upper thigh and the hips.

Anatomy: The ilioinguinal nerve, and the anterior branch of the obturator nerve.

Location: Sp-12/*Chongmen* is level with the upper border of the pubic symphysis, 3.5 AU lateral to the centerline, in the crease of the leg. It is located just at the outside edge of the femoral artery.

Anatomy: Sp-12/*Chongmen* lies over the superficial inguinal ring, essentially, a hole in the wall of the abdomen. A penetrating blow to this point threatens direct contact with the ilioinguinal nerve, and the genital branch of the genitofemoral nerve.

Comments: Sp-12/*Chongmen* is a meeting point of the Spleen and Liver meridians.

Mode and Usage: Strike these points diagonally downward, on a path that moves slightly outward. Attacks to this area will cause an opponent to bend over, and expose points on the back of the head to attack.

The Liver meridian is a Wood meridian and the Spleen meridian is an Earth meridian. Since Wood "penetrates" Earth, Li-12/*Jimai* and Sp-12/*Chongmen* work together according to the cycle of destruction.

Point Name: Sp-11/*Jimen*

Location: Posterior to the sartorius muscle, on the inner thigh, about one third the distance from the knee-joint to the groin.

Anatomy: The anterior femoral cutaneous nerve and the saphenous nerve.

Method & Usage: Strike this point to buckle the leg.

Comments: When this point is struck with a toe-tip kick (tsumasaki-geri), the effect is extreme. Some hours after the photographs detailing this kick were taken (1,2), the "victim" became ill, requiring the application of energy restoration techniques by George Dillman. Readers are urged to refrain from striking this point in this manner.

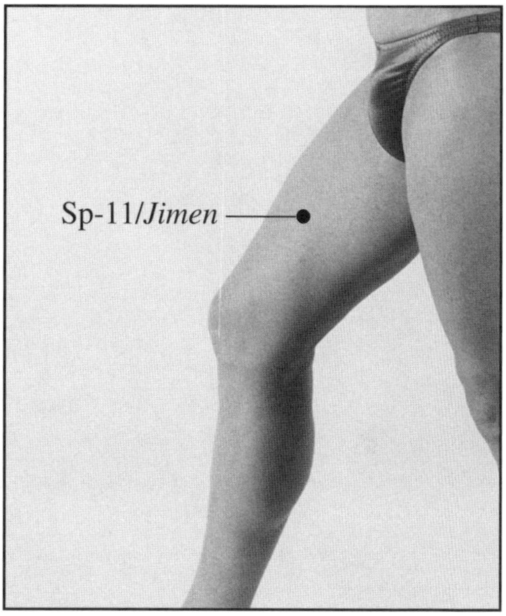

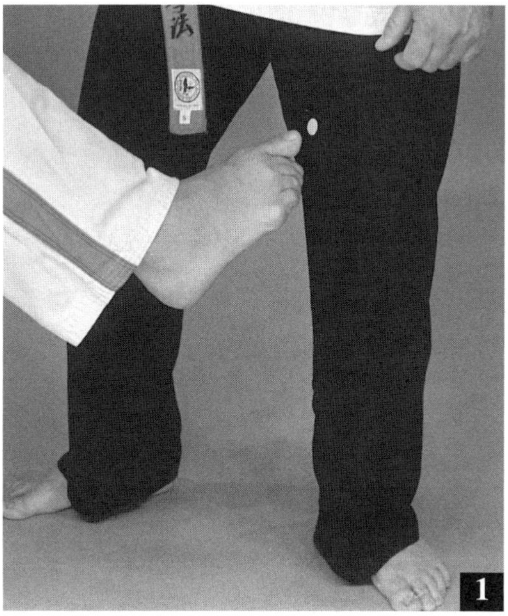

Author George Dillman demonstrating on Chris Martingilio.

Photo by Chris Thomas

Chapter Three: Naihanchi Shodan

INTRODUCTION TO NAIHANCHI

There are three kata in the Naihanchi series which have a long history in karate. Most styles include some version of one or more of them. In many old systems, Naihanchi kata are taught first. It is also well known that in ancient times great masters often only knew one single kata and more often than not it was Naihanchi.

The first Naihanchi kata has only 30 or so movements (the count can vary depending on how the sequences are broken down). It consists of only the horse stance, and the cross stance. Because of the simplicity of the kata, a great deal of nonsense has been said about it. Some have suggested that the kata movements are for fighting along the narrow walkways around rice paddies or for fighting on top of a wall, or for fighting in a narrow hallway. However, the movements of the kata cannot conceivably fit such interpretations. Furthermore, it is ludicrous to assume that developer of Naihanchi would painstakingly develop a form to fit so remote a contingency.

In addition to the ridiculous interpretations of Naihanchi which are given, students are often told, "Naihanchi is not a good kata for competition." And so, they complain about having to learn the form at all. In fact, no less than the late Masatoshi Nakayama wrote, "Since these [Naihanchi] kata are rather monotonous, turn the head briskly and strongly." What, turn your head briskly to stay awake? No wonder students find Naihanchi to be pointless.

Gichin Funakoshi reported that the first ten years of his karate training consisted of only the three Naihanchi kata. If the misconceptions about Naihanchi were true in Funakoshi's day, then certainly its sole purpose must have been to test a student's perseverance and determination. "You must prove yourself by spending the next ten years washing the toilet and practicing Naihanchi. If you survive this test, we will teach you real karate."

However, the problem is not with the kata, it is with those who have taught the kata. The truth is that the three Naihanchi kata are so practical and effective that it takes ten years of study to exhaust their concepts and knowledge (actually, it takes a lifetime of study, but ten years is a good start.) Together, the three Naihanchi kata contain the secrets to pressure point fighting which can be used to quickly and effectively defeat an opponent.

This text will present secrets and insights into Naihanchi shodan which should astound any martial artists with the wisdom to recognize what we are revealing. Nonetheless, we are still only scratching the surface. There is far more to learn than we can possibly include. But, more important than the interpretation of the kata presented here, are the principles which are applied. These principles are keys to unlocking the hidden meanings of any traditional form.

Naihanchi Shodan

NAIHANCHI SHODAN

Opening

1. Stand at attention with your feet together, heels touching.

2,3. Bow respectfully.

Movement # 1

4. Place the back of your right open hand in the palm of your left hand at about throat level.

5,6. Draw both hands inward, then down to about waist level. At the same time, pull your feet together and bend your knees slightly.

2

3

5

6

Movement # 2

7. Cross your left foot over your right, and drop your weight.

7

Movement # 3

8. Step with your right foot to the right into a horse stance, and sweep your right arm to the right, while drawing your left fist to your hip.

Movement # 4

9. Strike your right palm and your left elbow together.

Movement # 5

10. Stack your fists, left over right, at your right hip.

10

Movement # 6

11. Strike down and to the left with your left fist.

Movement # 7

12. Punch to the left with your right fist.

8

9

11

12

Movement # 8

13. Step to the left with your right foot, crossing right in front of left.

14. Step to the left with your left foot into a horse stance, and strike to the front with your right fist.

13

Movement # 9

15,16. Strike out with your left fist, then strike with both fists, left fist striking high, the right fist striking low.

Movement # 10

17,18. Pull your right forearm across your body, placing your fist under your left elbow, as you punch out at head level with a left snapping punch.

16

14

15

17

18

Movement # 11

19. Draw your left leg up, so your foot brushes the inside of your right knee.

19

Movement # 12

20. Set your left foot back down, and strike to the left diagonal with the left fist.

Movement # 13

21. Draw your right leg up, so your foot brushes the inside of your left knee.

Movement # 14

22. Set your right foot back down, and strike to the right diagonal with the left fist.

22

Movement # 15

23. Stack your fists, left over right, at your right hip.

Movement # 16

24. Strike with both fists to the left.

20

21

23

24

Movement # 17

25. Open the left fist and rotate the hand so your palm faces forward. At the same time, draw your right hand to the hip.

25

Movement # 18

26. Strike your left palm and your right elbow together.

Movement # 19

27. Stack your fists, right over left, at your left hip.

Movement # 20

28. Strike down and to the right with your right fist.

Movement # 21

29. Punch to the right with your left fist.

26

27

28

29

Movement # 22

30. Step to the right with your left foot, crossing left in front of right.

31. Step to the right with your right foot into a horse stance, and strike to the front with your left fist.

30

Movement # 23

32,33. Strike out with your right fist, then strike with both fists, right fist striking high, left fist striking low.

Movement # 24

34,35. Pull your left forearm across your body, placing your fist under your right elbow, as you punch out at head level with a right snapping punch.

33

31

32

34

35

Movement # 25

36. Draw your right leg up, so your foot brushes the inside of your left knee.

36

Movement # 26

37. Set your right foot down, and strike to the right diagonal with the right fist.

Movement # 27

38. Draw your left leg up, so your foot brushes the inside of your right knee.

Movement # 28

39. Set your left foot down, and strike to the left diagonal with the right fist.

39

Movement # 29

40. Stack your fists, right over left, at your left hip.

Movement # 30

41. Strike with both fists to the right.

37

38

40

41

Movement # 31

42. Draw your right foot up to your left foot, and place the back of your right open hand in the palm of your left hand at about throat level.

43. Draw both hands inward, then down to about waist level.

42

Movement # 32

44. Slide your left foot to the left, into a shoulder-width stance, and draw your fists to your hips.

45. Punch forward and down with both fists.

Closing

46. Draw your left foot inward, and stand at attention.

47. Bow respectfully.

45

43

44

46

47

Photo by Kim Foreman

Chapter Four: Naihanchi Bunkai

Practical Application of the Kata

Bunkai # 1

1. An attacker grabs you by the lapels and pulls you close.

2. Draw your arms up and inward to squeeze and control his forearms.

3. Place the back of your left hand on the left side of the attacker's face, covering his eye, and touching the points S-1/*Chengqi*, B-2/*Zanzhu*, M-HN-14/*Bitong*, M-HN-6/*Yuyao*.

4-6. Strike the back of your right hand into your left palm to knock your attacker out.

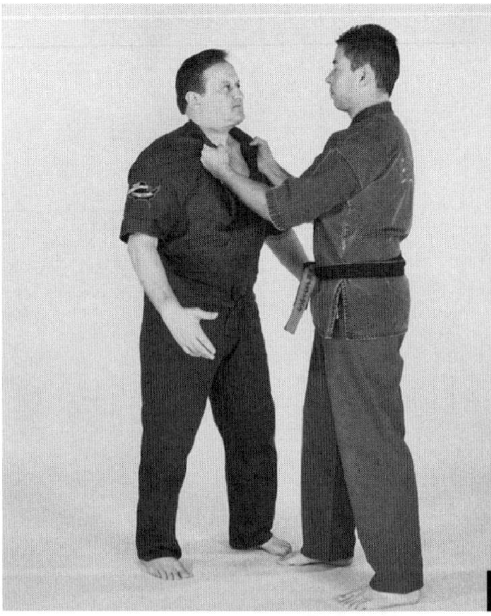

1

4

5

2

3

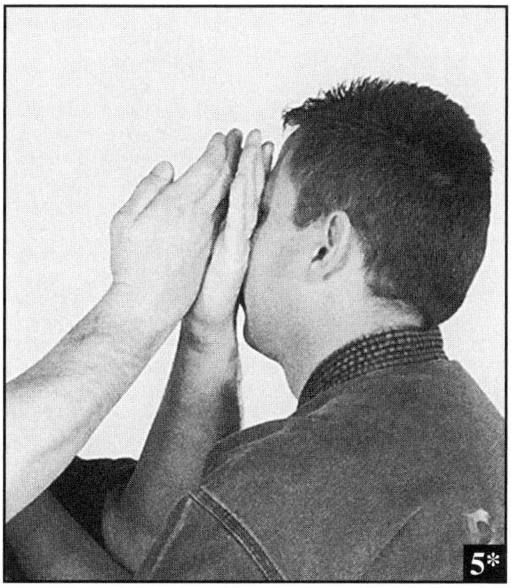

5*

6

Bunkai # 2

1,2. Sneak up behind your opponent, and bring your hands down over his eyes to obstruct his vision.

3. With your elbows held inward, rubbing against his shoulders at TW-15/*Tianliao* and GB-21/*Jianjing*, press down on the Anterior Nose Point/*Ganbi* to stretch the Anterior Ethmoidal Nerve.

4-6. Using a vibrating pressure on Ganbi, draw the attacker's head in to your chest, then slide him down to the floor.

1

4

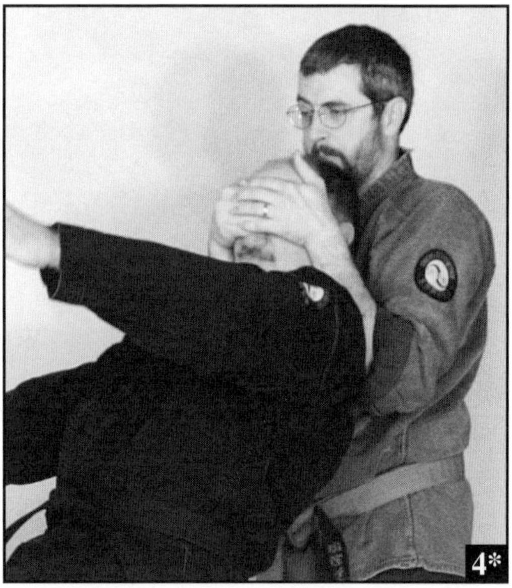

4*

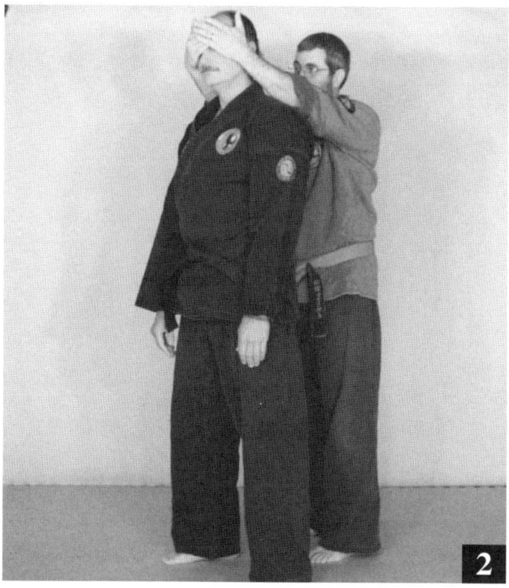
2

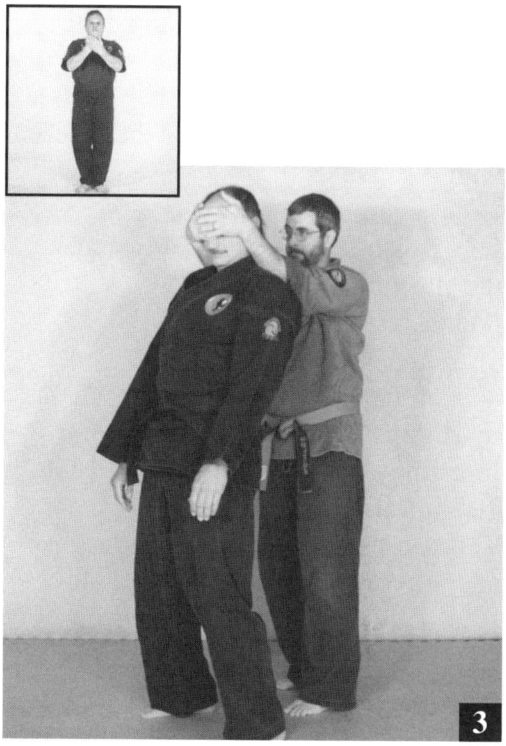
3

5

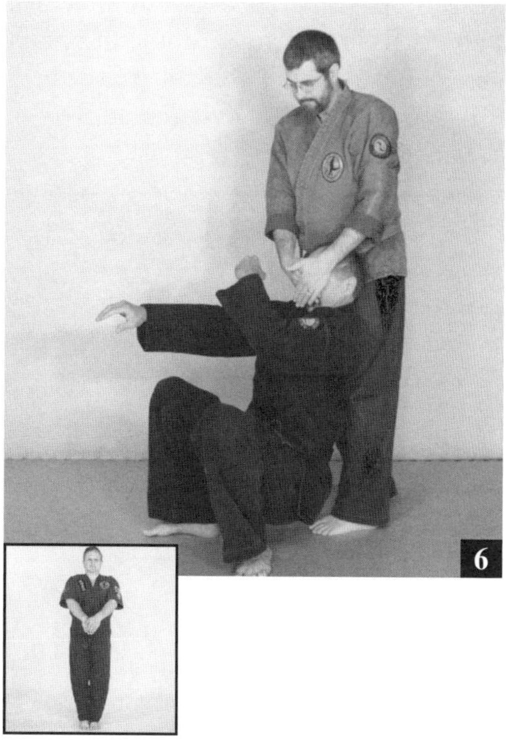
6

Bunkai # 3

1.An attacker seizes you by the lapels with both hands.

1

2,3. Brush your right forearm across the attacker's left forearm to stimulate point LI-7/*Wenliu.*

4. Continue the preceding movement by striking the attacker's right outer forearm near his elbow, at point LI-10/*Shousanli*, with your right arm. This causes him to turn to your right and fold over bringing his head close to your body.

5,6. Reach with your left hand to the far side of the attacker's head, and grab his hair firmly just in front and above his ear. As you grab, dig your knuckles into his scalp to activate a line of pressure points, including GB-4/*Hanyan*, GB-5/*Xuanlu*, GB-6/*Xuanli*, and S-8/*Touwei*.

4

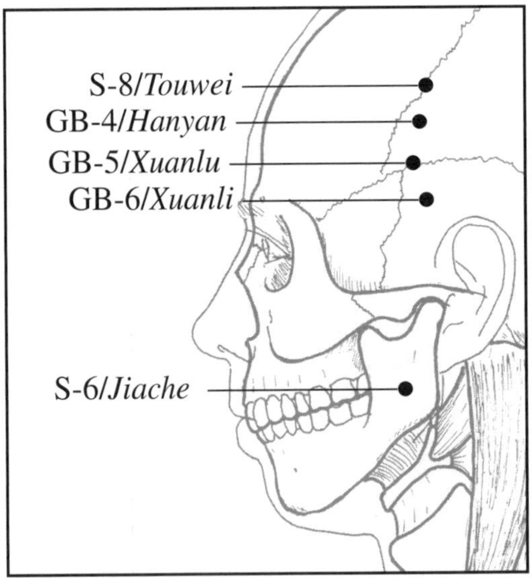

2

3

5

6

Bunkai # 3 (cont.)

7. Press the fingers of your right hand against pressure point S-6/*Jiache* on right side of the attacker's jaw.

8,9. Pressing with your right hand, and pulling with your left, spin the attack around, and sit him on the floor at your feet.

10. Pin the attacker's head against your right thigh with strong, pulsing pressure on S-6/*Jiache*.

7

9

Note: The progression from Large Intestine (Metal) points on the arm, to Gall Bladder (Wood) points on the scalp, to a Stomach (Earth) point on the jaw follows the principle of the 5 elements (Metal » Wood » Earth).

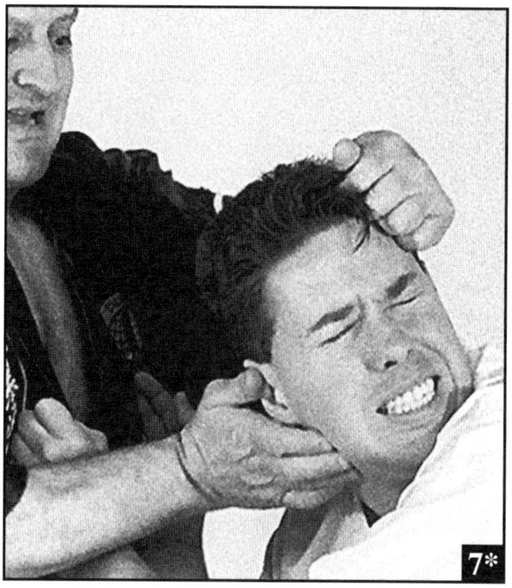

7*

8

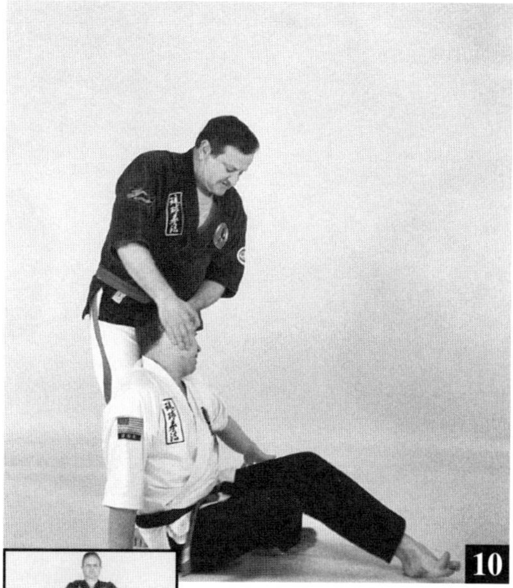

10

10*

Bunkai # 4

1. Your opponent grabs you by the lapel with both hands, pulling you in.

2. Bring both your arms up, cutting across LI-7/*Wenliu* on the outside of his forearms to press his elbows in towards his centerline.

3-4. Press or poke upward with the tips of your fingers on SI-17/*Tianrong*, behind the point of the jaw.

5-7. Drive your fingertips diagonally downward into Co-4/*Guanyuan*, just behind the knot of his belt to fold him over.

NOTE: *Co-4/Guanyuan is the alarm point of the Small Intestine meridian.*

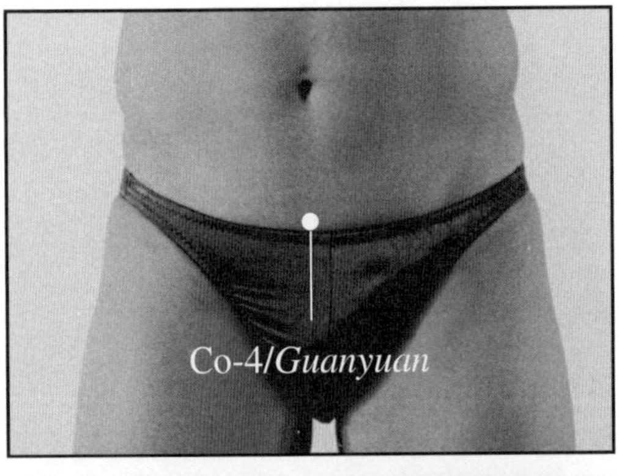

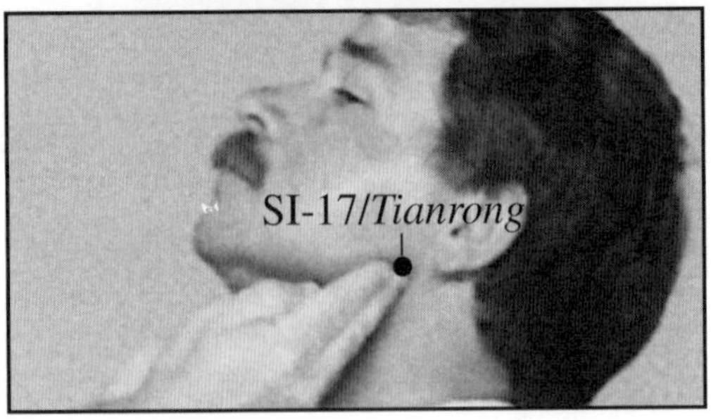

2

3

5

6

Bunkai # 5

1. An opponent grabs your left forearm at the elbow and wrist, and begins to drive you back.

2,3. With your right hand pin the attacker's left hand to your wrist. At the same time, drop your left elbow, and pivot on the balls of your feet 90° to your left into a cross stance.

4-6. Take advantage of the vulnerable position of the attacker's wrist, by applying rotational pressure on a 45° downward angle.

1

4

4*

2

3

5

6

Bunkai # 6

1

1. As an attacker pushes you with his right hand, bring both your hands over his hand, trapping it against your chest.

NOTE: *With the fingers of your right hand, lift your opponent's little finger and draw it behind his ring finger.*

2-4. Perform a cross-over step, left foot over right, and allow your body to turn naturally toward the right.

NOTE: *Your opponent is now caught in the basic tuité technique, palm turn.*

5. As the opponent moves to your right in order to release the pressure on his wrist, step out with your right leg into a horse stance and strike TW-17/*Yifeng* below the ear with a right back-hand strike.

NOTE: *The back-hand is not perfectly flat, but is cupped slightly so that the knuckles protrude and fit into the cavity behind the jaw where TW-17/Yifeng is situated.*

3

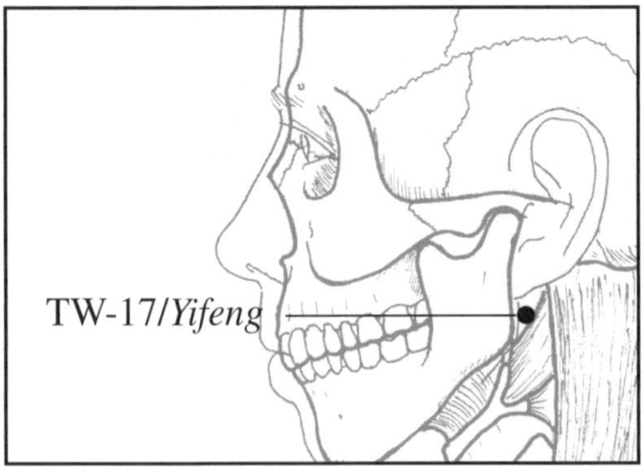

1*

2

4

5

Bunkai # 7

1. An attacker grabs your left forearm, and holds it down as he throws a right punch.

2. Pivoting around the attacker's grab, roll your left hand upward. At the same time, receive his punch by striking his forearm with your right hand at pressure point LI-7/*Wenliu*.

3-6. With your left hand, grab the attacker's right wrist as you step your right foot next to his left foot, and strike with your forearm to his neck at S-9/*Renying* & S-10/*Shuitu*.

2

2*

5

6

Bunkai # 8

1. Your opponent threatens with his right fist.

2,3. With a circular movement of your left hand, grab his wrist, twisting across the wrist pressure points.

4. Pull his captured right hand strongly to your left hip, and step towards him with your right foot into a horse stance.

5. Strike his GB-20/*Fengchi*, using your forearm at points TW-6/*Zhigou*, & TW-7/*Huizong*, TW-8/*Sanyangluo*.

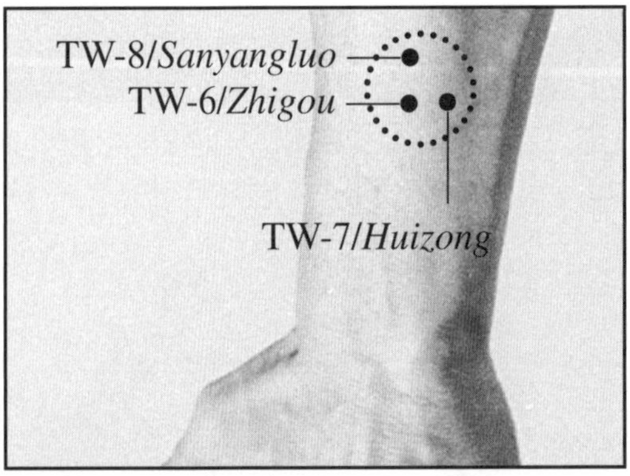

This is an advanced use of the principle of the Diurnal Cycle. Because *ki/chi* flows from the Triple Warmer Meridian into the Gall Bladder Meridian, you can strike with your Triple Warmer Meridian to his Gall Bladder Meridian to drive *ki/chi* easily into your target. The triangle of points TW-6/*Zhigou*, & TW-7/*Huizong*, TW-8/*Sanyangluo* is a particularly "hot" spot on the forearm.

2

3

5

5*

Bunkai # 9

1. As an attacker suddenly grabs your lapel, intent on punching you in the face, your hands will instinctively rise.

2,3. Pull your attacker's left palm tightly against your chest, pinning him where he grabbed you, and turn to your right (pivoting around his left wrist) as you drop into a horse stance.

NOTE: *Your right forearm cuts across the back of the opponent's forearm at TW-6/Zhigou, & TW-7/Huizong, TW-8/Sanyangluo.*

1

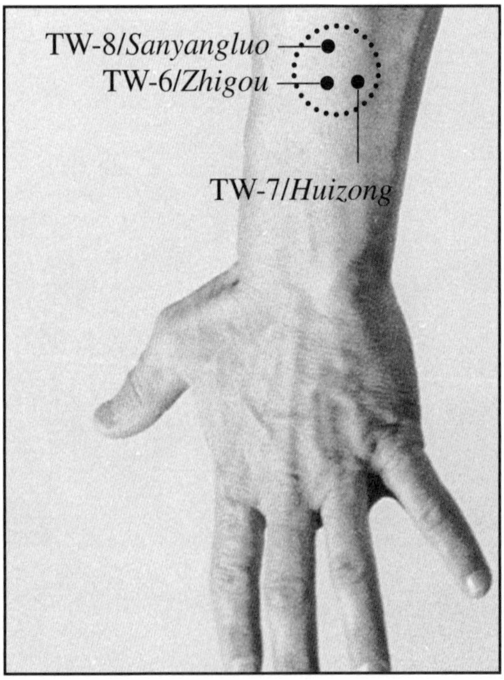

1*

2

3

2*

3*

Bunkai # 9 (cont.)

4-6. With your right hand, continue to pin the attacker's left hand to your chest, as you swing your left forearm across his face (and allow your arm to swing through and past).

NOTE: *Because the forearm strike is a gross motor skill, it primarily attacks an area rather than any one point. In photo # 5, the blow appears to be touching S-6/Jiache, SI-18/Quanliao, LI-20/Yingxiang.*

4

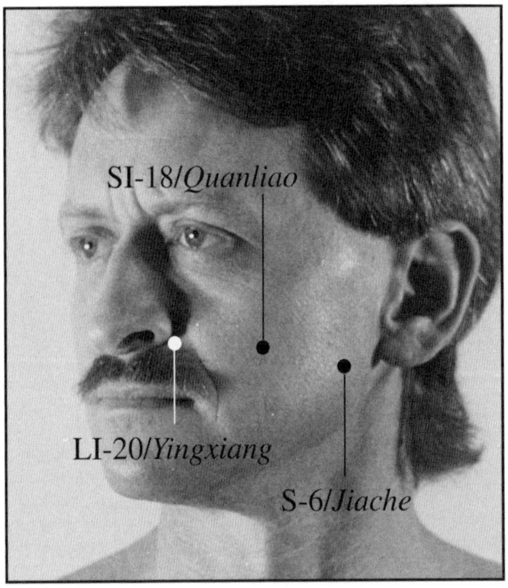

4*

5

6

5*

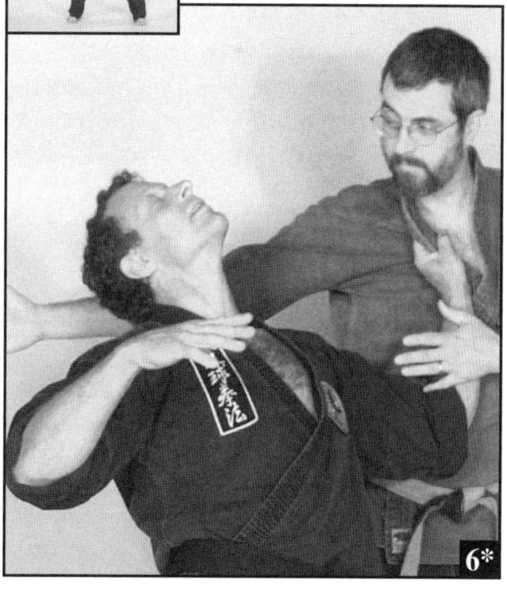

6*

Bunkai # 9 (cont.)

7. Bring your open right hand up against the left rear quadrant of the attacker's head as you punch with your left fist into his S-5/*Daying* pressure point.

7

NOTE: *Your right hand primarily has the job of anchoring and positioning the attacker's head so your left can easily strike the pressure point at the correct angle.*

8,9. Continue the motion of your punch, turning it into elbow strike aimed to the jaw, hitting S-6/*Jiache* or TW-17/*Yifeng* (depending on angle).

NOTE: *Be very careful not to perform the elbow strike with much force. Since his head is trapped between your hands, it cannot move to lessen the impact of your blow. As a result, he can be seriously injured by a hard elbow smash. Targeting the pressure points allows for a much softer technique.*

7*

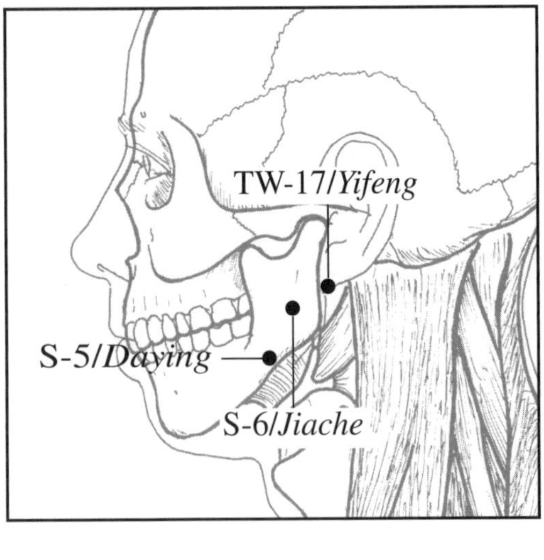

8

9

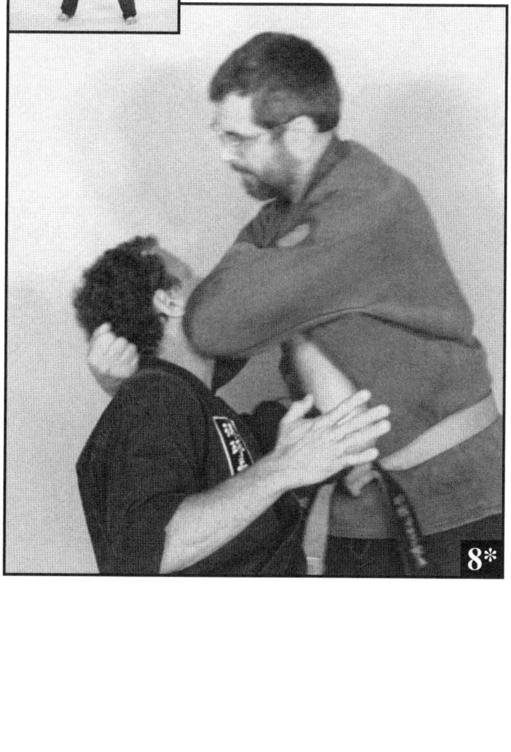

8*

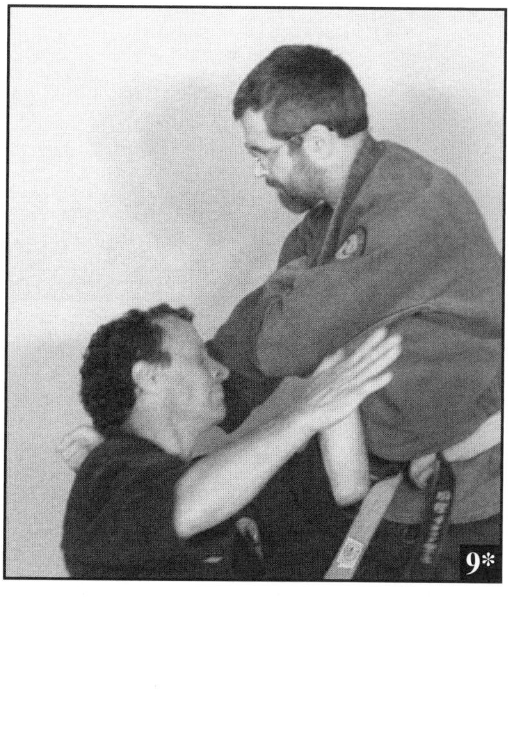

9*

Bunkai # 10

1. Your opponent grabs your left forearm with his right hand.

2. Grasp his right wrist with your right hand, trapping his hand to your arm.

NOTE: *Your fingertips dig into pressure point H-6/Yinxi and your thumb wraps around to press on P-6/Neiguan.*

4. Rotate your right elbow forward, turning his right hand in a palm turn.

5,6. Using the palm turn for control, bring your opponent's head into your elbow, striking below the ear at pressure point TW-17/*Yifeng*.

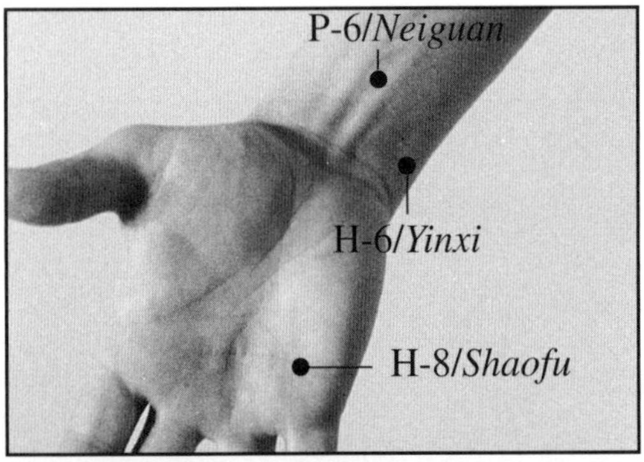

A palm turn activates H-8/*Shaofu* on the palm. A needle inserted through H-8/*Shaofu* exits the back of the hand at TW-3/*Zhongzhu*, since these two points are, at a deep level, connected. So, the Triple Warmer Meridian is activated by a palm turn. It is also activated by P-6/*Neiquan*, following the Yin/Yang principle.

2

3

4*

5

Bunkai # 11

1. An attacker grabs your right arm, just above the elbow, with his left hand.

2,3. Shift to your right, at a 45° angle to your opponent. As you make this move, smack the attacker with a right backhand, at K-21/*Youmen* & S-19/*Burong* on his abdomen.

4. Raise your right arm outside the attacker's left arm so that his left wrist rolls inward and bends slightly.

5. Grasp the attacker's left hand with your left hand, pinning it to your right arm. At the same time, fold your right arm over his captured wrist, rubbing across the back of his left forearm on points TW-6/*Zhigou*, & TW-7/*Huizong*, TW-8/*Sanyangluo*.

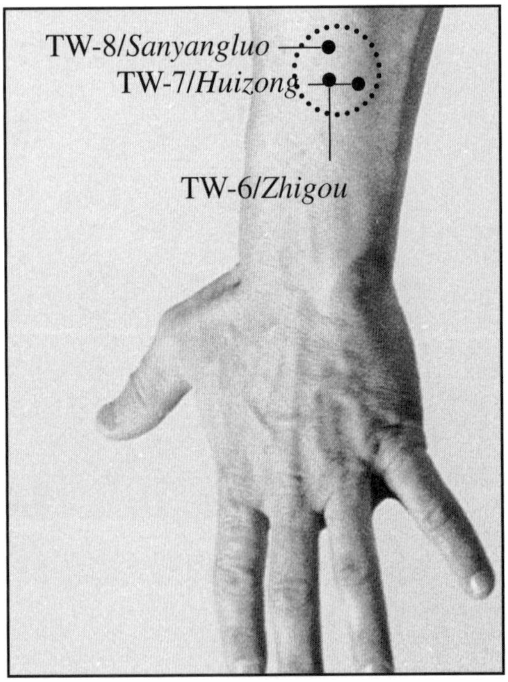

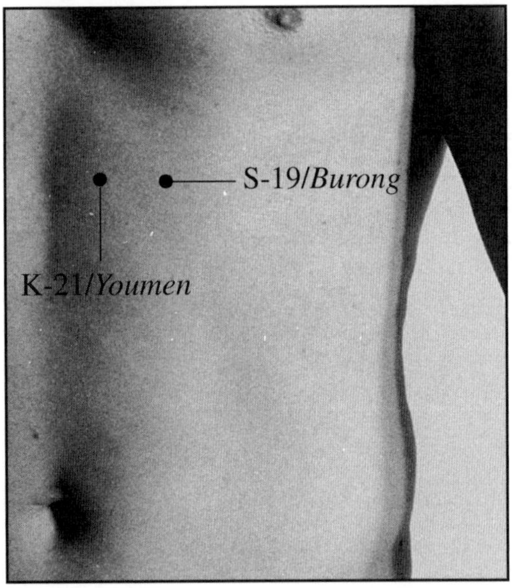

2

3

4

5

Bunkai # 11 (cont.)

6. Touch your right palm to your left elbow as you drop into a horse stance.

NOTE: *You have manipulated the attacker's arm into the tuité technique called a "Wrist Turn Press." This is also variously known as a Center Lock, an S-Lock, Dai Nikyo, etc.*

7,8. Drop your left elbow in order to change the orientation of the attacker's wrist from vertical to diagonal, then pull your right elbow strongly to your right hip.

NOTE: *Be extremely careful when practicing this technique as the change in orientation causes the wrist to become very vulnerable to injury.*

6

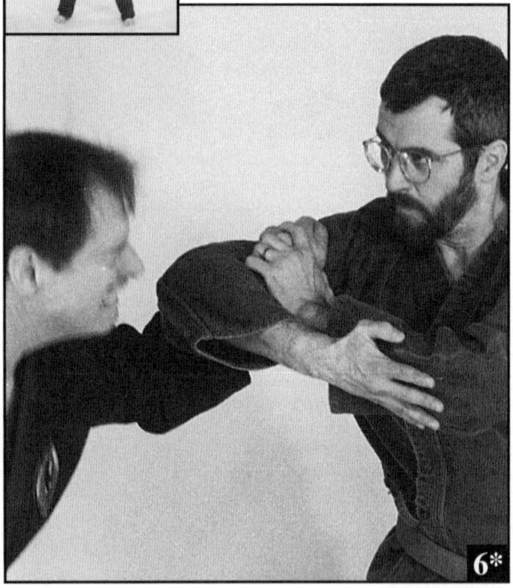

6*

7

8

7*

8*

Bunkai # 12

1. An attacker has seized your upraised wrists.

2. As you step forward with your left foot, and turn to your right. Pivot your left forearm around his grip so your elbow points toward his face, and his right wrist is bent and turned. Slide your right hand over his right wrist, rubbing firmly across TW-6/*Zhigou*, & TW-7/*Huizong*, TW-8/*Sanyangluo*.

NOTE: *His left hand is pinned to your right forearm by his own right wrist.*

3. Press downward with your left elbow on his right forearm as you pull strongly with your left hand

NOTE: *You are manipulating his right wrist in the tuité maneuver called a "Wrist Turn Press."*

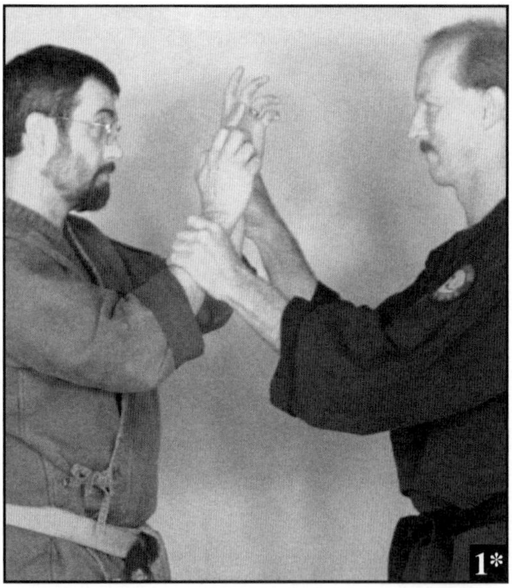

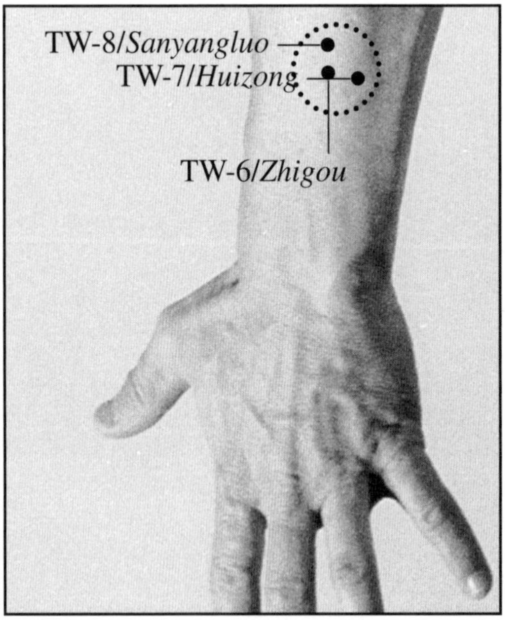

2

3

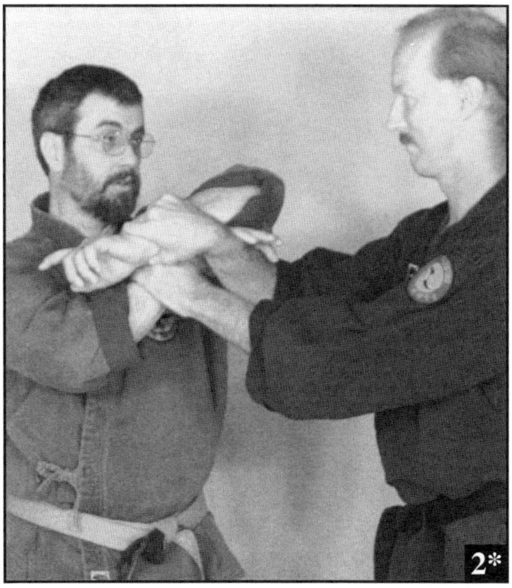
2*

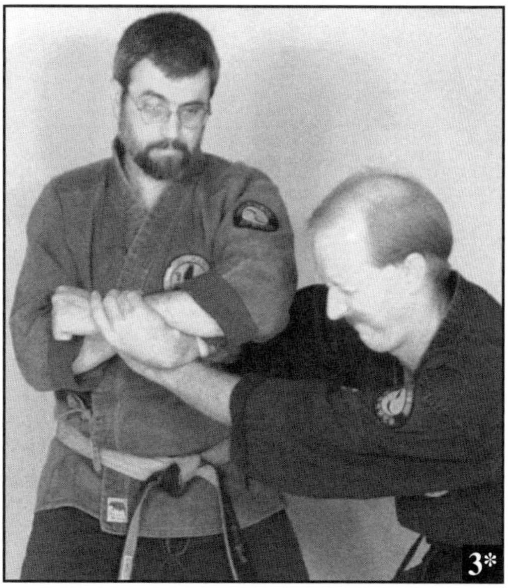
3*

Bunkai # 12 (cont.)

4. Drop into a horse stance and draw your hands to your right hip.

5. Still gripping strongly with your right hand, strike out with your left fist, to hit the attacker near the corner of the eye at GB-1/*Tongziliao* and TW-23/ *Sizhukong*.

NOTE: *Because the attacker's left hand is pinned in place by his own right wrist, he will not be able to free himself in time to stop your counter to his head.*

4

4*

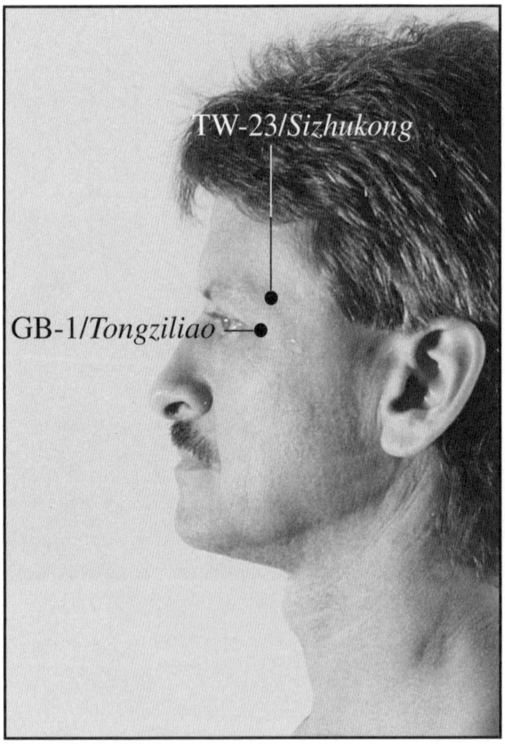

5

6

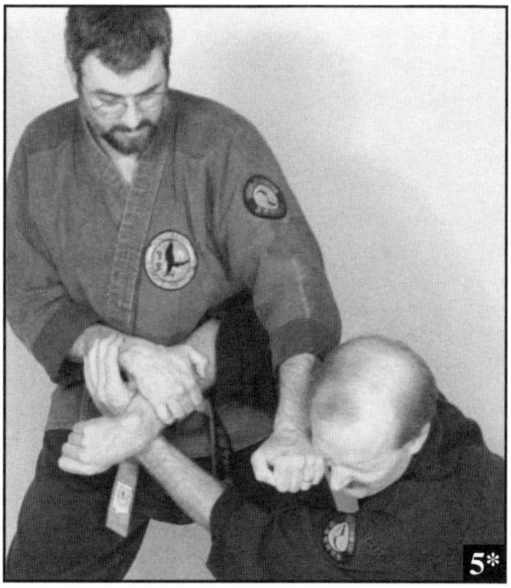
5*

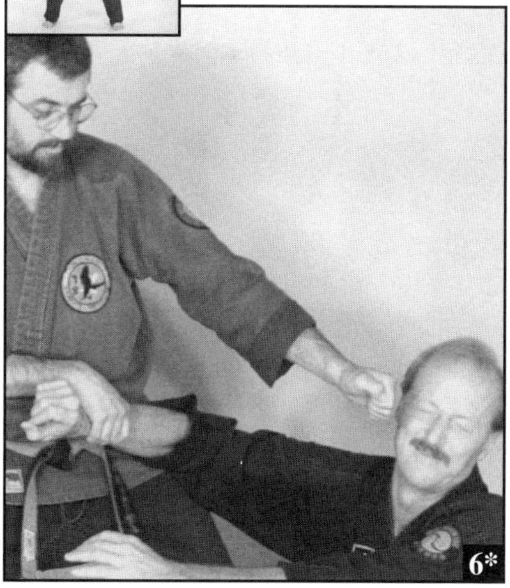
6*

Bunkai # 13

1. An attacker grabs your right wrist with his right hand.

2. Bend your right elbow *(he can't keep you from bending your own elbow).*

3. Press your fingers over his forearm, digging them across TW-6/*Zhigou*, & TW-7/*Huizong*, TW-8/*Sanyangluo*. With the foreknuckles of your left fist, rub up and down to activate TW-11/*Qinglengyuan*.

4. As his shoulder releases, drive him down into an arm bar.

1

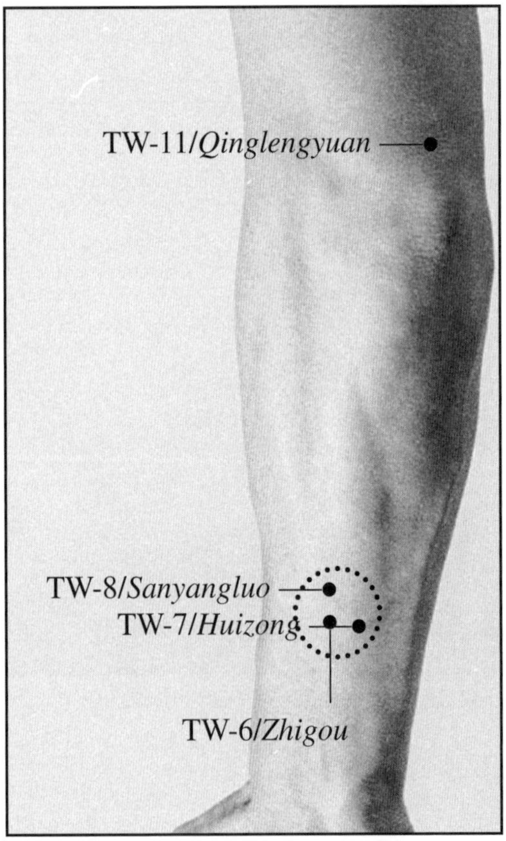

3*

2

3

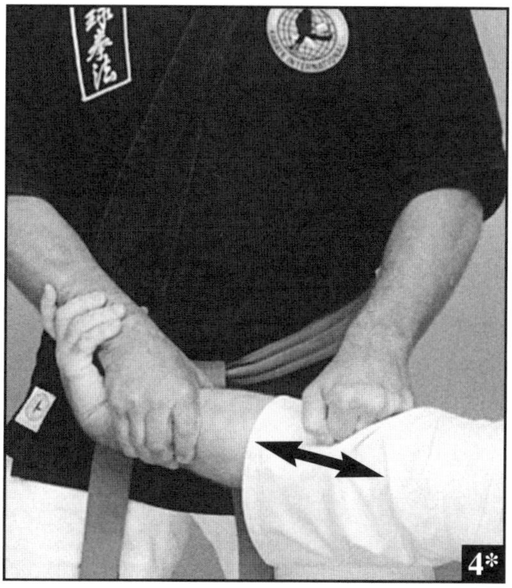
4*

4

Bunkai # 14

1. As an attacker grabs your lapel with his left hand, reach over with your right hand, pressing your thumb into H-6/Yinxi to weaken his grip.

2-3. Using both hands, twist his right hand over clockwise (from your point of view), manipulating him into the basic tuité position Wrist Reversal. In the final position, his right s aimed at his shoulder, and his fingers point up.

NOTE: *Your thumb presses on the back of the attacker's hand at M-UE-24/Luozhen, while your fingers press strongly into P-6/Neiguan.*

1

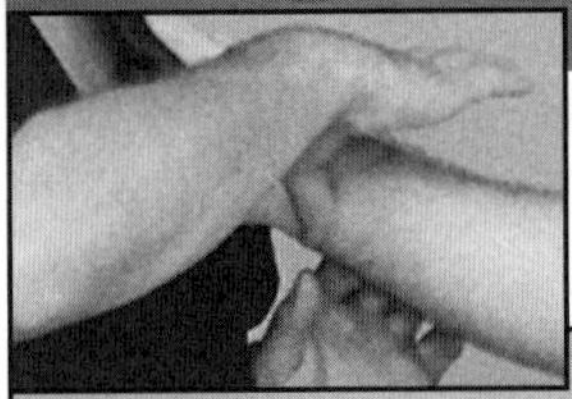

1*

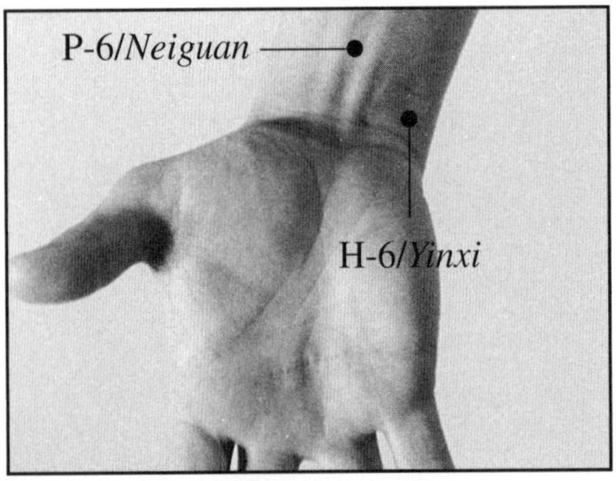

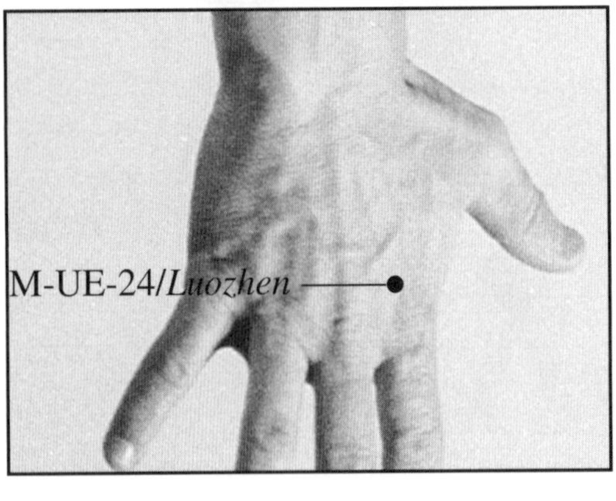

2

3

2*

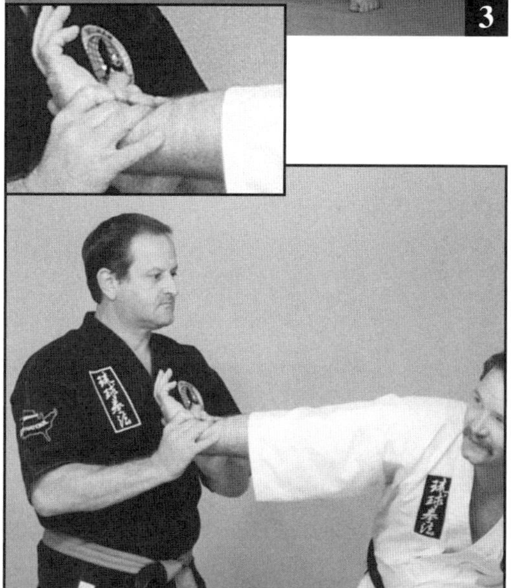

3*

Bunkai # 14 (cont.)

4. Step forward with your left foot, hooking it around the attacker's right foot as you assume a horse stance. Turn the attacker's hand further clockwise, as you pull it strongly to your right hip.

NOTE: *Allow your hands to slide on your attacker's hand so you are pressing your fingertips into H-8/Shaofu and squeezing your thumb across LI-2/ Erjian with your right hand, while twisting across P-6/Neiguan with your left.*

5-6. Strike with your left fist, hitting TW-17/*Yifeng* under the attacker's right ear.

4

4*

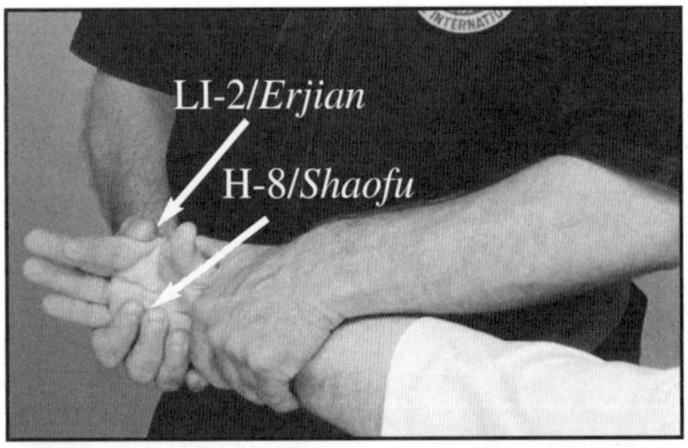

5

6

5*

6*

Bunkai # 15

1. When an attacker grabs your lapel with his left hand, grasp his wrist with your left hand, activating points SI-6/*Yanglao*.

2-3. Step to the left into a horse stance while punching with your right fist into the attacker's left arm at LI-13/*Shouwuli*.

NOTE: *When an attacker grabs with one hand, it is his other hand which represents a threat. Attacking the grabbing arm neutralizes the threat of a punch.*

4-6. Immediately strike the attacker on the back of his head at GB-20/*Fengchi* with a rising punch.

NOTE: *Enhance the strike by using a single-knuckle fist.*

1

4

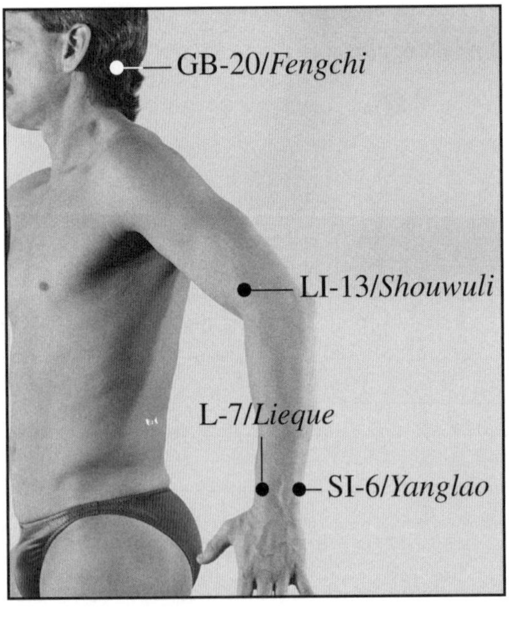

2

3

5

6

Bunkai # 16

1-3. As an attacker executes a straight left punch, slip to your right and capture his punch with your left hand, then draw his hand toward your left hip as you strike to his upper arm at point TW-12/*Xiaoluo* to fold him over.

NOTE: *The method of catching a punch is often called "Brush-Grab." It is covered in detail in "Appendix B: How to Catch a Punch," from* **Kyusho-Jitsu: The Dillman Method of Pressure Point Fighting**.

1

4-6. With your right hand, hold your attacker's left arm as you punch to his head, hitting GB-20/*Fengchi.*

NOTE: *To increase the effectiveness of the technique, tread lightly on the attacker's left foot as if trying to pin his fifth metatarsal (the small bone on the outer edge of the foot) to the ground. The pressure point affected by this is GB-41/Zulingqi.*

4

The Triple Warmer and Gall Bladder meridians are related by the diurnal cycle. Energy flows from Triple Warmer to Gall Bladder. This technique follows that sequence.

2

3

5

6

Bunkai # 17

1. The opponent grabs your lapel with his right hand, and threatens with his left.

2,3. With your right hand, punch the attacker in the crease of his hip, about 2" to the side of his groin, hitting Li-12/*Jimai* & Sp-12/*Chongmen* (inguinal crease cluster).

NOTE: *Striking Li-12/Jimai & Sp-12/Chongmen will cause your opponent to bend forward, with his face up (almost the same position as bowing before a kata). This action stretches out the nerves in the neck.*

4,5. With your left fist, strike upward, just inside the notch on the bottom of the jaw, hitting S-5/*Daying*.

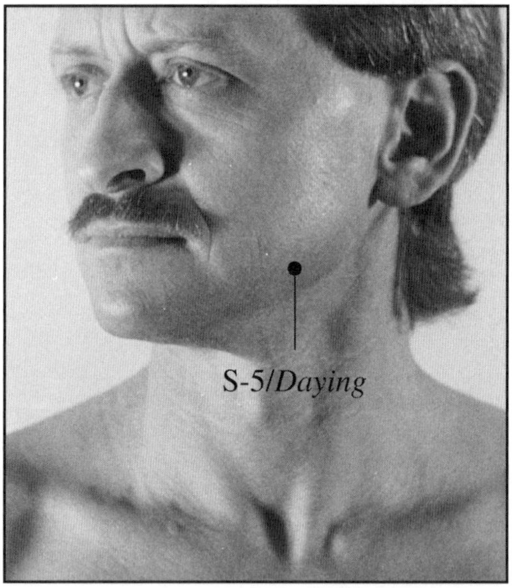

NOTE: *Execute this technique with a slightly broken timing, so the lower fist strikes an instant before the other. This technique utilizes two principles of kyusho-jitsu, the cycle of destruction (Liver/Wood & Spleen/Earth) and the principle of yin and yang (Spleen/yin to Stomach/yang).*

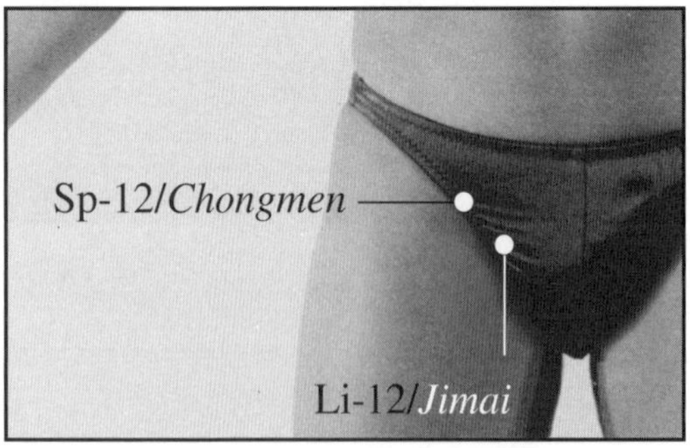

2

3

4

5

Bunkai # 18

1. An attacker seizes you by both lapels.

2. With your left arm, strike downward (and slightly inward) hitting both of the attacker's forearms, hitting pressure points LI-7/*Wenliu* and/or L-6/*Kongzui* (depending on how his arms are positioned).

3-6. Using the small knuckle of your right fist, punch upward, hitting the opponent under the eyebrow ridge at M-HN-6/*Yuyao*.

NOTE: *Only tap this point with your fist because; a) the eyebrow ridge is a very strong bone, and you could break your fist at the fifth metacarpal; b) you are basically attacking the point on the supraorbital nerve which is closest to his brain, making this a very serious attack.*

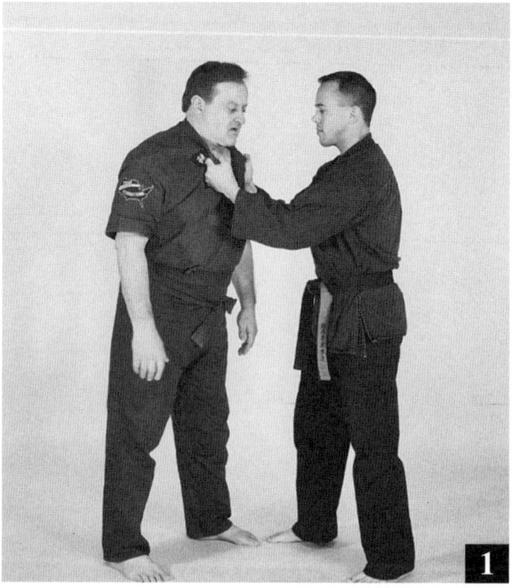
1

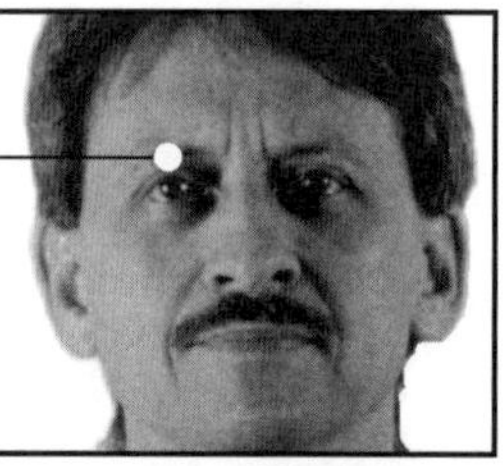

The pressure points on the arm, LI-7/*Wenliu* and/or L-6/*Kongzui*, are both Metal elements points. M-HN-6/*Yuyao* is a point related to the eye, making it a Wood element point. Striking Metal » Wood follows the 5 element rule.

4

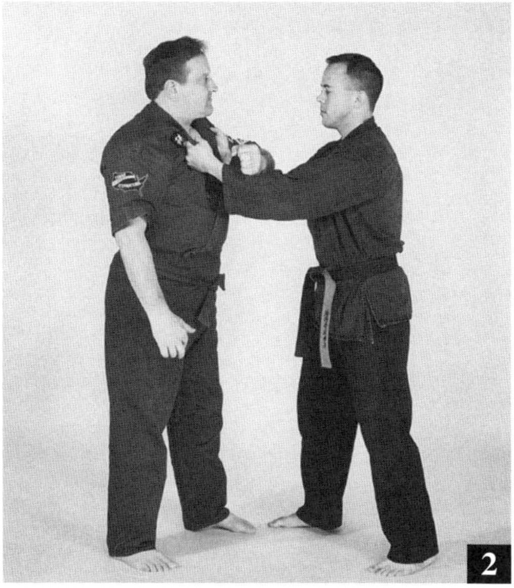
2

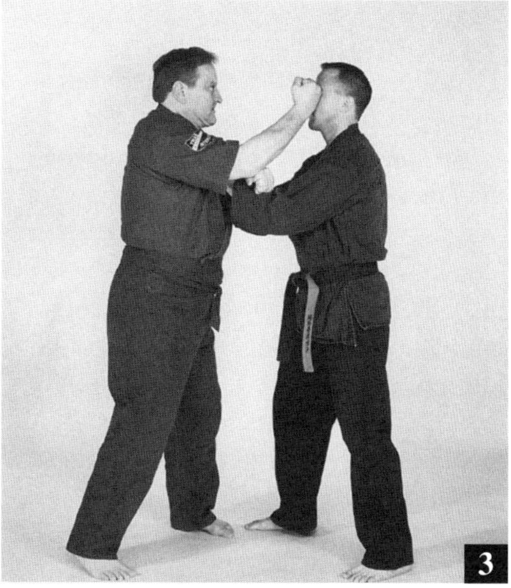
3

5

6

Bunkai # 19

1. An opponent grabs your lapel with his right hand.

2,3. With your left wrist strike the attacker's forearm at point LI-10/*Shousanli*. With your right fist strike his inner arm, just above the elbow, at pressure point H-2/*Qingling*.

4-6. Step outside the attacker's right leg with your left leg, as you press your left forearm close to your own belly to draw the attacker in close. Finish with a strike with your right fist to point GB-20/*Fengchi*.

1

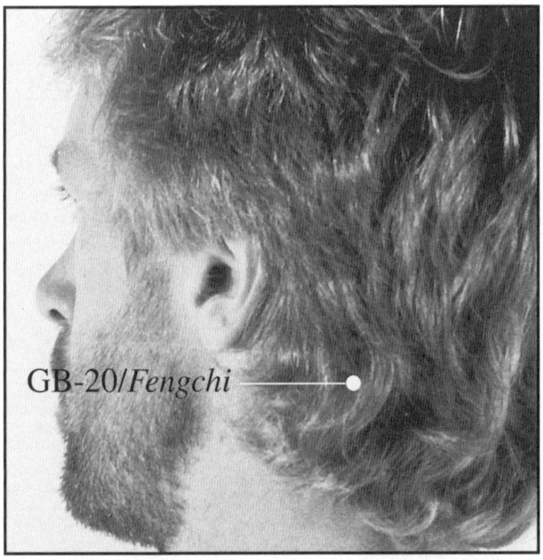

4

Heart meridian is Fire, Large Intestine is Metal, Gall Bladder is Wood. This sequence follows the 5 element principle.

2

3

5

6

Bunkai # 20

1. An assailant approaches from your left and places his right arm around your shoulder.

2,3. Turn to your left, stepping with your left foot onto the attacker's right foot at GB-41/*Zulingqi*, and striking with your left forearm into his ribs, hitting GB-24/*Riyue* & Li-14/*Qimen*.

4-6. Strike upward with your right fist hitting the eyebrow ridge at supraorbital foramen, the extraordinary point M-HN-6/*Yuyao*.

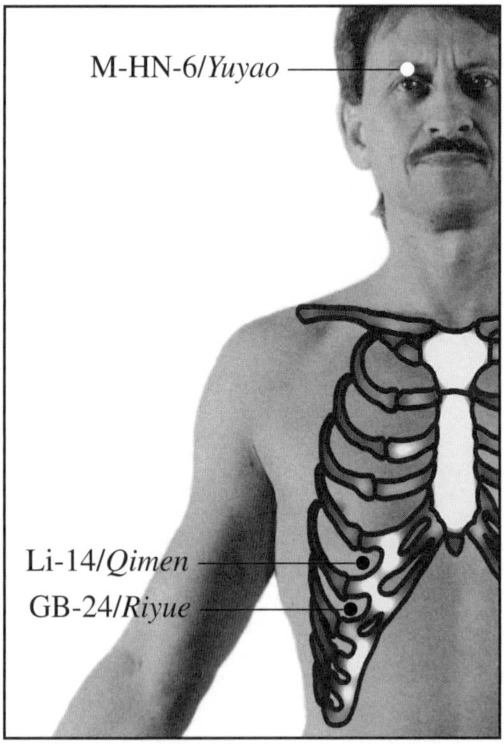

2

3

5

6

Bunkai # 21

1-2. As an opponent delivers a left punch, hook his forearm with your left hand, and grab across pressure points TW-6/*Zhigou*, TW-7/*Huizong*, & TW-8/*Sanyangluo.*

1

3. Strike upward with your right hand so that your forearm cuts across the opponent's left upper-arm at TW-12/*Xiaoluo.*

4-5. Continue the striking motion so that your right fist hits TW-17/*Yifeng* with a slight back-to-front hooking motion. At the same time, pull his left hand close to your body with a strong twist across TW-6/*Zhigou*, TW-7/*Huizong*, & TW-8/*Sanyangluo*.

4

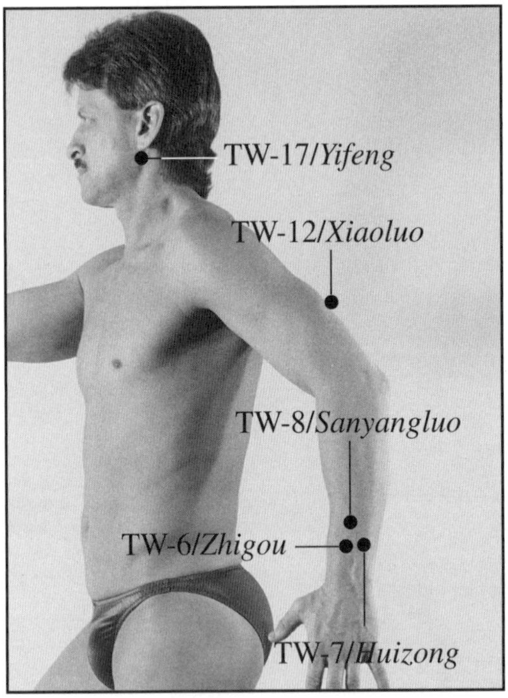

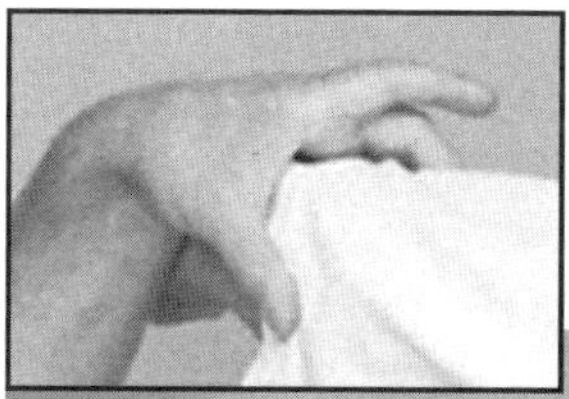

2

3

5

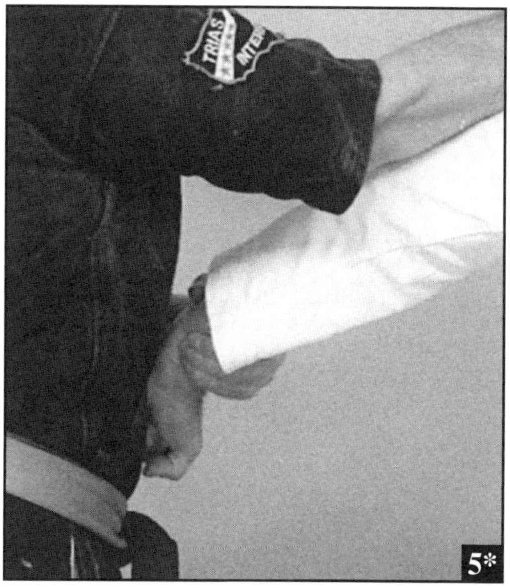

5*

Bunkai # 22

1,2. As your opponent punches with his right, move diagonally forward to your left, using your right forearm to control his attack.

3. With your left hand grasp his forearm, pressing your fingertips firmly into LI-10/*Shousanli*.

4,5. With your right fist, strike the attacker's right jaw at S-6/*Jiache*.

This technique is a variation on the familiar pattern "brush, grab, strike." The pressure point sequence follows the Diurnal Cycle, Large Intestine » Stomach.

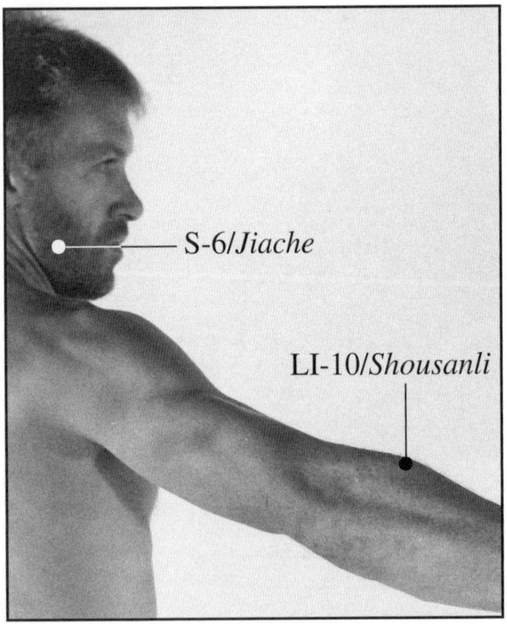

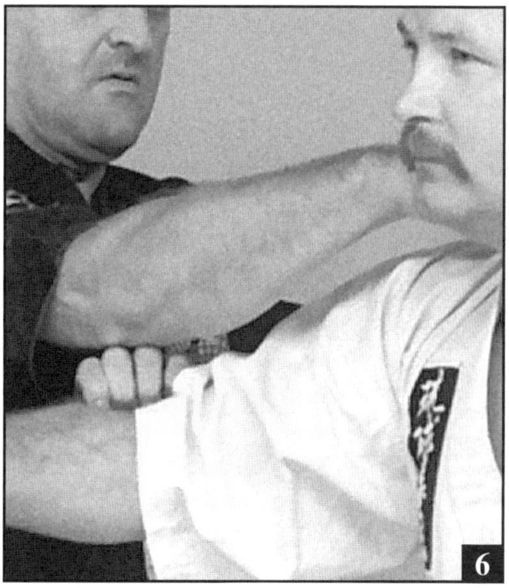

The distinctive movement of Naihanchi is the technique of bringing one foot up near the opposite inner knee. In our manner of performance, the raised foot lightly touches inside the knee. We will intentionally touch the ball of our raised foot to the pressure point Sp-9/*Yinlingquan*, and allow our heel to touch either Li-9/*Yinbao* or Sp-10/*Xuehai*. These are the points which the kata indicates as targets. We understand the application of the movement to be a kick aimed at one of these points (as you will see in the following examples).

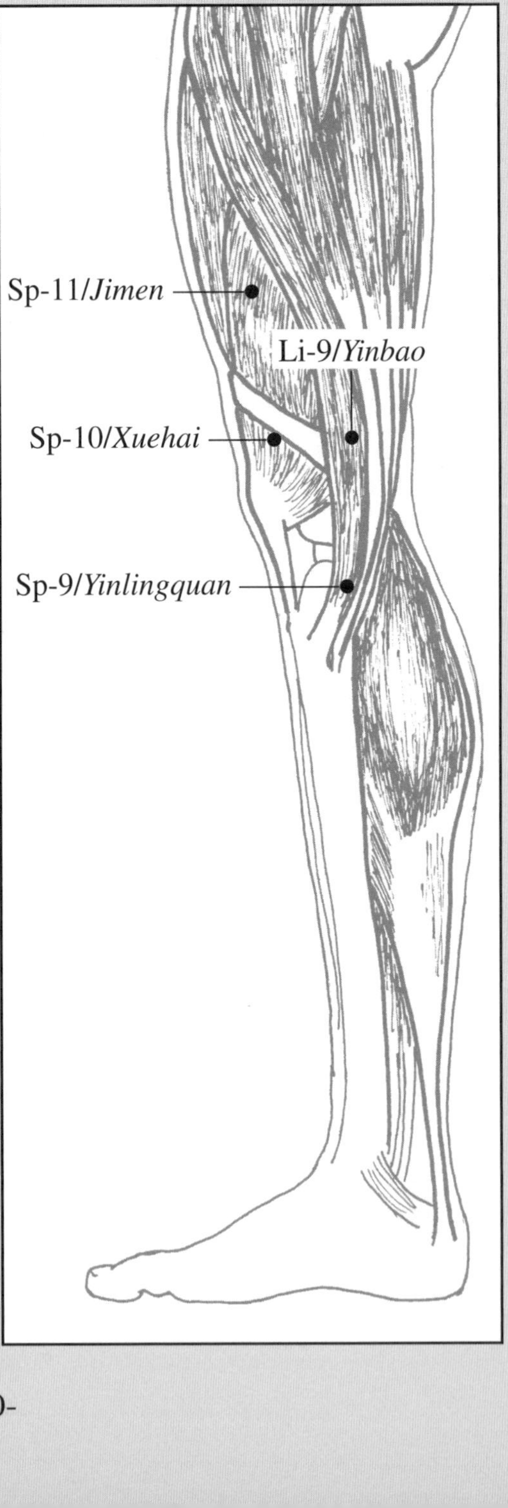

Some versions of the kata do not involve touching the raised foot to the points on the opposite leg. Instead, the foot is swept upward in front of the knee. This upward arc corresponds to the angle required to properly attack the point Sp-9/*Yinlingquan.*

It is worth noting that attacks to these points can cause injury to the knee joint. This occurs because the knee is buckled by the stimulation of the point, and collapses when body weight falls onto it. As a result, we often choose to kick Sp-11/*Jimen*, which lies slightly higher on the inner thigh, this is a very effective target, but has a lower risk of damaging the knee.

The method of kicking to the inside of the leg is quite easy to do, and requires minimal training. It is concealed in the kata by a representational – rather than literal – movement, probably to prevent beginners and outsiders from learning the technique. We find that this kick (which we call Naihanchi-geri, or "Naihanchi kick") can be successfully applied with almost any other movement in the kata.

Bunkai # 23

1. An opponent faces you in a threatening posture.

2-5. Preempt his attack by kicking against Sp-10/*Xuehai*, inside and above the knee, to drop him to the ground.

NOTE: *This kick is performed with a slight hooking action, catching the pressure point with the heal.*

1

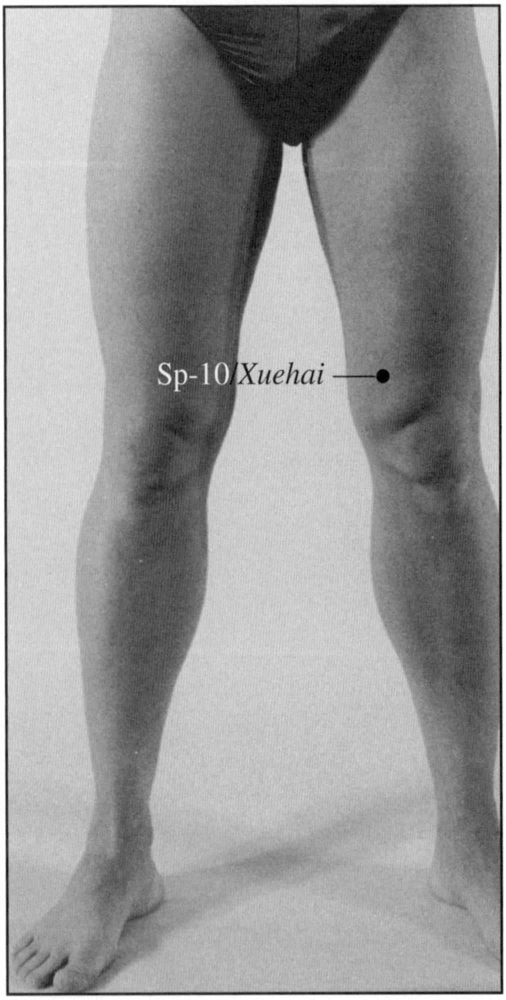

3*

2

3

4

5

Bunkai # 24

1. An assailant has grabbed you by both wrists.

2,3 Cross your wrists, left over right, and slip your right hand over the attacker's right wrist, rubbing across pressure points TW-6/*Zhigou*, & TW-7/ *Huizong*, TW-8/*Sanyangluo*.

4,6. Pull the attacker's right wrist strongly into your body, and push your left elbow forward slightly to put torque on the little finger side of his hand *(you are manipulating his right hand in the manner of the tuité technique called the Palm Turn).* At the same time, kick with your right leg to the inside of the attacker's left knee at Sp-10/*Xuehai* or Sp-11/*Jimen* to send him to the ground. Follow-up as necessary.

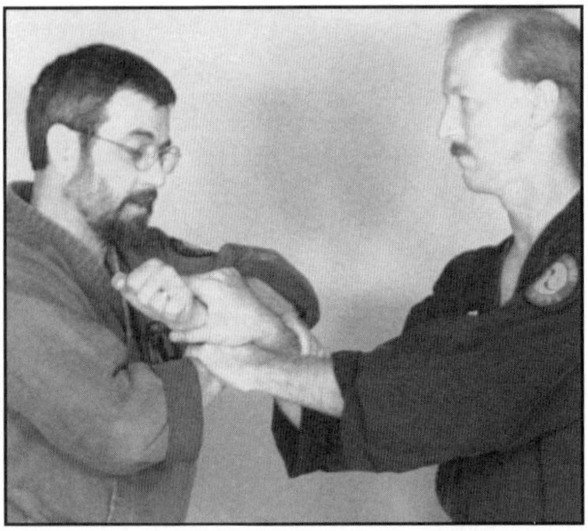

2

3

5

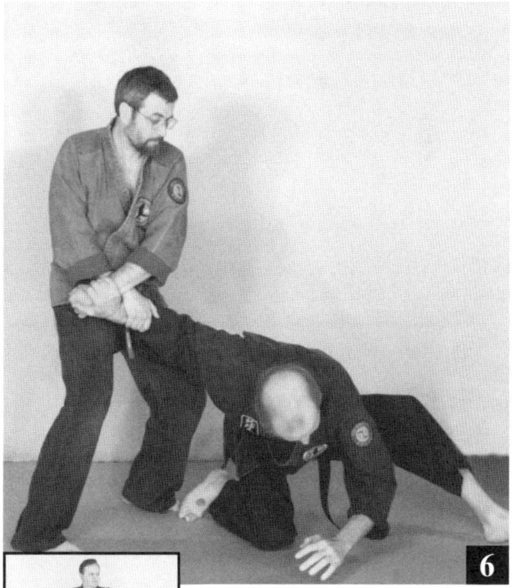
6

Bunkai # 25

1. As your opponent punches with his right, move diagonally forward to your left, using your right forearm to control his attack.

2-6. Attack three points at the same time – LI-10/*Shousanli* with your left fist, S-6/*Jiache* with your right fist, Sp-10/*Xuehai* with your right foot – to incapacitate your opponent.

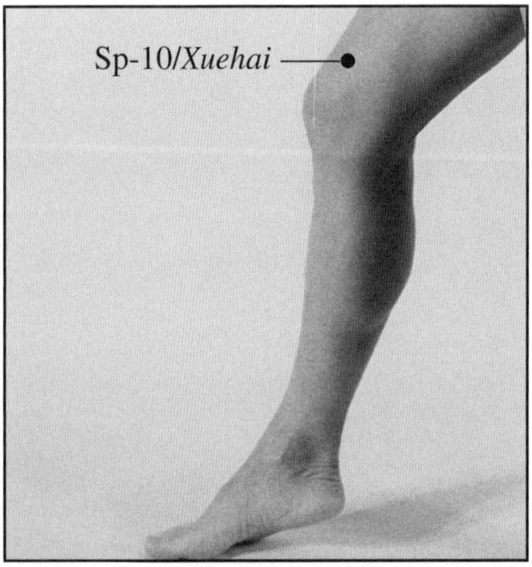

Attacking the Spleen meridian makes the Stomach meridian vulnerable following the rule of Yin/Yang. Attacking the Large Intestine meridian makes the Somach meridian vulnerable according to the rule of the Diurnal Cycle. This explains the dramatic results the technique produces.

2

3

5

6

Bunkai # 26

1. An assailant grabs your right wrist with his right hand.

1

2. Bend your elbow, and raise your right hand to rotate his arm.

3. Slide the fingers of your right hand over the attacker's forearm, activating points TW-6/*Zhigou*, & TW-7/*Huizong*, TW-8/*Sanyangluo*, and rub just above his elbow on TW-11/*Qinglengyuan* to bring his torso down.

4. Raise your right knee into his chest, smashing GB-23/*Zhejin*.

5,6. With your right foot, kick inside his left knee at Sp-9/*Yinlingquan*.

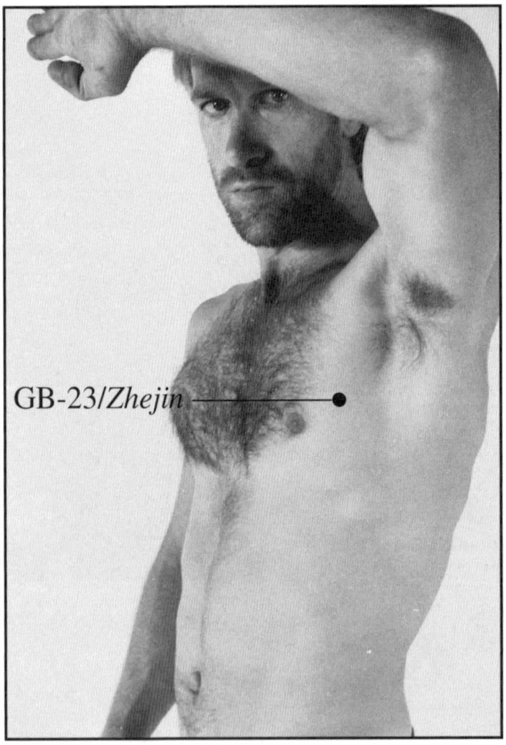

4

2

3

5

6

Bunkai # 27

1. An assailant grabs your upraised left wrist with his right hand.

2,3. Pull the attacker's right wrist strongly into your body with your right hand, and push your left elbow forward to put torque on the little finger side of his hand *(you are manipulating his right hand in the manner of the tuité technique called the Palm Turn).*

NOTE: *A kick can generally be broken down into three distinct movements: coil, extension, recoil. The conventional interpretation is that the point of contact for a kick is at the extension of the foot. In the preceding application, both the coil (as a knee strike) and the extension are interpreted as hits. And in this application, it is the extension and the recoil which are used. Such deep understandings of the application of basic movements are a hallmark of Ryukyu kempo.*

2

3

2*

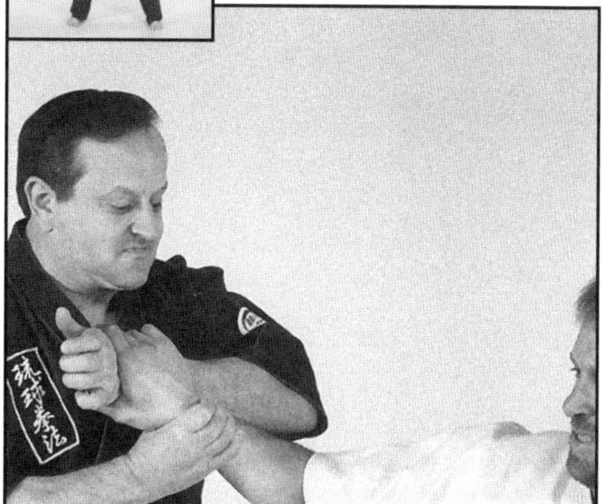

3*

Bunkai # 27 (cont.)

4. Kick out with your right foot hitting the attacker's left leg inside the knee at Sp-9/*Yinlingquan*.

5,6. Snap your foot back, striking inside his left knee at Sp-10/*Xuehai* with your heel.

4

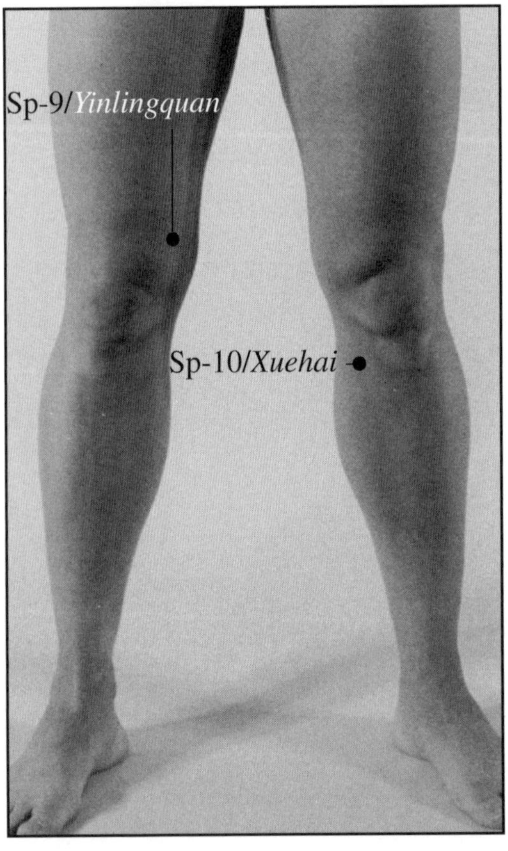

4*

5

6

5*

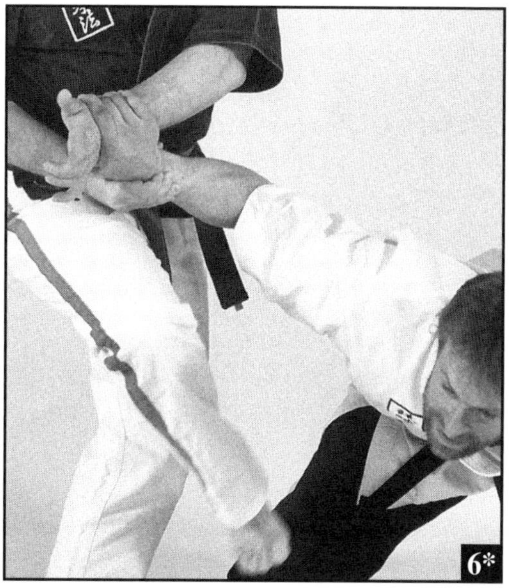

6*

Bunkai # 28

1. As an opponent attacks with a left lead punch, deflect it with your right palm, while reaching outside his forearm with your left hand.

1

2. Grasp his left wrist with your left hand and step forward with your right foot, hooking it behind his left ankle.

3-4. Tap with your right forearm on the attacker's left upper arm at TW-12/*Xiaoluo*, as you twist his palm to face upward.

***NOTE:** Pay special attention that your right thumb is pressing P-6/Neiguan on the attacker's left wrist.*

5-6. In a continuing motion, drive a right punch under the attacker's left ear at TW-17/*Yifeng*.

***NOTE:** Use horse stance to control his left leg and destroy his structure.*

4

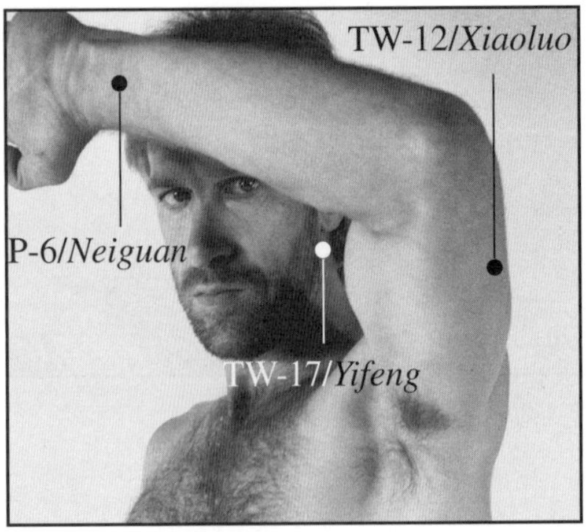

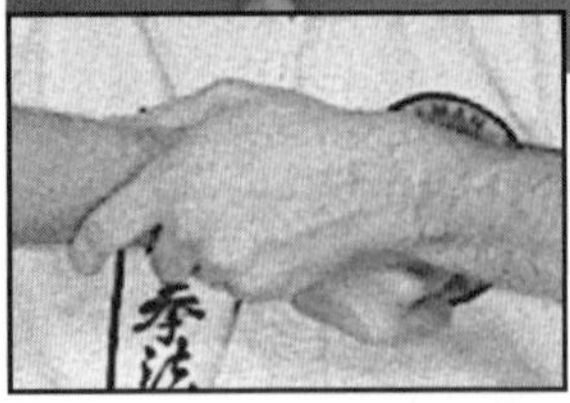

2

3

5

6

Bunkai # 29

1. As an opponent grabs your lapel with both hands, strike his forearms to collapse them inward, by hitting LI-10/*Shousanli*, on his left side, and LI-7/*Wenliu* on his right side.

2. As his body folds inward in response to your blows, step to your left and drop into a horse stance, as you pull his arms strongly inward, to pin him against your torso.

3. Keeping his arms trapped by your right hand, strike out with your left fist, hitting through S-5/*Daying* on the left side of his jaw. *(This does not need to be a strong blow, but it must go through the point, both to properly activate the target, and to cause the attacker's head to rock away and then back into the following action.)*

2

3

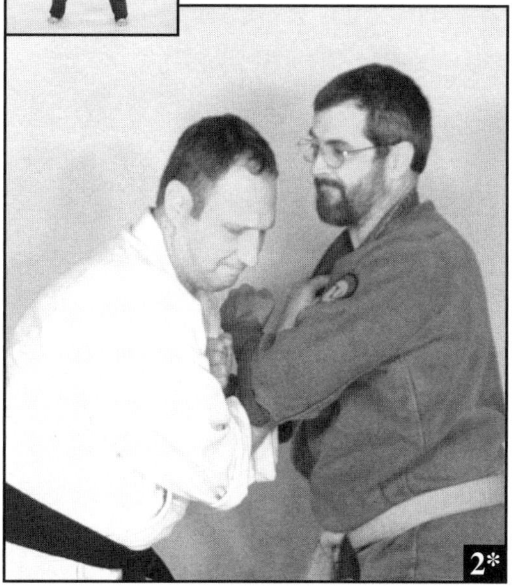
2*

3*

Bunkai # 29 (cont.)

5-6. Allow your right hand to ride out in the same motion as your left strike, and punch the attacker's head as it rocks back, hitting S-5/*Daying* a second time.

NOTE: *Alternately, S-6/Jiache for one or both strikes in place of S-5/Daying.*

4

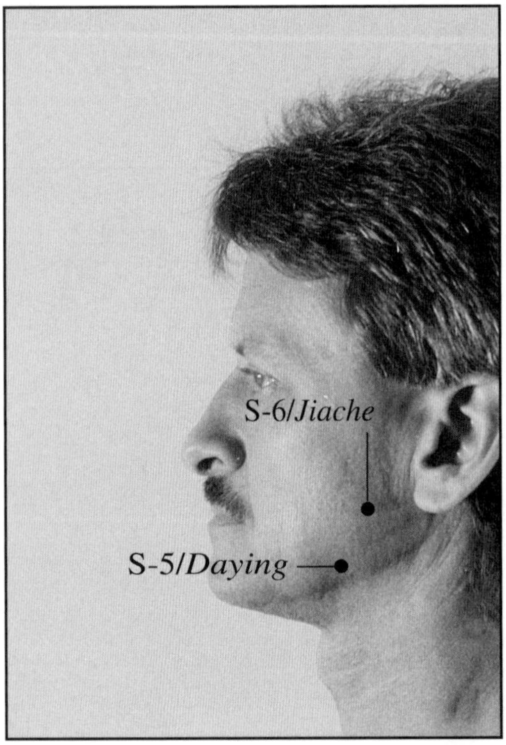

4*

5

6

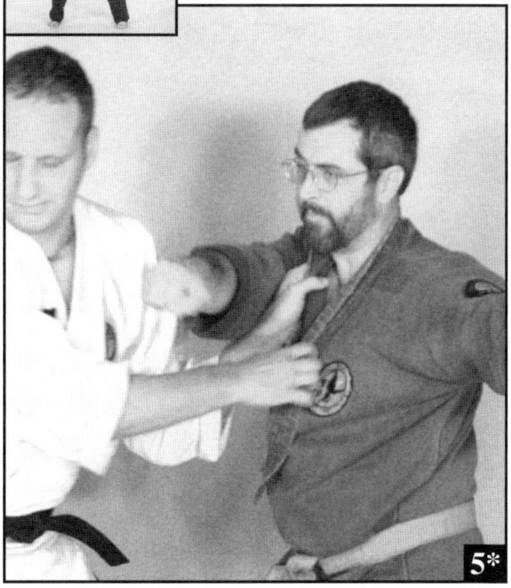
5*

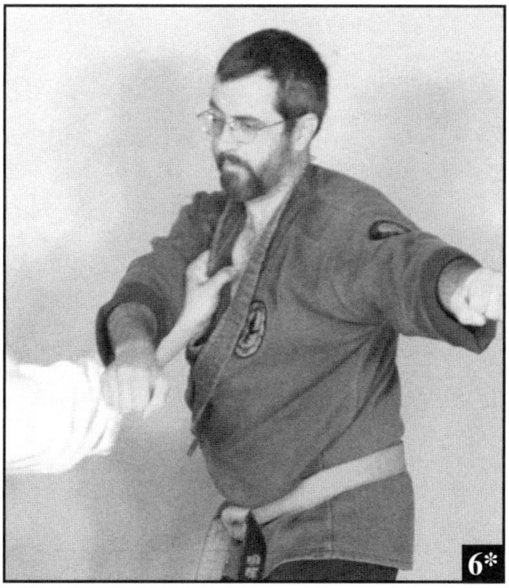
6*

Bunkai # 30

1. An opponent grabs you with his left hand, preparing to punch with his left.

2. With your left fist, strike his right forearm at pressure point LI-10/ *Shousanli* to expose the side of his jaw.

3. Strike out using a strong twisting movement of your left fist to attack his jaw on the right side at S-6/*Jiache*.

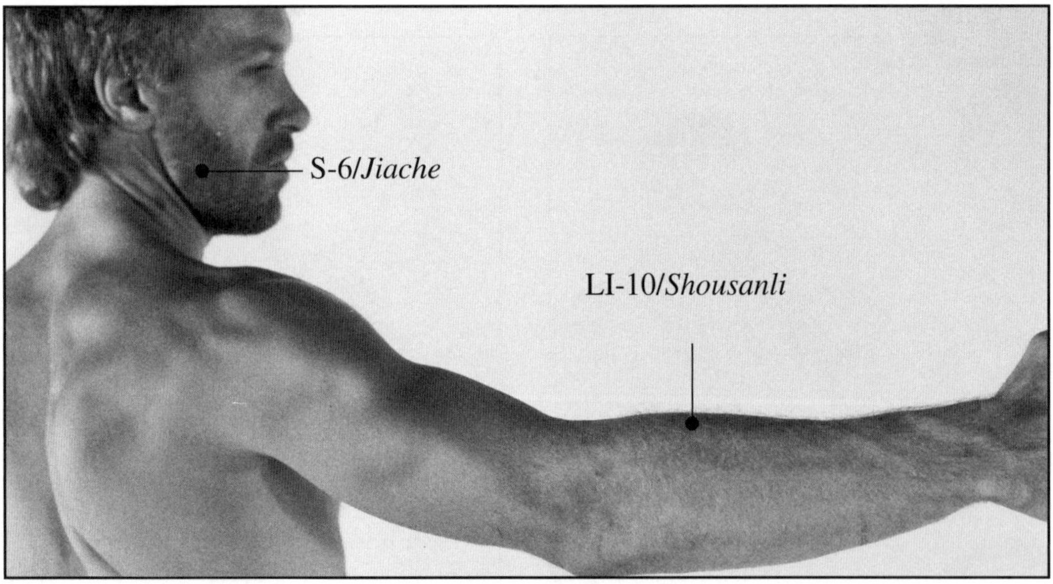

2

3

4

5

Bunkai # 31

1-2. As an attacker strikes out with a right jab, move forward and to the left, as you deflect his fist with your left palm.

1

3-4. Grasp his right wrist with your right hand, squeezing strongly into the wrist pressue points H-6/*Yinxi* & L-8/*Jingqu*, and shuffle step forward to hook your left foot behind his right ankle.

5-6. Strike the left side of the attacker's chin with your left fist, hitting M-HN-18/*Jiachengjiang* (the mental foramen).

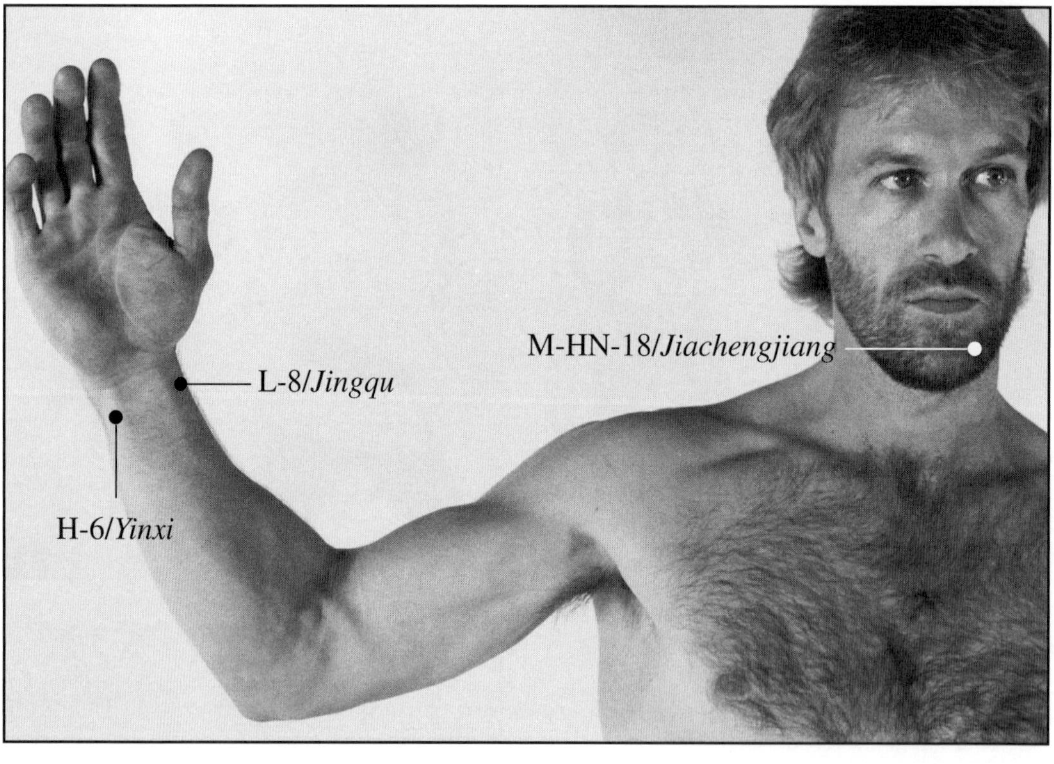

2

3

5

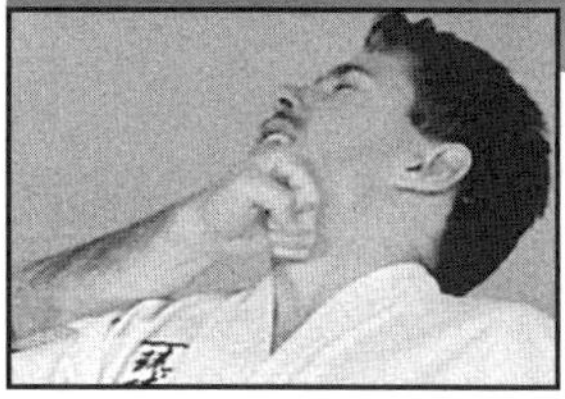

6

Bunkai # 32

1. As an attacker reaches with his right hand, meet it with your left palm.

2-3. Grasp across his fingers with your left palm *(do not raise your elbow as you do this).* At the same time, cut your right hand along the outside of the attacker's right wrist, rubbing across SI-6/*Yanglao.*

NOTE: *Manipulating SI-6/Yanglao releases the wrist.*

1

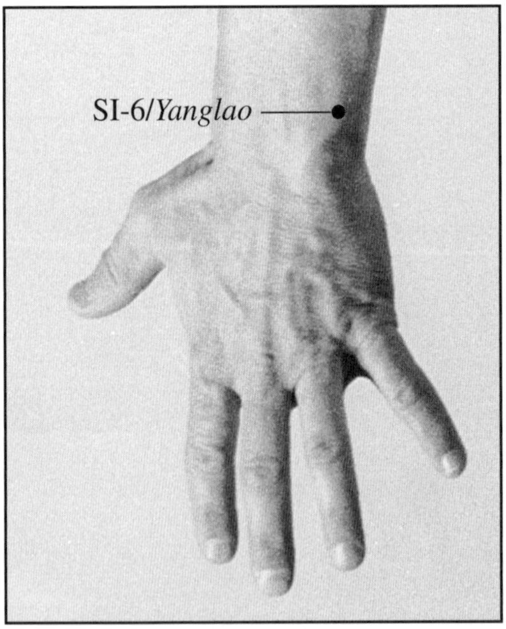

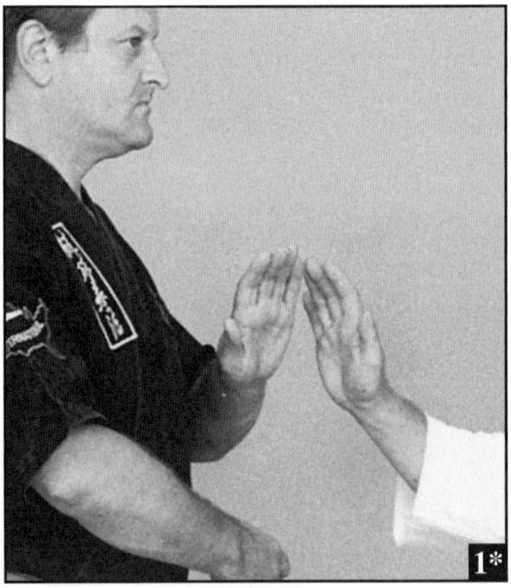
1*

2

3

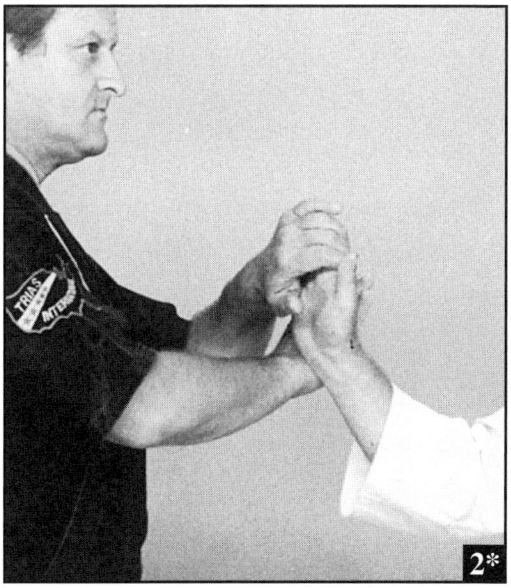

2*

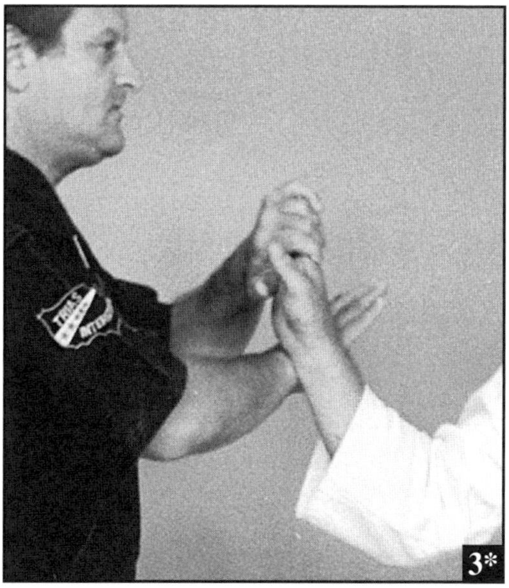

3*

Bunkai # 32 (cont.)

4-5. Hook your right hand behind his wrist, grasping across TW-6/*Zhigou*, & TW-7/*Huizong*, TW-8/*Sanyangluo* as you twist his fingers clockwise (viewed from above).

NOTE: *You have manipulated the attacker's right hand into the tuité technique Palm Turn. Done properly, a Palm Turn especially activates the Heart, Small Intestine and Triple Warmer meridians.*

6. Holding the attacker's wrist strongly with your right hand, strike with your left fist to TW-17/*Yifeng* below the attacker's right ear.

4

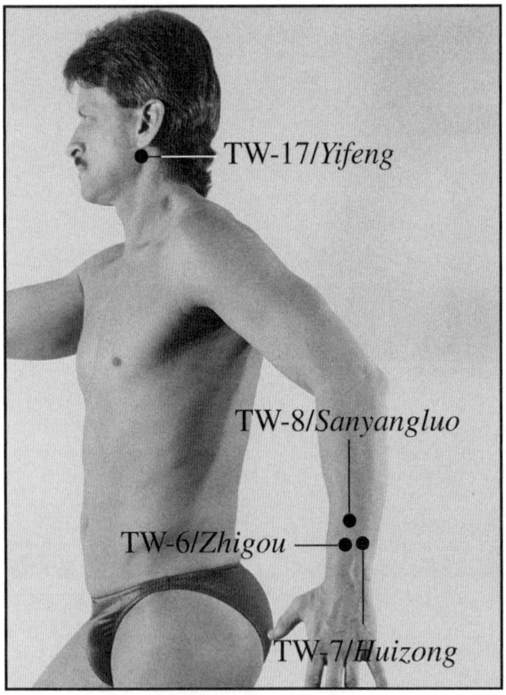

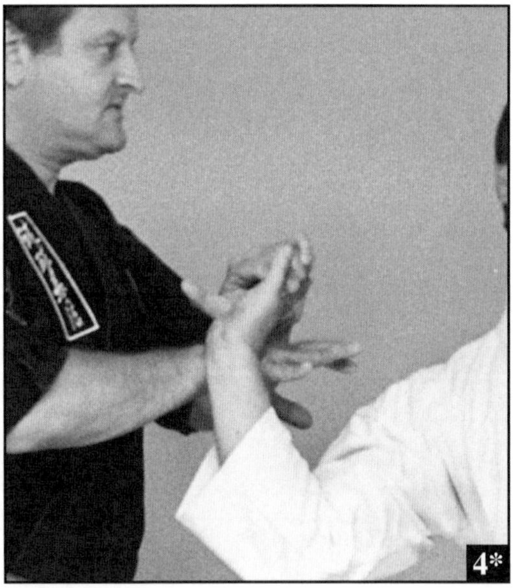

4*

5

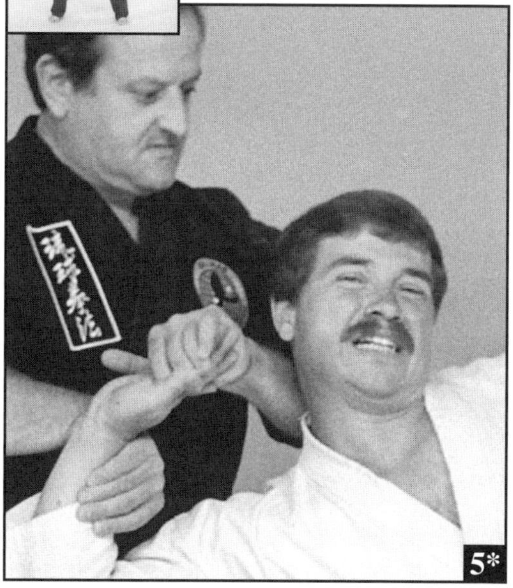

5*

6

6*

Bunkai # 33

1. An attacker grabs your lapel with his left fist, threatening a right punch.

1

2-4. Without hesitation, grasp his left wrist with your right hand across TW-6/*Zhigou*, TW-7/*Huizong*, & TW-8/*Sanyangluo (with your fingers)*, P-6/*Neiguan (with your thumb)*, and strike with the back of your left hand to TW-17/*Yifeng*.

NOTE: *Your left hand should be cupped slightly so that your knuckles can slip into the cavity under the attacker's ear to reach TW-17/Yifeng.*

4

5-.6 Immediately turn your left hand over, and grasp the attacker's left ear to bring him to the ground.

NOTE: *The "backhand strike" and the "double punch" form bookends for Naihanchi Shodan. This is an indication of their particular usefulness to handle many situations.*

2

3

5

6

Bunkai # 34

1-2. As an attacker reaches for you, move forward and slightly to the left, as you deflect his right hand with your left hand, slide your right hand along the outside of his right forearm.

1

3. Grasp his right wrist with your right hand (seizing pressure points H-6/*Yinxi* & L-7/*Lieque*), as you reach up with your left hand to grab the attacker by the hair at Scalp Point Cluster (B-7/*Tongtian*. B-8/*Luoque*, GB-17/*Zhengying*, GB-18/*Chengling*).

NOTE: *The knowledgeable reader will see that this movement is the same as the familiar pattern "brush, grab, strike" with a hair grab occurring in place of the final strike.*

1*

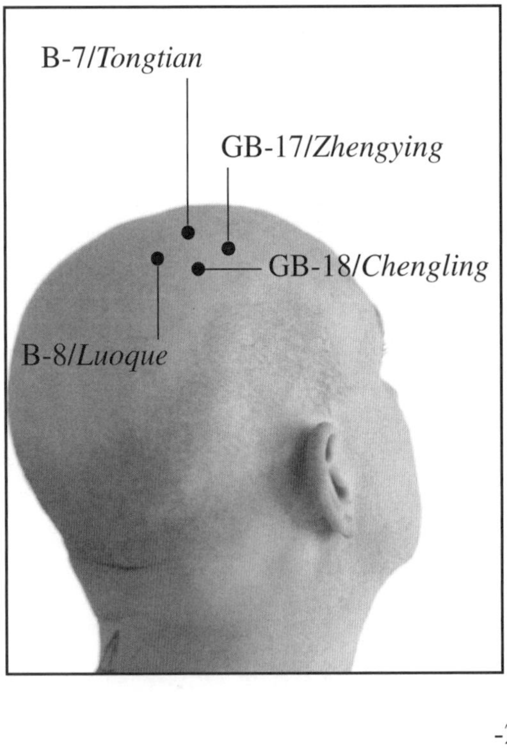

2

3

2*

3*

Bunkai # 34 (cont.)

4-10. Using a spiraling motion, manipulate the attacker's head to destroy his balance and bring him to his knees. *(Photos continue on the following pages.)*

NOTE: *This technique depends heavily on the tuité principle of "Confusion" for more on the principles of tuité refer to* **Advance Pressure Point Grappling: TUITÉ**.

4

4*

5

6

5*

6*

Bunkai # 34 (cont.)

7

8

7*

8*

9

10

9*

10*

Author George Dillman teaching pressure point method in the home of martial artist and action star Chuck Norris.

Photo by Kim Foreman

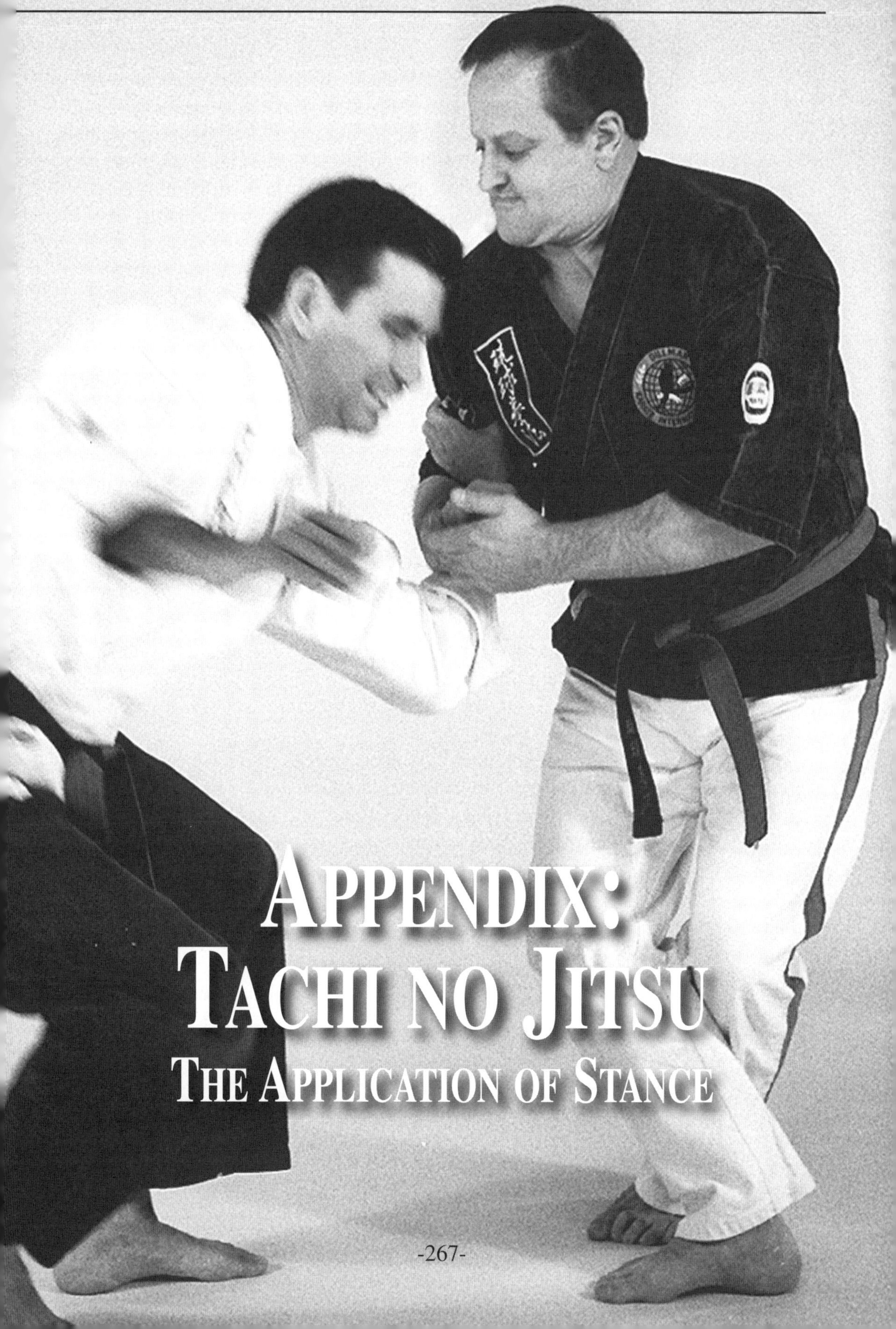

Appendix: Tachi no Jitsu

The Application of Stance

One of the features which distinguishes the classical martial arts from combat sports (like boxing) is the use of stances. Fixed positions can seem counter-productive when one considers the dynamic nature of combat, yet their importance remains beyond question among those who have studied the old methods. Part of what makes stances so important is the unique manner in which different stances manifest different facets of internal energy (ki/qi). These energetic qualities can enhance the effectiveness of pressure point techniques in surprising ways.

When we talk about stances we speak of 9 stances in particular (though each stance may have a number of variations, as well as some intermediate versions [called *emergent stances*] which blur the distinction between one stance and another). These nine stances are the five **Primary Stances** (horse, cat, cross, open horse, front), and the four **Secondary Stances** (reverse cat, crane, hourglass, kneeling).* Each stance possesses a specific elemental quality (Earth, Metal, Water, Wood, Fire) and a specific polarity (yin/yang).

The difference between primary and secondary stances is found in the relationship between the stance polarity and the elemental polarity. For example, the element fire is yang polarity, so the primary fire stance is yang polarity, making it Yang-Fire. But, just as in the body where there is a Yang-Fire as well as a Yin-Fire, there is a secondary Fire stance which has the polarity yin – Yin-Fire. The element Earth, however, is neutral (ground) in polarity. So, Earth is yin-yang potential; it becomes yin or yang in an encounter with other specific energies. (To borrow language from quantum physics, yin and yang are superposition states of Earth, until the "yin-yang potential" collapses into "yin or yang actual" at the moment of interaction). As a result, the primary Earth stance is it's own secondary stance.

In addition to elemental and polarity values, stances also have cardinal directions, and some specific ways in which they displace energy in the body. Together, these facets of stance provide a depth of meaning for classical arts, and suggest many interesting areas of study. At best, we can only introduce these concepts, then leave it to the reader to explore them in greater detail.

*Hourglass stance is almost universally known as Sanchin stance; horse stance is often referred to as Naihanchi stance; open horse stance is sometimes called Seiuchin stance; cross stance is sometimes called Chinto stance. These alternate designations are derived from the names of kata in which the respective stances are prominently featured.

The 9 Stances

Reverse Cat Stance

Front Stance

Kneeling Stance

Cat Stance

Horse Stance

Open Horse Stance

Crane Stance

Cross Stance

Hourglass Stance

5 PRIMARY STANCES

Horse stance has the polarity value "neutral," or "ground," which is why it is taught first. The body is balanced side to side. The feet and knees point directly ahead.

In the lower leg, the meridians Spleen (Earth), Liver (Wood), Kidney (Water) crisscross, so there is no clearly defined aspect of the leg which corresponds to a particular meridian. But, at the knee joint and inner thigh, the meridians have straightened out. As a result, in the horse stance, with the feet parallel and the knees pointing forward, the Spleen (Earth) points Sp-9/*Yinlingquan*, Sp-10/*Xuehai*, Sp-11/*Jimen* on each leg are facing each other. This is part of what defines horse stance as having the elemental value Earth.

Horse stance, being neutral and Earth element expresses all cardinal directions, especially (and exclusively among the stances) the diagonals (NE, SE, SW, NW).

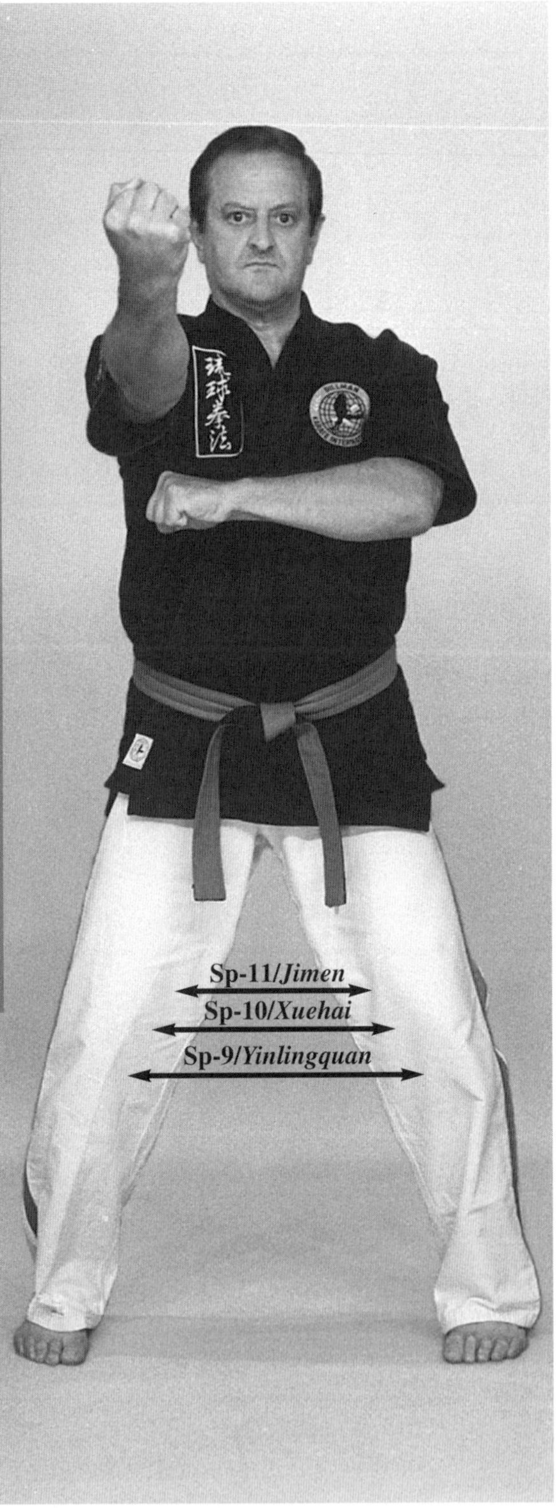

Cat stance has the polarity value "predominant yin." The feet are placed in the manner of a check mark (✔) with the lead heal raised.

As one adopts a cat stance, the body contracts in all directions (i.e., squeezes together and sinks down) as metal does when it cools (cooling and contracting are yin characteristics). Accordingly, cat stance has the elemental value Metal (Yin-Metal). The Cardinal Direction for cat stance is from the west (facing east).

5 PRIMARY STANCES (cont.)

Cross stance has the polarity value "extreme yin." The stance is formed by physically connecting K-8/*Jiaoxin* on the back leg with B-58/*Feiyang* on the front leg which gives it the elemental value Water (Yin Water). Like water, the body sinks and twists when assuming the stance.

An examination of kata shows that the cross stance is used sparingly and briefly. This is because adopting a stance accesses the elemental energy of the body. That particular energy becomes available <u>for</u> attack, but also vulnerable <u>to</u> attack. In the case of Water energy, it is the kidneys which become vulnerable, and the kidneys are the receptacles of *yuan qi*, the original life force of the body. For this reason, one does not remain in cross stance, but moves quickly out of it.

The Cardinal Direction for cross stance is from the north (facing south).

Open horse stance has the polarity value "predominant yang." The knees and feet point outward on the diagonals, reminiscent of the spreading roots of the tree. The position of the knees aligns the points Li-7/*Xiguan*, Li-8/*Ququan*, Li-9/*Yinbao* across from each other. This alignment gives open horse the elemental value Wood (Yang-Wood). A tree possesses a harder aspect (the outer bark) and a less hard aspect (the wood). Likewise, the open horse stance is particularly strong to the rear (with the back corresponding to the bark, and the front corresponding to the inner wood), and so, is often used in defenses against attacks from behind.

The Cardinal Direction for open horse stance is from the east (facing west).

5 PRIMARY STANCES (cont.)

Front stance has the polarity value "extreme yang." In front stance, the back leg pushes forward and the weight is on the forward leg. The silhouette of the stance is an expanding and rising cone, like the blast from a cannon, which reveals the elemental value of front stance, Fire (Yang-Fire).

The Cardinal Direction for front stance is from the south (facing north).

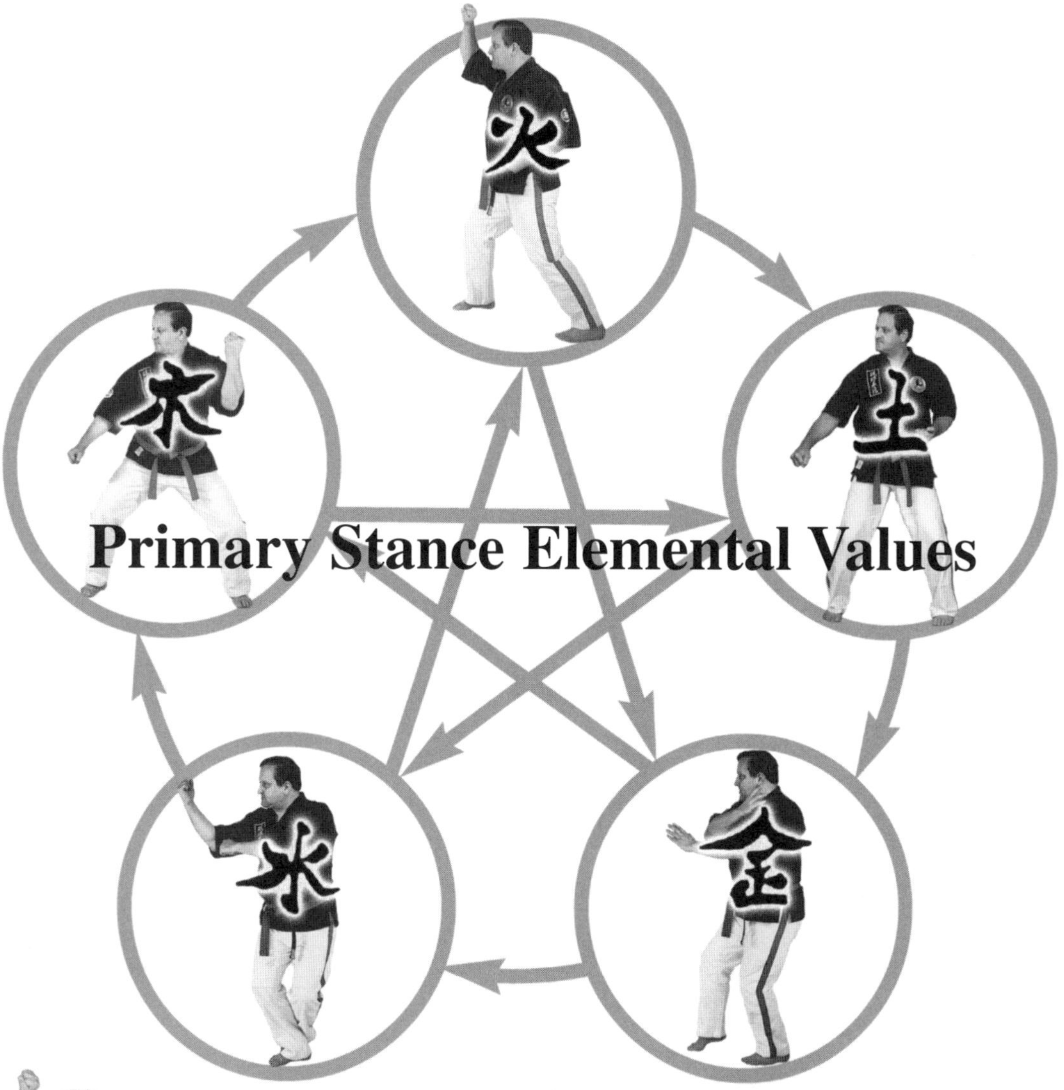

Front Stance (zenkutsu-dachi) Yang-Fire

Open Horse Stance (shiko-dachi) Yang-Wood

Horse Stance (kiba-dachi) Earth

Cat Stance (neko-dachi) Yin-Metal

Cross Stance (kosa-dachi) Yin-Water

Stance Cardinal Directions

NOTE: In the southern hemisphere the Cardinal Directions for front stance and cross stance are reversed. At the equator, front stance and cross stance possess simultaneous north and south orientations. At the equator the difference between cat stance and open horse stance is at it's greatest – the distinction between them disappears at the poles.

The use of Cardinal Direction with stance is problematic in combat, since it is not practical to be thinking constantly about which direction you are facing. However, when engaging in energy training (kiko [Jp], chi-gung [Ch]) it is most effective to face the correct direction.

Horse stance, as neutral and Earth element expresses all cardinal directions, but especially the diagonals. This does have a practical and evident fighting application – horse stance is especially strong for directing force along diagonal lines (relative to the stance). Throughout this book, the observant reader will see the frequent use of diagonal lines in conjunction with horse stance (1,2,3).

1

2

3

USING STANCE ELEMENTAL VALUES

The easiest way to use the elemental value of a stance is to use the same element to attack the same element. This can be thought of in the homeopathic sense of "like cures like." So, if one is attacking the Triple Warmer meridian (1-3) by pressing on TW-3/*Zhongzhu* with one hand while striking TW-23/*Sizhukong* with the other fist, one would use a fire stance. In this way, Triple Warmer meridian points accept Fire energy as "friendly" because Triple Warmer is a Fire element meridian. The points do not resist the input of Fire energy from an attack, and are easily overwhelmed when it turns out to be "unfriendly" Fire energy (one might call this "Chi in sheep's clothing," or, as one black belt cheerfully quipped, "Trojan chi.").

1

The second method of using the elemental value of the stance is to follow the cycle of destruction. So, when attacking a point on the Triple warmer meridian (such as TW-17/ *Yifeng*), adopt the stance with the elemental value Water, because Triple Warmer is Fire (4-6).

This method can be combined with the above, by using the same energy for the initial attack, then finishing with a cycle of destruction method.

4

2

3

5

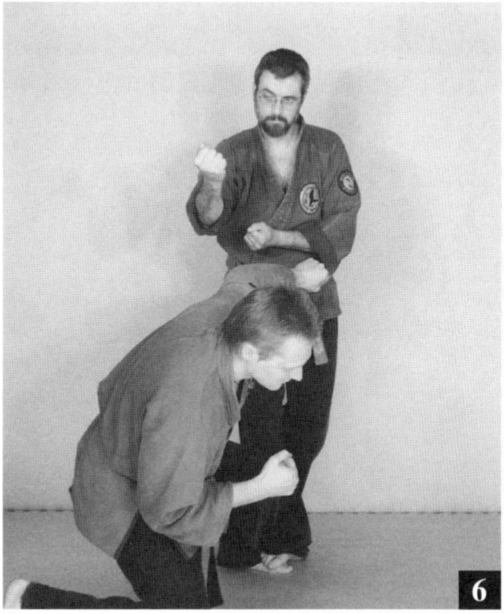
6

ELEMENTAL TRANSMUTATION OF STANCE

Stance energetics are not static. Hitting a stance causes the corresponding energy to elevate in a burst. But, this burst is short lived, and the energy quickly drops below the baseline resting state. If this energy burst is graphed as a wave, the shape closely resembles the action potential for a nerve. If you stay in a particular stance for a long period of time (as when practicing *chi-gung/kiko*) the specific elemental energy will slowly rise and grow. But, in fighting, the burst of energy must be immediately used. Generally, the count of one-two is all the time available to capture that wave. However, as with nerves, the energetic burst can be repeated if there is a sufficient stimulus. Typically, this stimulus is the stomping of the foot (the entire foot or just the heel). Foot stomps are a common feature of kata, and can be thought of as "resetting" the elemental value of the stance.

Stance energetics also undergo a *transmutation*. For clarity, let us consider cat stance as an example. Hit a cat stance and Metal energy immediately rises. The elevation of Metal causes a nearly simultaneous sedation of Wood energy (which drops sharply below baseline). As the burst of Metal energy is (quickly) fizzling out, Water energy rises, having been nourished by Metal. At the same time, the Water energy nourishes the Wood, cancelling out the sedating effect which occurred initially. This cancelling effect stops the interaction (or it would continue cycling through the body endlessly). It should be noted that the sedation of Wood happens virtually instantly, while the rise of Water takes a bit longer. This is because destruction is always faster and easier than creation.

From a practical combative perspective, cat stance starts out as Metal, then transmutes into Water. The rhythm of this transmutation is the familiar triplet found in many places in kata. The rhythm is "1,2 and 3," which, in the example of Cat stance means "Metal, Metal, and Water."

Front Stance	Open Horse Stance	Horse Stance	Cat Stance	Cross Stance
Fire, Fire & Earth	*Wood, Wood & Fire*	*Earth, Earth & Metal*	*Metal, Metal & Water*	*Water, Water & Wood*

Stance Transmutation Curves
(Example: Cat Stance)

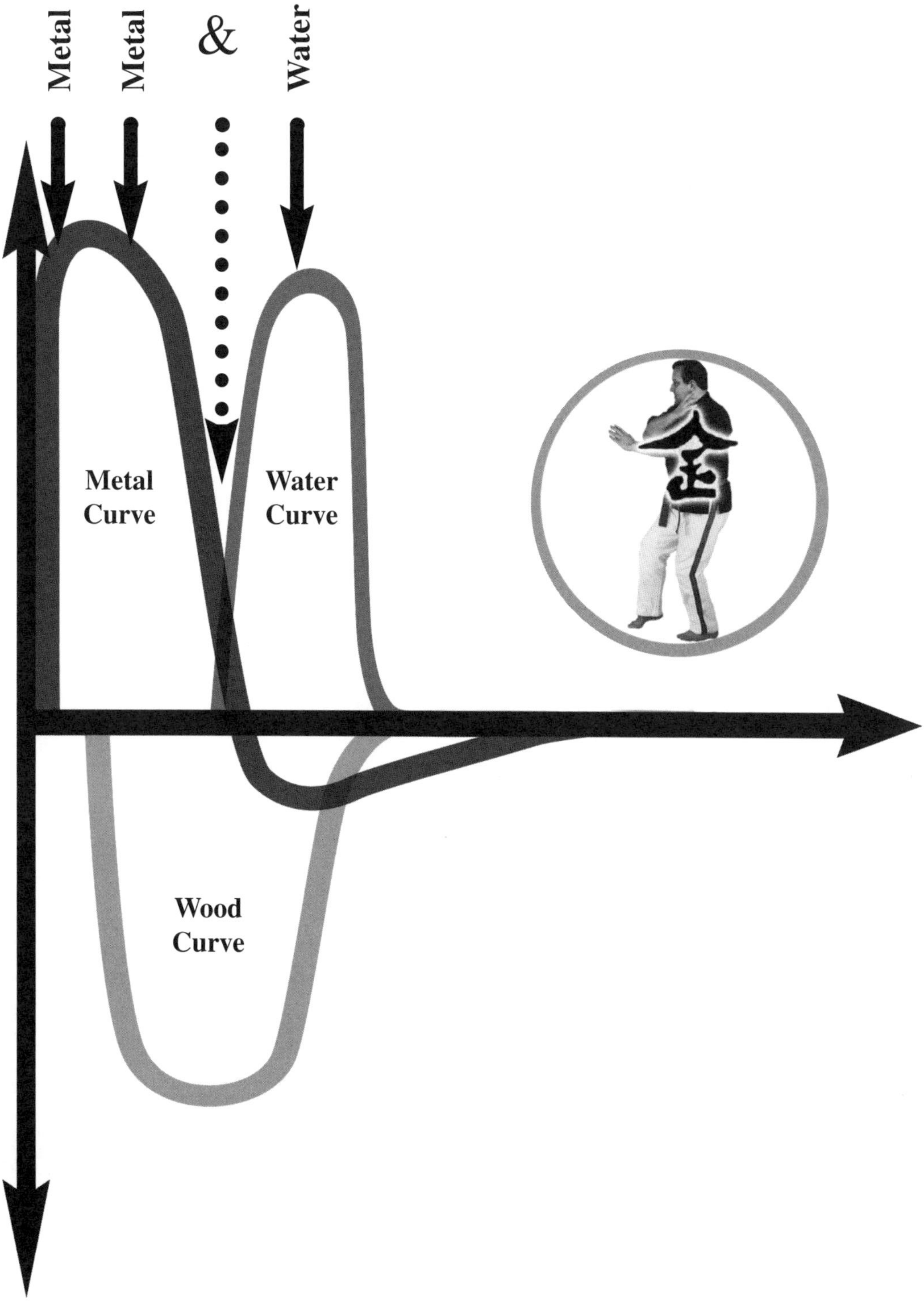

ELEMENTAL TRANSMUTATION OF STANCE (cont.)

The kata Naihanchi Nidan contains a classic example of the use of the foot stomp to reset the energetic value.

1

1,2. In the kata performance, the right foot is lifted, then stomped to the floor as the right fist strikes downward onto the left palm.

3. In application, when an opponent grabs your lapels with both hands, you step to your right and drop into a horse stance as you strike the opponent's right forearm at LI-10/*Shousanli* to turn his body and expose his neck.

4. Lay the back of your open left hand on the left side of the attacker's neck so your first two knuckles lie over S-9/ *Renying* & S-10/*Shuitu*.

5,6. At this point, because of the time required to control and position your opponent, the burst of Earth energy which accompanied your taking a horse stance is depleting. But, since S-9/*Renying* & S-10/ *Shuitu* are Earth points, Earth energy is highly effective against them. So, following the kata, you lift your right foot and stomp it down (resetting the Earth energy of the stance) as you punch into your own palm, driving the knuckles of your left hand into the pressure points on his neck.

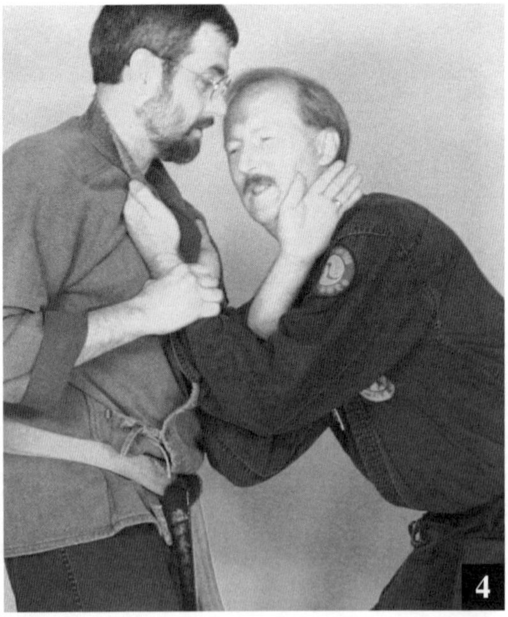

4

2

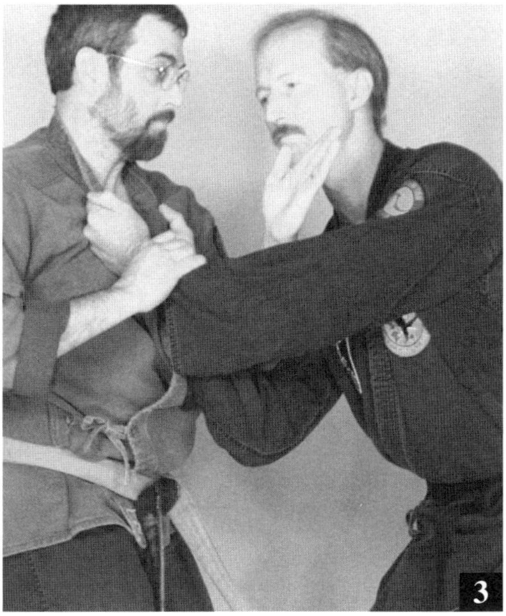
3

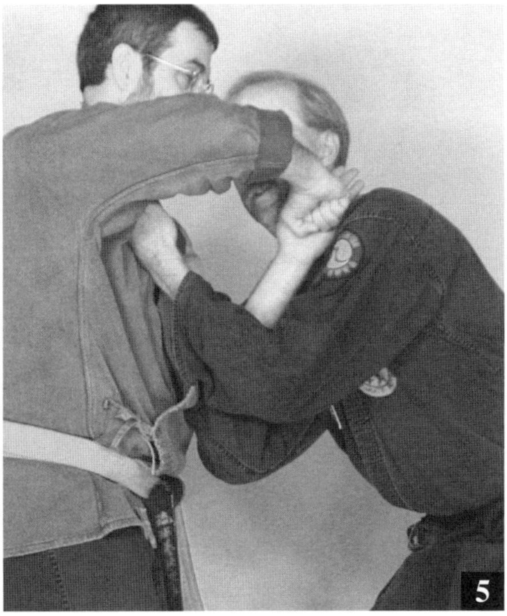
5

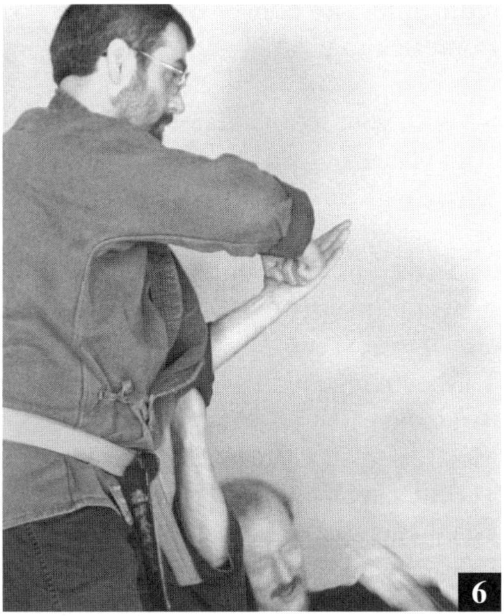
6

ELEMENTAL TRANSMUTATION OF STANCE (cont.)

The kata Pinan Shodan contains a classic example of the use of stance transmutation in the application of a triplet.

1

1. Assume a left cat stance, as you swing both fists upward.

2. Strike forward with your right fist while you draw your left fist back and over your right forearm.

3. Pulling your right fist strongly back to your hip, strike with your left fist.

4. In application, when an attacker grabs your lapel with his left hand and punches with his right, drop into a cat stance and bring your arms up, so your left obstructs his attack, and your right fist swings around behind his left ear, hitting pressure point TW-17/*Yifeng* from back to front.

4

5. With your left hand hold the attacker in place, and strike again to TW-17/*Yifeng* with your right fist.

6. Strike out with your left fist a third time at pressure point TW-17/*Yifeng*.

This technique works because the first two strikes to TW-17/*Yifeng* are with Metal energy because of the cat stance. The attacker's body is able to resist Metal energy at a Fire point (TW-17/*Yifeng*), but is entirely unprepared for the third strike to come as Water energy once the stance has transmuted.

2

3

5

6

Stance Polarity (Yin/Yang)

Front Stance (zenkutsu-dachi) Extreme Yang	Open Horse Stance (shiko-dachi) Predominant Yang	Horse Stance (kiba-dachi) Neutral	Cat Stance (neko-dachi) Predominant Yin	Cross Stance (kosa-dachi) Extreme Yin

Energetic Entry & Exit locations

Downward arrows indicate "Heavenly (Yang) Chi" which enters from above, while upward arrows indicate "Earthly (Yin) chi" which arises from below.

Wider arrows indicate major entry or exit points, while narrower arrows indicate minor entry or exit points.

ENERGETIC MANIPULATION

Energy in the body is manipulated by posture and this can be used in combat. To understand the basics of energy manipulation we think in terms of 6 energy transfer locations (this is a useful, but simplified description of the dynamic energetic interactions of the body). Each of these locations represents an entry point and an exit point for energy (think of a 9 volt battery with a positive and negative pole). These six locations are, the palms of the hands, the soles of the feet, the crown of the head, and the perineum.

The crown of the head is a major energetic entry location (at point GV-20/*Bahui*), and a minor exit location.

The perineum is a major energetic exit location (at C-1/*Huiyin*), and a minor energetic entry point.

The palms of the hands are a major energetic exit location at the point P-8/*Laogong*, and a minor energetic entry.

The soles of the feet are a major energetic entry location at the ball (K-1/*Yongquan*) and minor energetic exit at the heel.

The two yin stances – cat stance and cross stance – in particular have useful energy manipulation, which have specific application in fighting. This is due the characteristic they share, that one heel is raised.

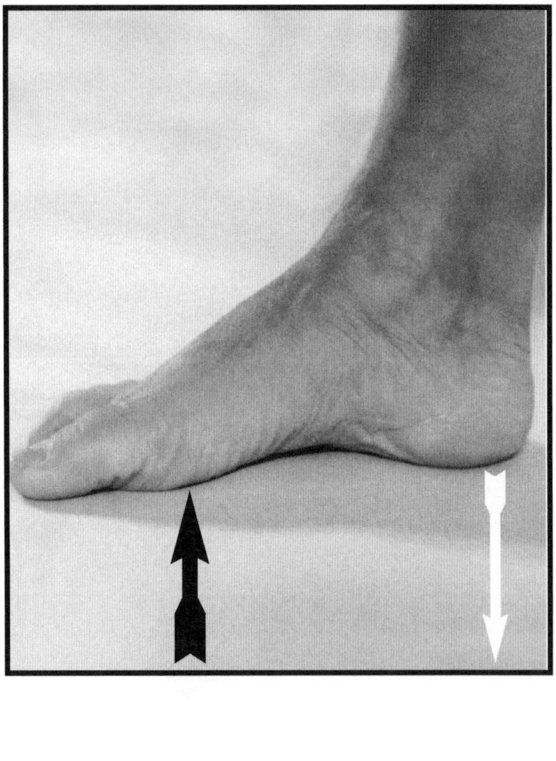

Energy exits through the heel and enters through the ball of the foot at K-1/*Yongquan*. In cat stance, one heel is raised, so energy can enter, but cannot exit on that side. As a result, the energy "backs up", filling the opposite hand (legs and arms are related across the body). Because one hand is suddenly loaded with energy, the body becomes unbalanced. To correct this, the opposite hand undergoes a relative inversion – which means that its polarity (yin/yang) immediately reverses.

This feature of cat stance is important in the application of gender specific techniques.

ENERGETIC MANIPULATION (cont.)

The application of cat stance in gender specific technique is easy to demonstrate with strikes directed to S-5/*Daying*. Because the Stomach meridian, which is yang polarity, splits at this point, the energy there is "turbulent" and very strongly yang. The most effective strikes to this point utilize yin values. But, the energy at S-5/*Daying* has right side and left side characteristics. In males, the right side is yang, the left side yin. In females this is reversed.

Palm strikes and blows with the fist also have polarity values. For males, the right palm is yang and the left palm yin, the right fist yin and the left fist yang. For females this is reversed. These characteristics produce an equation for attacking S-5/*Daying*. When striking a male opponent's left side S-5/*Daying* (yin side/yang) a male would use his right palm or his left fist (male yang hand). On the opponent's right side (yang side/yang), a male would use his left palm or right fist (male yin hand).

Likewise, a female striking a male's left side S-5/*Daying* (yin side/yang) would use a right fist or left palm (female yang hand). When striking to the opponent's right side (yang side/yang), a female would use a left fist or right palm (female yin hand).

Adopting a cat stance allows for all of these characteristics to be reversed. This can seem complicated at first, but classical kata training makes it much easier to remember and apply.

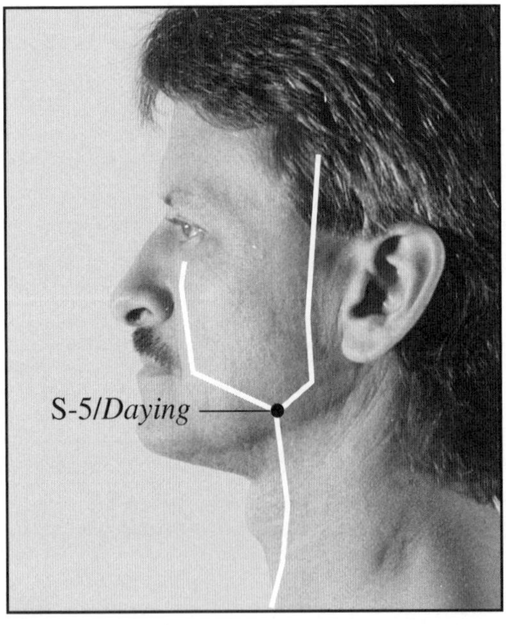

1. A female using a right palm to strike a male at his left side S-5/*Daying* is only moderately successful because her right palm is yin hitting his yin side.

2-3. When she adopts a right cat stance, her right palm inverts into a yang strike with profound effect.

1

2

3

ENERGETIC MANIPULATION (cont.)

Male: Right palm (yang hand) to right side S-5/*Daying* (yin side/yang).

Male: Left fist (yang hand) to right side S-5/*Daying* (yin side/yang).

Female: Right fist (yang hand) to right side S-5/*Daying* (yin side/yang).

Female: Left palm (yang hand) to right side S-5/*Daying* (yin side/yang).

Male using cat stance: Right fist (inverted yang hand) to right side S-5/*Daying* (yin side/yang).

Male using cat stance: Left palm (inverted yang hand) to right side S-5/*Daying* (yin side/yang).

Female using cat stance: Right palm (inverted yang hand) to right side S-5/*Daying* (yin side/yang).

Female using cat stance: Left fist (inverted yang hand) to right side S-5/*Daying* (yin side/yang).

ENERGETIC MANIPULATION (cont.)

Cross stance, like cat stance, has one heel raised, so energy in that leg "backs up" to the opposite hand. Because the legs cross, connecting Bladder and Kidney meridians, energy traveling down and out the front leg is shorted across to the rear leg, captured and pulled back up. Finally, the point where the legs cross lies directly below the perineum at C-1/*Huiyin*, so that energy exiting from that point to connect to the ground is also captured and pulled back up. The result is that the entire upper body floods with energy and creates a form non-muscular strength to overcome an opponent. This flood of energy also makes the body (for a moment) invulnerable to many types of attacks. (Invulnerability methods are sometimes called "iron body" or "iron shirt".)

1-3. When an opponent grabs your arm above the elbow, the simple act of bending your elbow and drawing it into your strength can put him down. However, in this demonstration, the attacker has focused his internal energy on his gripping hand, so that even using two hands his structure does not break.

ENERGETIC MANIPULATION (cont.)

1-4. Even with internal energy focused on the grab, simply by stepping into a cross stance the opponent's resistance gives way and he is easily dropped.

ENERGETIC MANIPULATION (cont.)

1,2. A wrist turn press joint technique can easily drop the opponent.

3,4. However, if the opponent steps into a cross stance, he is able to resist the wrist turn press, even though his hand is already positioned for the technique.

5,6. The protective effect of the cross stance can be neutralized by simply touching the opponent's leg with one foot.

***NOTE:** The result of this counter-for-counter is that the wrist turn press is, in the end, even more painful and effective.*

1

4

5

2

3

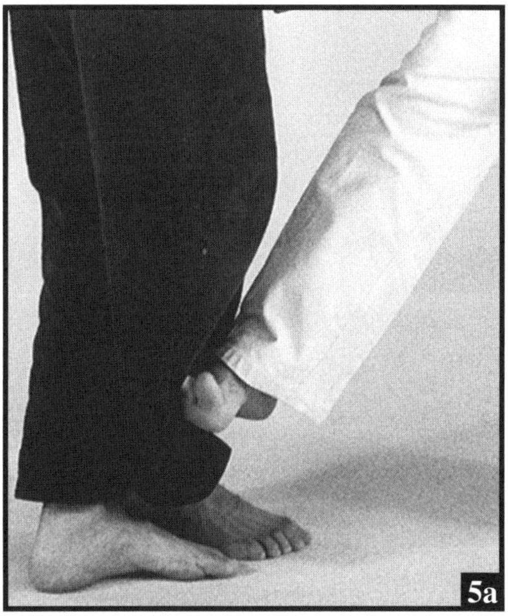
5a

6

SPECIAL NOTE 1

The Principle of energetics found in crossing the legs, has an analog in the arms.

1,2. A kick to the thigh at Sp-11/*Jimen* can easily stagger an opponent.

3,4. However, if the opponent crosses his wrists, he is able to take multiple kicks without much effect.

5-7. This can be neutralized by simply touching the opponent's forearm with one hand.

NOTE: *The result of this counter-for-counter is that the kick is, in the end, even more painful and effective.*

1

4

5

2

3

6

7

SPECIAL NOTE 2

When an opponent grabs on, it is possible to use his own stance – his connection to the ground – against him. By leaping into the air to strike, the effect is similar to a lightening rod. Energy entering your body through the top of your head cannot exit into the ground, so it exits through the opponent. This greatly amplifies the effect of the technique.

1-3. When an opponent grabs with two hands, leap into the air and strike to the forehead at GB-15/*Toulinq*.

1

2

3

4 SECONDARY STANCES

Kneeling stance is the secondary Fire stance, Yin-Fire. To assume a kneeling stance, begin in a front stance (Yang-Fire) and simply drop down (sinking is a yin characteristic). Secondary stances are used in ways similar to primary stances. As an example, when entering energy into a Yang-Fire meridian like Triple Warmer, front stance can be used (Yang-Fire) because like receives like. However, using Yin-Fire energy is even more effective because the meridian is both open to accepting the energy (Fire) and compromised by it's opposing polarity (yin). So to attack Triple Warmer from a Yin-Fire stance (kneeling stance) is profoundly effective. This principle of application applies to all the secondary stances.

Kneeling stance occurs in a few old kata, including some (but not all) versions of Gojushiho, Chinto, Pinan Godan, Wansu (Empi).

4 SECONDARY STANCES (cont.)

Reverse cat stance is the secondary Metal stance, Yang-Metal. The body weight is on the front leg, with the foot and knee slightly turned outward, and the back foot is raised onto the ball. The angle of the front foot in reverse cat stance is virtually identical to the angle of the rear foot in cat stance.

Reverse cat stance is found in most versions of Seisan kata.

Crane stance is the secondary Water stance, Yang-Water. The rear leg hooks behind the knee of the front leg, so that Sp-6/*Sanyinjiao* on the rear leg comes into contact with B-54(B-40)/*Weizhong* on the front leg.

Crane stance is found in some versions of Chinto and Wansu kata.

4 SECONDARY STANCES (cont.)

Hourglass stance (commonly known as Sanchin stance) is the secondary Wood stance, Yin-Wood. The feet are turned inward and the hips are sunk into the inguinal crease. Muscular tensions is concentrated in the inner thigh.

Hourglass stance is frequently used in kata from the Naha tradition (Goju-ryu, Uechi-ryu), as is the Yang-Wood stance, open horse. However in the Shuri tradition of Okinawan martial arts, the Wood stances are less common.

Primary and Secondary Stances: Structural Comparisons

Yin-Fire stance drops down from Yang-Fire stance.

Yang-Water and Yin-Water stances differ only in the position of the back leg.

Yin-Wood stance turns the feet in, and Yang-Wood turns the feet out.

Yang-metal and Yin-Metal stances reverse the front and rear foot positions.

Elemental Transformations

Primary and Secondary Stance Elemental and Polarity Values

SPECIAL NOTE 3
Variant & Emergent Stances

We have described nine stances, but the human body is capable of assuming an almost limitless number of postures. As a result, there can be variations for each stance, variations which still possess the energetic qualities we have described the distinctive leg touch movement in Naihanchi is a Yang-Water stance, because K-1/ *Yongquan,* on the ball of the raised foot, touches the base leg at Sp-9/ *Yinlingquan*, which is the water point of the Spleen meridian. This completes with Water "circuit."

In contrast to the stance variations are the emergent stances. These are postures which blur the energetic distinctions of stance we have discussed. A common one legged stance in which the raised leg is not touching the support leg (shown below) is an emergent stance. It lies in the transition between Metal stance and Water stance, and would be termed "emergent Water stance." The familiar back stance (*kokutsu-dachi*, below top) of Japanese karate lies in the transition between Earth stance and Metal stance ("emergent Metal stance"). Similarly, the stance known as the "immovable" stance (*fudo-dachi*, below bottom) lies in the transition between Fire stance and Earth stance ("emergent Earth stance").

Emergent stances do not fully manifest an element until the third beat of the elemental transmutation we have described (pgs. 280-285). So, while cat stance transmutes as "Metal, Metal, & Water," back stance transmutes as "Emergent Metal, Emergent Metal, & Full Metal."

Photo by Kim Foreman

Jean-Paul Bindel with authors George Dillman and Chris Thomas. Jean-Paul Bindel and Paul Bowman are the senior DKI instructors in Europe.

A gathering of DKI master instructors.

Will Higginbotham, Senior Monk De Jing, and George Dillman, in the cemetery at the Shaolin Temple. **Photo by Sterling Johnson**

Bibliography & Sources

BEIJING COLLEGE OF TRADITIONAL CHINESE MEDICINE, et. al
ESSENTIALS OF CHINESE ACUPUNCTURE
Pergamon Press, Ltd., 1981

BISHOP, Mark
OKINAWAN KARATE
A & C Black (Publishers) Ltd, 1989

DEADMAN, Peter, AL-KHAFAJI, Mazin, BAKER, Kevin
A MANUAL OF ACUPUNCTURE
Journal of Chinese Medicine Publications, 1998

DILLMAN, George A., THOMAS, Chris
KYUSHO-JITSU: THE DILLMAN METHOD OF PRESSURE POINT FIGHTING
Dillman Karate International, Publishers, 1992
ADVANCED PRESSURE POINT FIGHTING OF RYUKYU KEMPO
Dillman Karate International, Publishers, 1994
ADVANCED PRESSURE POINT GRAPPLING - TUITE
Dillman Karate International, Publishers, 1995
LITTLE JAY LEARNS KARATE
Dillman Karate International, Publishers, 1997
PRESSURE POINT KARATE MADE EASY
Dillman Karate International, Publishers, 1999
HUMANE PRESSURE POINT SELF-DEFENSE
Dillman Karate International, Publishers, 2002

GUYTON, Arthur C., M.D.
TEXTBOOK OF MEDICAL PHYSIOLOGY (7th ed.)
W.B. Saunders, Co, 1986

HOKAMA, Testsuhiro, translated by Joe Swift
TIMELINE OF KARATE HISTORY: PRE-HISTORY TO 2000
Ozato Print Co., 2007

HOLLINSHEAD, W. Henry, Ph.D.
ANATOMY FOR SURGEONS: VOLUME 1 THE HEAD AND THE NECK (2nd ed.)
Harper & Row, Publishers, Inc., 1968

JAY, Wally
SMALL-CIRCLE JUJITSU
Ohara Publications, Inc., 1989

MABUNI, Kenwa
KOBO JIZAI KARATE KEMPO, SEIPAI NO KENKYU
Nakasone Genwa Kobukan, 1934

McCARTHY, Patrick
THE BIBLE OF KARATE: BUBISHI
Charles E. Tuttle Company, 1995
THE BUBISHI: A TRANSLATION AND ANALYSIS (3rd ed.)
International Ryukyu Karate Research Society, 1994

MILLER, Ronald D., M.D.
ANESTHESIA: ATLAS OF REGIONAL ANESTHESIA PROCEDURES (5th ed.)
Churchill Livingstone, 2000

MOTOBU, Choki,
OKINAWAN KEMPO KARATE-JITSU
translated by Oyata & Wagner
Ryukyu Imports Inc., 1977
OKINAWAN KEMPO
translated by Ken Tallack
Masters Publications, 1995

NETTER, Frank H., M.D.
ATLAS OF HUMAN ANATOMY
CIBA-GEIGY Ltd., 1989

PRESAS, Remy
MODERN ARNIS: THE FILIPINO ART OF STICK FIGHTING
Ohara Publications, 1983

SHANGHAI COLLEGE OF TRADITIONAL MEDICINE
ACUPUNCTURE: A COMPREHENSIVE TEXT
Eastland Press, 1981

TERRY, Charles, MD; BARCLAY, David; PATTERSON, Terry, PhD; STECKER, Mark; MD.
PHYSIOLOGIC STUDY OF PRESSURE POINT TECHNIQUES USED IN MARTIAL ARTS
Journal of Sports Med Phys Fitness 1999; 39: 328-35

THOMAS, Chris
PRESSURE POINT TECHNIQUES: A TEAM OF DOCTORS TRIES TO FIND OUT HOW SAFE THEY ARE
Black Belt Magazine (USA) September, 1998
IS SAFE PRESSURE POINT PRACTICE POSSIBLE?
Martial Arts Illustrated (U.K.) Vol. 12, No. 5, October, 1999

WEISS, Al & WEISS, David
OFFICIAL HISTORY OF KARATE IN AMERICA THE GOLDEN AGE: 1968-1986
Pro-Action Publishing, 1997

WILSON-PAUWELS, AKESSON, STEWART
CRANIAL NERVES: ANATOMY AND CLINICAL COMMENTS
B.C. Decker, Inc., 1988

KYUSHO-JITSU: The Dillman Method of Pressure Point Fighting

by George A. Dillman
with Chris Thomas

272 pages, soft cover, $34.95
ISBN 978-0-9631996-1-4

Kyusho-jitsu, or pressure point fighting, has long been a closely guarded secret of the martial arts. Taught to almost no one, the art was in danger of disappearing forever. In this revolutionary book, world famous karate instructor George A. Dillman with noted martial arts authority and writer Chris Thomas openly reveal the secrets of pressure point fighting to western martial artists of all styles. **KYUSHO-JITSU: The Dillman Method of Pressure Point Fighting** contains 272 pages of vital information, and is considered a classic among martial arts books, it has forever changed the way karate is understood.

"This kyusho-jitsu is a wonderful technique. I was also impressed by the unique methods of *kappo* (revival)."

Chosei Motobu, son of Choki Motobu and *soke*, of Motobu-ryu karate-jitsu

---

Little Jay Learns Karate

Written by: Chris Thomas

Illustrated by: Dan Rosandich

Created by: George A. Dillman
& Kimberly Dillman Foreman

48 pages, soft cover, $9.95
ISBN 978-1-889267-01-2

This delightful and thought-provoking story helps to introduce the ethical concepts which are a part of all traditional martial arts training. It provides the perfect entry for conversations between parents and children who are interested in studying karate. School teachers have found **Little Jay Learns Karate** to be especially useful for helping young students discover the joys of reading because the topic of karate draws their interest and the wise story holds their attention.

"My nephew was thrilled with *Little Jay Learns Karate*. It's a fun book and a good introduction to the principles of the martial arts"

Michael Hauge, screenwriter, and author of *Writing Screenplays That Sell.*